W9-DDI-233

AMERICAN GRAPHIC ART

SERIES IN AMERICAN STUDIES

Editor-in-Chief: Joseph J. Kwiat

PROGRAM IN AMERICAN STUDIES

UNIVERSITY OF MINNESOTA

AMERICAN GRAPHIC ART

By FRANK WEITENKAMPF

With a New Introduction by
E. MAURICE BLOCH
PROFESSOR OF ART HISTORY
DIRECTOR, GRUNWALD GRAPHIC ARTS FOUNDATION
UNIVERSITY OF CALIFORNIA, LOS ANGELES

JOHNSON REPRINT CORPORATION
NEW YORK AND LONDON
1970

62644

INTRODUCTION

When his *American Graphic Art* first appeared in 1912, Frank Weitenkampf could report that some aspects of the subject had already been treated by a number of well-known authorities in the field. An ambitious publication of the Gesellschaft für Vervielfältigende Kunst of Vienna, *Die Vervielfältigende Kunst der Gegenwart,* issued in four volumes between 1887 and 1903, included considerations of the contemporary woodcut and etching in America as well as a section on lithography which was contributed by Weitenkampf himself. Within the same period William Spohn Baker, Philip Gilbert Hamerton, J. Ripley W. Hitchcock, Sylvester Rosa Koehler, William James Linton, and David McNeely Stauffer produced biographical dictionaries and special studies on wood-engraving, etching, and engraving in this country. Author-artists such as Francis Hopkinson Smith and Joseph Pennell also wrote extensively about the art of illustration with emphasis on the American contribution.

What was still lacking, however, was a general handbook which concerned itself not only with the technical development of the various graphic media but, perhaps more importantly, with the evolution of the professional illustrator, caricaturist, and the commercial artist. Weitenkampf undertook this task and unquestionably his personal interest in the varied aspects of the subject, along with his enormous store of knowledge of the men and events connected with it, made him the logical man to undertake it. The book filled a vital reference need at the time and, twelve years afterward, he prepared a new edition, revising the contemporary sections and adding a bibliography, as well as reorganizing and refining a large portion of the text. To this day this little volume remains our chief source of information on many individual artists; in the case of some general sections it is still the most reliable text of its kind in the field. It is the latter edition which is here reprinted.

In his prefatory "explanation" to the second edition Weiten-

v

kamp pointed out that he had deleted some facts and names of artists which he no longer believed were important to an essential understanding of the development of the graphic arts in this country. Most of the names of contemporary artists dropped from the new edition were obviously of men whose reputations had somewhat faded in the intervening years although even Weitenkampf felt that in terms of any future history and reevaluation of the period they would unquestionably still play a role. The omission of these men, however, made way for a new generation of artists. The eliminations were actually few by comparison with the many new names now added to the roster. As early as 1912 Weitenkampf noted the work of John Sloan, Childe Hassam, and John Marin; by 1924 he could observe the rise of Edward Hopper, Rockwell Kent, Kenneth Hayes Miller, Mahonri Young, George Overbury "Pop" Hart, Arthur William Heintzelman, William and Marguerite Zorach, W. Auerbach-Levy, Adolph Dehn, Peggy Bacon, Kerr Eby, and Edward Borein.

The structure of the two editions remained essentially the same with chapters devoted to the development of each graphic process as well as chapters dealing more specifically with illustration, caricature, the comic paper and the daily press, the bookplate, and applied graphic art.

Frank Weitenkampf's career as a scholar and writer spanned a period of some seventy years. He was author and co-author of at least six books apart from catalogues and other separate pieces. His contributions to periodicals appeared first in 1887 and continued with ever-increasing regularity until 1959, well past his ninetieth year. Of the approximately seventy-five articles, at least half were concerned with American graphic art and artists. His interests in prints were actually very broad and often developed in areas well beyond the demands of his position as Curator of Prints at the New York Public Library. His particular devotion to the art of the illustrator and the caricaturist is such an instance, revealed in the many excellent articles he wrote on the subject and in the reference files which are still considered among the invaluable assets of the Library's

Print Department. Since his own career had begun during the golden era of American illustration Weitenkampf had occasion to come into contact with many of the editors and publishers of illustrated books and magazines and knew many of the artists personally. Glimpses in vignette of some now half-forgotten illustrators of once great fame like Reginald B. Birch, Harry Fenn, Thure de Thulstrup, and Francis Hopkinson Smith, come to life again in another of Weitenkampf's books, *Manhattan Kaleidoscope,* published in 1947.

The full range of Frank Weitenkampf's knowledge actually encompassed the entire history of the art of illustration, however, and this was repeatedly demonstrated in the important exhibitions he assembled at the New York Public Library, all based on the collections he helped form there. This knowledge also culminated in the appearance in 1938 of another of his valued handbooks, *The Illustrated Book,* in which he once again discussed the position of the American graphic artist and illustrator.

It is a privilege to be asked to prepare some words by way of introduction to this reprinting of an important work by Frank Weitenkampf. I came to know him first during my student days and later as a museum curator and can still recall vividly many of the conversations we had on printmakers and illustrators. My deepest impressions are of his phenomenal memory for facts and of the great enthusiasm for prints which he enjoyed sharing with the young people who came his way. Those are also characteristics he reveals in much of his writing. He belonged to a now almost vanished generation of creative scholars and curators whose devotion to the graphic arts, coupled with great taste and farseeing good judgment, set the standards of quality upon which most of the great public collections were formed. Those collections, along with the published works of these men, provide present and future generations of scholars with a foundation for study and learning as well as serving as examples which they may well strive to emulate.

E. Maurice Bloch

Frank Weitenkampf:
A Selective List of Publications
Relating to American Graphic Art,
1927–1959

"John Greenwood: An American Born Artist in 18th Century Europe, with a Checklist of His Etchings and Mezzotints," *Bulletin of the New York Public Library*, XXXI (August 1927), 623–634.

"A. B. Frost," *Arts*, XV (March 1929), 168–172.

"American Wood Engraving Today," *International Studio*, XCIV (December 1929), 52–56.

"Country Life in American Prints," *Print Connoisseur*, XI (October 1931), 295–316; XII (January 1932), 50–56.

"Winslow Homer and the Wood Block," *Bulletin of the New York Public Library*, XXXVI (1932), 731–736.

The Illustrated Book. Cambridge, Mass.: Harvard University Press, 1938. Sections on American graphic art in 19th and 20th century: pp. 122–126, 135, 141–142, 178–184, 194–205, 231–233.

Nevins, Allan, and Frank Weitenkampf. *A Century of Political Cartoons in the United States from 1800–1900.* New York: C. Scribner's Sons, 1944.

"Early American Landscape Prints," *Art Quarterly*, VIII (Winter 1945), 40–67.

"Political Cartoons as Historical Documents," *Bulletin of the New York Public Library*, L (March 1946), 171–176.

"New York State in National Politics: Notes for a Cartoon Record," *New-York Historical Society Quarterly*, XXX (April 1946), 77–91.

Manhattan Kaleidoscope. New York and London: Charles Scribner's Sons, 1947.

"F. O. C. Darley, American Illustrator," *Art Quarterly*, X (Spring 1947), 100–113.

Early Pictures of North American Indians: A Question of Ethnology. New York: The New York Public Library, 1950.

Political Caricature of the United States in Separately Published Cartoons: An Annotated List. New York: The New York Public Library, 1953.

"Emergence of the American Illustrator," *Art Quarterly,* XVIII (1955), 394–402.

"American Illustrators of Shakespeare," *Bulletin of The New York Public Library,* LX (February 1956), 70–72.

"New York and the Illustrated Weeklies," *New-York Historical Society Quarterly,* XLII (July 1958), 300–308.

"American Illustrators Abroad," *Art in America,* XLVII (Summer 1959), 328–333.

AMERICAN GRAPHIC ART

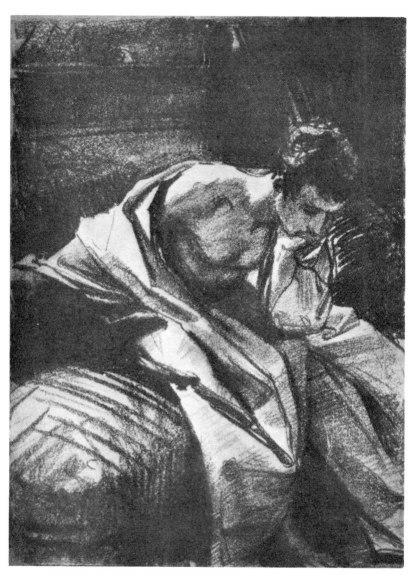

STUDY
Lithograph by John S. Sargent

AMERICAN GRAPHIC ART

By F. WEITENKAMPF, L. H. D.

CURATOR OF PRINTS, NEW YORK PUBLIC LIBRARY;
AUTHOR OF "HOW TO APPRECIATE PRINTS," "THE
ETCHING OF CONTEMPORARY LIFE," ETC.

NEW EDITION REVISED AND ENLARGED

With Illustrations

THE MACMILLAN COMPANY

NEW YORK   MCMXXIV

Printed in the United States of America by
THE FERRIS PRINTING COMPANY, NEW YORK.

To M.

A WORD OF EXPLANATION

THE history of American painting and sculpture has been written more than once. That of the reproductive graphic arts as a whole remained to be told. There are such monographs as W. J. Linton's excellent and partly polemical record of American wood-engraving and Ripley Hitchcock's very useful volume on etching in the United States, both published in the eighties of the last century. There is, too, D. McN. Stauffer's alphabetical record of our engravers on copper, an invaluable book of reference. But the present work is the only connected and comprehensive account of American graphic art, from the early products, of such a strong historical interest, to the most recent efforts at original expression, as we see them in the present revival of painter-etching, and in the individual adoption of the wood-block and the lithographic stone as painter-media.

The object is to group scattered facts in a brief but clear review of the whole field of American graphic art. It is not intended to present a detailed list including every artist who may have practised any of these arts in this country, but to offer a survey that will bring out salient or characteristic personalities and tendencies.

The first issue of this book (1912) was a quite detailed record. It included a number of facts and names which might conceivably, sometime, help some very special investigator,—who may, for the matter of that, still find and consult the book in our public libraries. Others would not find these facts of especial use in forming a picture of the development of the arts in this country,— if, indeed, they would not find them a sort of undergrowth to make the woods of information less easy to traverse. They were therefore dropped, without much regret, in the preparation of this second edition, which, it is hoped, has gained in compactness and clearness, and which, moreover, brings the story down to the present day.

Thanks are due to the publishers of Scribner's Magazine, the Print Connoisseur, the Century Magazine and the American Printer for permission to reprint certain passages from my contributions to those magazines.

CONTENTS

CHAPTER   PAGE

       A WORD OF EXPLANATION   vii

    I   ETCHING: EARLY ATTEMPTS AND THE NEW YORK ETCHING CLUB
        PERIOD   1

   II   ETCHING: THE PRESENT REVIVAL   24

  III   ENGRAVING IN LINE AND STIPPLE: THE EIGHTEENTH CENTURY .   43

  IV   LINE AND STIPPLE IN THE NINETEENTH CENTURY   61

   V   MEZZOTINT (THE ART OF ROCKER AND SCRAPER)   87

  VI   AQUATINT AND SOME OTHER TINTS   99

  VII   WOOD-ENGRAVING   112

VIII   THE "NEW SCHOOL" OF WOOD-ENGRAVING   126

  IX   PAINTER-WOOD-ENGRAVING   138

   X   LITHOGRAPHY: A BUSINESS, AN ART   152

  XI   THE ILLUSTRATORS   179

  XII   CARICATURE   206

XIII   THE COMIC PAPER AND THE DAILY PRESS   228

XIV   THE BOOK-PLATE   251

XV   APPLIED GRAPHIC ART: FROM BUSINESS CARD TO POSTER . .   266

BIBLIOGRAPHY   291

INDEX   299

ix

ILLUSTRATIONS

Study. Lithograph by JOHN S. SARGENT . . . . Frontispiece

FACING PAGE

Battle of Bunker's Hill. Etching by JOHN BAKER. 2
(*Courtesy of Print Connoisseur.*)

Mud Boats on the Thames. Etching by CHARLES A. PLATT 9
(*Courtesy of F. Keppel & Co.*)

Theatre Royal, Haymarket. Etching by JOSEPH PENNELL 11
(*Courtesy of F. Keppel & Co.*)

The Poe Cottage, Fordham, New York. Etching by C. F. W. MIELATZ 12

Summer at Easthampton. Etching by MRS. MARY NIMMO MORAN . . 13
(*Courtesy of F. Keppel & Co.*)

Mother and Baby. Dry-point by MARY CASSATT 14

Old Mills, Coast of Virginia. Soft-ground etching by JAMES D. SMILLIE . 16

A Bit of Mount Vernon St., Boston. Etching by CHARLES HENRY WHITE 26
(*Courtesy of Harper & Brothers.*)

The First Snow. Etching by MAHONRI YOUNG. 29
(*Courtesy of American Magazine of Art.*)

Ralph Waldo Emerson. Etching by OTTO J. SCHNEIDER 34

Japanese Priest. Dry-point by CADWALLADER WASHBURN 34

Jonathan Mayhew. Line-engraving on copper by PAUL REVERE . . 45

The Boston Massacre. Engraving by PAUL REVERE 51
(*Courtesy of Print Connoisseur.*)

Federal Hall. Engraving by AMOS DOOLITTLE 52
(*Courtesy of Kennedy & Co., and Print Connoisseur.*)

Andrew Jackson, after Sully. Stipple engraving by J. B. LONGACRE . 62

Ariadne. Line-engraving, from a painting by John Vanderlyn, by A. B.
DURAND 73

Cotton Mather. Mezzotint by PETER PELHAM 87

Sir Thomas Lawrence, after a painting by himself. Mezzotint by JOHN
SARTAIN 93

Evening, Raquette Lake. Mezzotint by J. D. SMILLIE. 97
(*Courtesy of Charles Scribner's Sons.*)

New York from Governor's Island. Aquatint, after W. G. Wall, by JOHN
HILL 102

FACING PAGE

Old Dam. Aquatint by JAMES D. SMILLIE 105

Richard Mather, by JOHN FOSTER. The first known wood-engraving
executed in the colonies 112

The Last Arrow. Wood-engraving after J. G. Chapman, by J. A. ADAMS. 119

The Haywain, after John Constable. Wood-engraving by TIMOTHY
COLE 134
(*Courtesy of The Century Co.*)

Girl and Peonies, after Irving R. Wiles. Wood-engraving by HENRY
WOLF 136
(*Courtesy of Harper & Brothers.*)

Wood-engraving. From a book-plate by G. W. PLANK . . on page . . 138
(*Courtesy of Charles Scribner's Sons.*)

Lower New York. Wood engraving by HENRY WOLF 140
(*Courtesy of Print Connoisseur.*)

Sleigh Ride. Wood Engraving by J. J. LANKES . . . . . on page. . 142
(*Courtesy of Charles Scribner's Sons.*)

New York from the Manhattan Bridge. Wood Engraving by RUDOLPH
RUZICKA, ... on page. . . 143
(*Courtesy of Charles Scribner's Sons.*)

Head-piece from "Journeys to Bagdad," by Charles S. Brooks. Wood
engraving by A. ALLEN LEWIS, ... on page. . . 145
(*Courtesy of Charles Scribner's Sons.*)

Two of the earliest known lithographs produced in the United States.
Both by BASS OTIS 152

Washington. Lithograph by REMBRANDT PEALE 154

One of the "Campagne Sketches," a series of lithographs by WINSLOW
HOMER 167

Flower-girl. Lithograph by WILLIAM M. HUNT 168

View on the Seine. Lithograph by H. W. RANGER 169

Limehouse. Lithotint by J. A. M. WHISTLER 170

Morning. Lithograph by BOLTON BROWN 174
(*Courtesy of Charles Scribner's Sons.*)

Little Arkansas River. Lithograph by BIRGER SANDZEN 175
(*Courtesy of Charles Scribner's Sons.*)

Autumn. Lithograph by ARTHUR B. DAVIES. 176
(*Courtesy of Print Connoisseur.*)

The Cards. Lithograph by ALBERT STERNER. 177
(*Courtesy of Charles Scribner's Sons.*)

FACING PAGE

Tenement Roofs. Lithograph by JOHN SLOAN 178
    (*Courtesy of Charles Scribner's Sons.*)

A Scene from "Oliver Twist." A Scene from Cooper's "Leather Stock-
    ing Tales." Illustrations, engraved on steel, from designs by FELIX
    O. C. DARLEY 182

"There never was anything the least serious between us." Illustration
    for Henry James's "Julia Bride," by W. T. SMEDLEY 192
    (*Courtesy of Harper & Brothers.*)

Viewing the Battle of Bunker Hill, by HOWARD PYLE 198
    (*Courtesy of Harper & Brothers.*)

Illustration for "To-morrow's Tangle," by ARTHUR I. KELLER . . . 202
    (*Courtesy of Bobbs-Merrill Co.*)

America Swallowing the Bitter Draught. Engraving by PAUL REVERE . . 208
    (*Courtesy of Print Connoisseur.*)

A Caricature of the War of 1812, by WILLIAM CHARLES 214

One of the Anti-Tweed caricatures in *Harper's Weekly*, by THOMAS NAST 233

Cartoon, *Puck*, April 28, 1886, by JOSEPH KEPPLER 233
    (*Courtesy of Puck.*)

Book-plate of George Washington 252

A Group of Modern Book-plates by E. A. ABBEY, W. E. FISHER, W. F.
    HOPSON, E. D. FRENCH, S. L. SMITH, G. W. EDWARDS 259
    (*Courtesy of Charles Scribner's Sons.*)

AMERICAN GRAPHIC ART

AMERICAN GRAPHIC ART

CHAPTER I

ETCHING: EARLY ATTEMPTS AND THE NEW YORK ETCHING CLUB PERIOD

THE first strong impulse toward the practice of painter-etching came with the founding of the New York Etching Club in 1877. There was a preliminary period of preparation, marked by the efforts of Falconer, Cole, Warren and Forbes.

In the eighteenth century, Joseph Wright's portrait of Washington (1790) was probably the first etching executed by a painter. This profile was evidently copied in the one by Joseph Hiller, Jr. (1794), described by Charles H. Hart, who saw four impressions on the backs of playing cards, and found the original plate. St. Memin etched two large views of New York City, and a business card for Peter Mourgeon, *copper-plate printer from Paris.* One may extract from Dunlap's "History of the Arts in the U. S.," or Stauffer's work, or Ripley Hitchcock's little volume on "Etching in America" (1886), names such as that of Pigalle (1797), who did title-pages, John Rubens Smith, or Francis Kearny. Dunlap himself executed a frontispiece for a "dramatic trifle," published in 1797 or 1798 (a portrait of Wignell in the rôle of Darby). Printed directions for etching existed here as early as 1794, in the Philadelphia edition of an English work, "The artist's assistant in drawing, perspective, etching, engraving, mezzotinto-scraping, &c." A copy of this book was in Washington's library.

The *Theatre in Chestnut Street, Philadelphia*, signed *Gilbert Fox Aquafortis,* was presumably done about 1800. We enter the new century with Alexander Lawson, the engraver, who "had points made for etching and tried that." Benjamin West signed a few plates, as did Thomas Middleton, an amateur. W. Birch's "Country Seats of the United States" (1808) are to be noted, as is the crude view of the Battle of New Orleans, signed *Francis Scacki.* William Charles executed in soft-ground etching and roulette, for Rees' Cyclopedia, two facsimiles of drawings by Poussin. And in the thirties John Baker drew *The Battle of Bunker's Hill* and *Washington Crossing the Delaware.* Also, Dr. John Redman Coxe experimented in etching on glass with fluoric acid, executing a little landscape published in the "Emporium of Arts and Sciences" (Philadelphia), 1812.

This early history is little more than a record of names and attempts. There is hardly anything that can be regarded as painter-etching. The art was mostly applied to portraiture and other practical ends, and was usually not employed in its purity, but as a basis for line-engraving.

There was an early attempt to use etching as a reproductive art. Robert W. Weir about 1820 "copied some of Rembrandt's etchings so close as to be with difficulty detected," and he "was on the eve of turning my attention

BATTLE OF BUNKER HILL
Etching by John Baker

seriously to the publication of etchings from various old pictures in the possession of different gentlemen in New York, but . . . it fell through after the first or second plate was finished."

England, from which so much of our art influence came in those days, furnished models for us in caricature and book-illustration by etching. Etched caricature of the period of the third and fourth Georges had a weak reflection here in the productions of William Charles; and, later, George Cruikshank was imitated, in the "Scraps" issued in the thirties and forties by David Claypoole Johnston. The Dickens period of illustration by etching, in England, had likewise its imitation here. Yeager reetched the Cruikshank plates for the American editions of "Harry Lorrequer" and other books, and Frank Bellew illustrated John T. Irving's "The Attorney" (1853) in the manner of Phiz.

One must not look in this early work for any of the characteristics of etching that we have learned to appreciate. As Hitchcock points out, the etchings shown at the early Academy exhibitions in New York no more deserved the name than did the engravings of Smillie. Dunlap spoke of etching as a mere "auxiliary to engraving," and that is precisely what it was in his day and long afterward, used as a first stage in line-engraving on steel. John Gadsby Chapman's predisposition to measured precision, joined to a liberal use of the ruling machine for the skies, resulted in plates of a neat execution that have much of the formality of bank-note art. George Loring Brown in "Etchings of the Campagna" (1860), like

Chapman affected a similar finish and tone; but his effects were richer. Emanuel Leutze, E. J. Kuntze and Hermann Carmiencke did some etchings. A valuable review of this introductory period was offered in the exhibition in the Boston Museum of Fine Arts in 1881, which included work by Dunlap, Johnston, R. W. Weir, W. Franquinet (1845), W. W. Weeks (1845), Thomas G. Appleton (1847), Henry B. Gay (1849), Chapman, William Wilson (1849) and Edwin White (1849).

Whistler began his French set in 1858, but there was no immediate response here to the appeal that his works constituted. It remained for the next generation to appreciate fully such works as his *Kitchen, Vieille aux Loques* and *Black Lion Wharf*. After them came his Venice plates, of a vivacity, a sureness of vision, a sense of adjustment of means, a pre-eminent mastery in selection, an exquisiteness of execution that have placed him in the front rank of the etchers of all time. It is not necessary to summarize what has been written of him by the Pennells, Bacher, Menpes, Theodore Duret or Miss E. L. Cary. Two definitive catalogues of his plates have been issued, one by Howard Mansfield for the Caxton Club of Chicago (1909), the other by E. G. Kennedy for the Grolier Club of New York (1910), the latter illustrated with a reproduction of each etching.

From the eighties to the present, the influence of Whistler has been felt. Meanwhile, however, we are regarding the sixties, and witnessing somewhat different tendencies.

The late S. R. Koehler pointed out that the rising

French influence in art, after the middle of the century, bringing the note of individualism, was the real factor of importance in the development of painter-etching here.

In 1866 Cadart, the Paris publisher of etchings, held an exhibition of French etchings in New York City (Derby Gallery—Chauncey L. Derby, 625 Broadway), and formed an American branch of the French Society of Etchers. A number of artists were interested, Victor Nehlig, Edwin Foɩbes, J. M. Falconer, Charles H. Miller, J. Foxcroft Cole among them. Forbes, artist-correspondent during the Civil War, diɑ a series of *Life Studies of the Great Army,* drawn by him on the grounded copper; the biting and printing left to other hands. Falconer, who had made his first attempt in 1849, showed, as Koehler says, "an open eye for the poetry of decay," in his views of streets and old buildings in New York, Boston and other cities. An earlier impulse toward original etching is noted by Henry Russell Wray, in his "Review of Etching in the United States" (1893). He records that as early as 1860 or '61, John Sartain illustrated the process of etching, by practical demonstration, for Thomas Moran and S. J. Ferris.

The attention paid to etching as a means of expression for the painter gradually increased. The little landscapes of A. W. Warren, simple in method, showing much of what etchings should have, are among the most satisfactory results of this period. In 1872 Henry Farrer entered on the path since followed with such success by Pennell, Mielatz and others, by bringing out a series of views of New York. Farrer had an idyllic vein, a preference for sunset effects with the simple, direct expression of mood which they permit. Also I have seen three plates by Wyatt Eaton, two heads and a study of a plant (1877). These are not startling facts. There were neither daring innovations nor brilliant achievements. But there was some creditable accomplishment and the soil was being prepared. Ripley Hitchcock comments on the too heavy inking of Forbes's *Life Studies*, lacking the refinements mastered in Paris, and on the too dry printing of Warren's landscapes, which, says he, appeared to much better advantage when intelligently reprinted in later years, losing much of their hard, dry character. This throws light on the defective knowledge here, at that time, of an important factor in the production of prints. Sidney L. Smith told me that the first "retroussage" printing was done in Boston in the early seventies. Estes and Lauriat, wanting to have an etching by Rajon after Bonnat printed, turned over the electro to Daniels, a well-known copper-plate printer. He printed with a "clean wipe," as one does from a visiting card plate. But the original had been "retroussaged," a method then unknown here; Daniels worked out the matter by himself.

At the Philadelphia Centennial Exhibition of 1876, the etchings included a number of plates by Americans,— G. L. Brown, Forbes, Peter Moran, S. J. Ferris, Volkmar. The medal was awarded to Peter Moran, of whose prints a dealer published twelve sets. Publication of etchings was undertaken here much earlier, however. By Emil Seitz, for instance, and Hitchcock records that

F. B. Patterson (who endeavored to interest C. S. Reinhart and E. A. Abbey) "issued a portfolio of Farrer's New York views in 1872." "By degrees," Hitchcock adds, "print collectors began to look for modern etchings." Notwithstanding all this, when the Fairmount Park Art Association (Philadelphia), having purchased the *Dying Lioness,* issued an etching of the group by Peter Moran, it was met by most of the subscribers with forcible disapproval. They had expected an engraving,. asked "what is an etching," and generally considered themselves swindled.

On May 2d, 1877, at the first meeting of the New York Etching Club, three men joined in the production of a little plate for the instruction of their fellow-artists. James D. Smillie "grounded" the plate; R. Swain Gifford drew the design; and Dr. Leroy M. Yale, physician and enthusiastic etcher, worked the press. The print appears as a frontispiece in Ripley Hitchcock's "Etching in America," and the original plate is in the New York Public Library.

For a number of years the exhibitions of the club, with the catalogue illustrated with etchings, formed an interesting pendant to the annual display of the American Water Color Society in the Academy building at 23d Street and Fourth Avenue, New York. A number of artists emphasized the variety of effect possible to the etching needle. There was much creditable attainment that we can look back on with a satisfaction that does not need the apologetic attitude of patriotism.

Interest in painter-etching crystallized around similar

organizations in other cities. The Boston Etching Club, founded in 1881, held its first exhibition in 1883, with a catalogue etched throughout, text and illustrations; among the members were E. H. Garrett, F. T. Merrill, F. G. Attwood and J. E. Baker. The Scratchers' Club, of Brooklyn, born in 1882, under the auspices of G. W. H. Ritchie, Walter M. Aikman, Carleton Wiggins, Benjamin Lander, Stanley Middleton, lived for a few years. "Sometimes," says Mr. Aikman, "one of the members would have a plate to 'bite,' and our friend George W. H. Ritchie pulled the proofs. We never had an exhibition for the simple reason that we never made enough plates to hold one." In Cincinnati and Philadelphia organizations were established in 1880. The Etchers' Club in the former city included H. F. Farny; M. Louise McLaughlin, ceramic artist, who wrote a little treatise on etching; Emery H. Barton; Elizabeth Nourse and Caroline Lord. The Philadelphia Society of Etchers held its first exhibition in 1882–83, and an etching class was formed in the Philadelphia Sketch Club. The membership list of the Philadelphia Society included P. Moran, S. J. Ferris, Pennell, Parrish, B. Uhle, J. Neely, Jr., W. J. Le Fevre, Hermann Faber, H. R. Poore. The catalogue of this first Philadelphia show, "devoted exclusively to painters' etchings," included 1,070 numbers, of which 356 by American artists. The Boston exhibit of 1881 comprised 548 pieces by 106 American artists (including one plate by George Inness), covering the country from New England to California, the latter represented by Virgil Williams and pupils. In the same year (1881) the Royal Society

MUD BOATS ON THE THAMES
Etching by Charles A. Platt

of Painter Etchers in London held its first exhibit, to which American artists contributed. Interest was stimulated also by Sir Seymour Hadden's lectures in 1882–84 in New York, Philadelphia, and other cities. "In quick mastery of detail and ready adaptability," said Hitchcock, "it would be hard to surpass our etchers; but want of originality, lack of the personal inspiration behind the executing instrument, the timidity or presumption of inexperience, and want of training—in drawing, for example—are betrayed upon the copper plate as easily as upon the canvas. . . . But criticism is met by one fact. All this production of etchings has been evolved from nothing within a very few years. A new field has been opened in American art." Among those who devoted themselves to the art were Stephen Parrish, whom Hamerton characterized as "sincere and straightforward"; Charles A. Platt, whose deft sureness in the precision of line or the juicy emphasis of dry-point, and judicious and delicate suggestion, were shown especially in his treatment of water; Charles A. Vanderhoof; C. H. Miller (in whose summary *A Sun Shower* much depends on the printing; clean-wiped, it would be a mere skeleton); Thomas R. Manley, who found interest in such subjects as the Hackensack meadows, and gave completeness of pictorial effect without insistence on detail, and who in recent years brought into play a new process, breaking up the line into dots; and Alexander Schilling, whose delightful little landscapes are of a suggestiveness akin to that of Pissarro or Raffaëlli. Other names come to mind: W. C. Bauer, W. Goodrich Beal, Prosper L. Senat,

Carlton T. Chapman. The bulk of the really note-worthy work was in landscape. River and harbor scenes were depicted by Farrer, Platt and others. Coast scenes, similarly bringing water and land into juxtaposition, by Pennell, Mielatz, Moran, Parrish, Charles E. Whittemore. J. C. Nicoll laid more weight on the water itself, as, for example, in his *In the Harbor*. In such a plate, or in two or three attempts by M. F. H. de Haas, we get more of the feeling for, and understanding of, the sea. Figure subjects were done by J. Fagan, F. M. Gregory, W. H. Shelton, J. W. Beatty, Joseph Lauber, F. W. Freer. Alfred Brennan, deft pen-draughtsman, showed picturesque qualities. John Ames Mitchell's Paris plates (the series *A travers l'Exposition 1878* and a scene on the stage of the Opera House) show a lively style, gracefully humorous, as were his pen-sketches subsequently in "Life." Most of these men did not work in the spirit of painter-etching, striving for a completeness of effect that gives their work the appearance of having been done after paintings. Many, in fact, were drawn to reproductive etching, even Winslow Homer (*Saved* and *The Life Line*), whom one might have expected to develop into a true painter-etcher. I. M. Gaugengigl paraphrased some of his paintings of eighteenth century subjects in a free, swinging style. F. S. Church repeated the world of mermaids, nymphs, and love-sick lions of his paintings, with a happy, light manner in harmony with the playful spirit of his subjects. Robert Koehler made a "rather free" reproduction of his painting *The Social-*

THEATRE ROYAL, HAYMARKET
Etching by Joseph Pennell

ist. And Walter Shirlaw repeated on copper the succulent richness and decorative quality of his illustrations.

Expression of American life was practically absent in the work of our figure etchers, if we except plates such as those in which Thomas Hovenden so well copied his paintings of negro character (*Dem was good old Times,* etc.), or those in which T. W. Wood attempted to translate his own canvases.

Animal subjects, even less frequently met with, included a few plates by J. Foxcroft Cole, and sheep-pieces by J. A. S. Monks. Noteworthy are the cattle-pieces of Peter Moran, in which completeness of effect is joined to a free and vigorous line, elaboration to the "discretion which knows where to stop," wrote Mrs. Schuyler Van Rensselaer.

Quantitatively it is in pure landscape etching that the greatest amount of noteworthy effort appears, with much attention to fine composition and picturesque effect, that stamps much of it as the work of practiced painters. There is the "nervous vitality" of Thomas Moran, whose prints are marked by boldness in conception and vigor in execution, and, as Koehler puts it, "with a successful indication of color effect." The more placid temperament of H. D. Kruseman van Elten made choice of subjects likely to be popular (*Twilight on the Housatonic* et al.). Among John H. Hill's best plates is one after his father, John W. Hill, a happy rendering of a landscape, with cattle fording a stream. B. Lander, too, was devoted to detail and tone, a statement that would cover also, more or less, Thomas C. Parrish and others of these days.

There is richness of color in Samuel Colman's scenes, etched in strong lines with dry-pointed tones, in an artistic spirit that stimulates the imagination. R. Swain Gifford, while attracted by motives in the Orient, Venice and Holland, made his strongest appeal in the expression of the mood of the scenery of the New England coast. He attained his effect with few lines, lightly yet firmly set down. James D. Smillie, a master of technical media, had to counteract the influence of years of formal line-engraving, and of commissions to do reproductive work not always worthy of his powers. To the end of his long and useful life he was his own severest critic. Whenever he had the opportunity to produce *con amore,* the result was apt to be a joy to the eye. For example, his flower-pieces, drawn in dry-point directly from nature, among them a bunch of pansies of remarkable variety and gradation. Pennell is known particularly as an etcher of city views, and of great industrial centres, a draughtsman of astounding sureness of eye and hand. He has quick resourcefulness, and a simplicity and directness born of the ability, so necessary in etching, to select, and resulting in what some one has called a "wise reticence in line." Mielatz was identified closely with the picturesque qualities of the city, especially of New York City. These, often unnoticed, he saw clearly and also with frequently a freshness of view that invests them with the interest of a new scene. Huneker well said of him, "His line is firm, virile, lean, even ascetic, rather than rich or luxurious," yet Mielatz was then doing his views at Georgian Court, Lakewood, which are noteworthy for vivacity and

THE POE COTTAGE, FORDHAM, NEW YORK
Etching by C. F. W. Mielatz

SUMMER AT EASTHAMPTON
Etching by Mrs. Mary Nimmo Moran

richness. In the maturity of his powers he thus struck out into new fields, both by method and in choice of subject.

A large proportion of these artists worked in pure etching, but other aids were occasionally resorted to. For example, by Thomas Moran, and by his wife, Mary Nimmo Moran, who used the roulette in various plates, and "Scotch stone" (a substance used to reduce plates) in *Twilight, Easthampton.* Parrish sometimes roughened his plates by acid or other means, S. J. Ferris employed roulette and stipple, and *Road to the Beach,* by C. F. W. Mielatz, an indefatigable experimenter, is executed in roulette, aquatint and soft-ground etching. The last-named process was employed by J. D. Smillie, C. A. Vanderhoof, Henry Farrer, Kruseman van Elten, and more recently by Mary Cassatt, A. T. Millar, George Senseney, and Mielatz (*Pell Street Balcony,* marked by what Huneker called "his delicate sense of color sparingly indulged in"). The somewhat unfortunate effect of double printing in the sky of J. C. Nicoll's *In the Harbor* is caused by a double needle, and the late Dr. Yale occasionally used a half-dozen or so of needles set in one handle. The use of such short cuts is always of questionable appropriateness.

A noteworthy factor in the production of many of these men is their efficiency as printers. Whistler's penciled "imp" is a familiar addition to proofs of his plates, and some of the last photographs taken of him show him at the press. Not a few of the younger men realized the importance of the printer's art.

The fair sex contributed a notably large proportion of our etchers.   In some cases, too, in a more serious spirit than that which inspired Hood when he wrote of etching:

"It scarce seems a ladylike art that begins
With a scratching and ends with a biting."

Their work was shown separately at the Boston Museum in 1887, and at the Union League Club, New York City, in 1888, with a catalogue for which Mrs. M. G. Van Rensselaer wrote an introduction.   Of this number were Miss Cole (sister of Thomas), who experimented with the etching needle as early as 1844, Eliza Greatorex (who delineated the picturesque side of New York City), Mrs. Anna Lea Merritt (figure subjects), Mrs. E. L. Pierce Getchell, Mrs. J. H. Twachtman ("whose few little plates are treated with surprising freedom and lightness," wrote S. R. Koehler), Ellen Oakford, Gabrielle D. Clements, Blanche Dillaye, Margaret W. Lesley (Mrs. H. K. Bush-Brown), Mary Cassatt and Mrs. Moran.   The best of their work deserves praise unmodified by any reference to sex.   Mrs. Moran, a virile talent, had energetic emphasis and bold directness, with a sure eye for pictorial effect.   Her *Autumn, Edge of Georgica Pond, Easthampton,* is of a sunny lightness. Miss Mary Cassatt has helped us to see the beauty in the child without calling in the adventitious aid of silly prettiness or saccharine sentimentality.   Her dry points, with wise restraint of linear expression, robust in method and sensitive in feeling, are among the best work produced in this field by Americans.

MOTHER AND BABY
Dry-point by Mary Cassatt

While this wide-spreading movement was witnessed here, Whistler[had]found his Venice, a city of picturesque bits of canal, of inviting doorways and cool arches, light balconies and graceful architectural ornament. Such he showed her in delightfully airy and sunny impressions, without paraphernalia of dogal grandeur and civic or ecclesiastical display and circumstance which lent its pomp to the Venetian scenes of painters such as Bellini. With Whistler in Venice were Frank Duveneck, Otto Bacher, Theodore M. Wendel (of a "delicate and charming style") and others. Charles A. Corwin, George E. Hopkins and H. M. Rosenberg, in Italy at about the same time, produced isolated plates, akin to each other in manner and subject. The Whistler influence has been felt to most recent times. Duveneck did three plates of the Ducal Palace, Riva, so much in Whistler's manner that they were actually taken for that artist's work.² 'Bacher executed etchings of unusual force, concerning which Seymour Haden said (of the Venice set) : "The whole of it, accessories and all, evinces a strong artistic feeling. Bold and painter-like treatment characterizes it throughout." S. R. Koehler notes that he "passed unmoved the Walhalla . . . and then stopped to make a loving study of a rickety old wooden bridge." Koehler adds that later, under the influence of Whistler, Bacher's manner "o'erleaped itself and degenerated into wildness. And yet it is impossible to close oneself against the telling effect of these plates. A stormy life surges in them." S. L. Wenban, an Ohio artist who did much of his work in Munich, and whose somewhat Haden-like *A Bavarian*

Forest won high praise at the *Salon,* was addicted to detail, yet broad in manner. His work offers such contrasts as his *Rushing Brook,* of a Klinger-like hardness and precision, and the remarkably free and airy *Brook in Winter.* J. Alden Weir went his own experimental way in a number of interesting and striking landscapes and some portraits. Wrestling with the process, he subjugated it to more than one subject or mood. And when he aimed at completeness of effect, it was tone he had in view, not detail of form. He did not specialize; anything was welcome to his inquiring spirit. John H. Twachtman echoed the delicate impressions of evanescent light and color effects of his paintings in a few etchings. Robert F. Blum produced some twenty plates, among them his own portrait and *The Hag,* of a peculiar richness and snap. Blum produced one plate (*The Modern Etcher,* 1883: a portrait of W. M. Chase, who himself did a *Jester* and two or three other plates), by a process of photographing a pen-and-ink drawing on to a specially prepared ground. The result was a pen-and-ink drawing rather than an etching. The movement found support in the "American Art Review," edited by Sylvester Rosa Koehler, which was issued at Boston during 1880–82, and published etchings by a number of American artists. The "American Art Review" went out of existence, but the seed was sown, and a number of sumptuous volumes were published in limited editions, and often in various forms to suit different pocketbooks (e. g., with "vellum proofs" at $100, "satin proofs" at

OLD MILLS, COAST OF VIRGINIA
Soft-ground etching by James D. Smillie

$50 and "Japan proofs" at $35, all three with "remarques"—"remarques" must have had a rare attraction for the budding amateur—and "regular impressions on etching paper" at $12.50). There were brought out during 1884–90, "Original Etchings by American Artists," "Some Modern Etchings," "Recent American Etchings," "American Etchings," "Notable Etchings by American Artists," "Representative Etchings by Artists of To-Day in America," and "Selected Etchings," each volume with text by either S. R. Koehler or Ripley Hitchcock. Among artists represented in these publications, whose names have not already been mentioned, are J. •Wells Champney, Gabrielle D. Clements, Elliott Daingerfield, Wm. St. John Harper, Joseph F. Sabin, S. A. Schoff, Charles Volkmar, Frank Waller.

Beside the many names mentioned in connection with this "New York Etching Club period," there are a considerable number more: A. H. Bicknell, C. H. Eaton, John H. Niemeyer, William Sartain, M. J. Burns, C. C. Curran, Edward Loyal Field, Louis K. Harlow, F. Leo Hunter (facile workers for publishers, the last three), Roland Rood, Theodore Wust, H. Bolton Jones, Robert v. V. Sewell, Carroll Beckwith, R. C. Minor (whose *The Close of Day* has an unassuming, reposeful mood), Robertson K. Mygatt, R. Cleveland Coxe, and Leigh H. Hunt, who has found subjects in many places, and fixed them on copper with a fine and sober sense of composition. About this time also was formed the "Society of American Etchers," which had for one of its objects the

limitation of editions, "every proof being guaranteed by
the stamp of the Society."

There were even some incursions into the field of book-
illustration: Samuel Colman's plates for Alice Durand
Field's "Palermo" (1885), and Dean Sage's "The
Ristigouche and its Salmon Fishing" (Edinburgh, 1888),
with etchings by Platt, Henry Sandham and Mrs. A. L.
Merritt.   The last-named illustrated a volume on her de-
ceased husband, and Goethe's "Faust" (1888) and "Hermann and Dorothea" (1889) were issued in Philadelphia,
with etchings by Hermann Faber.   Publications of the
Bibliophile Society of Boston have contained etched portraits by W. H. W. Bicknell (known by his larger portraits of Lincoln and Franklin) and James Fagan.

Etching has also been called to the service of the inter-
est in local and national history.   S. Hollyer illustrated
New York City and Robert Shaw delineated, for the
Colonial Society of America, buildings and places promi-
nently identified with the colonial history of our country.
Etching was used for portraits by H. B. Hall, Max and
Albert Rosenthal, and with particular sureness of hand
and richness of effect by S. A. Schoff.   Thomas Johnson
etched a number of portraits including those of Lincoln,
Walt Whitman (with hat), Cardinal Manning, Theo. L.
De Vinne, and S. P. Avery.   In our day, Jacques Reich
has issued a number of carefully executed portraits of
American statesmen, Washington, Jefferson, Franklin,
Webster, Lincoln, Cleveland, McKinley among the num-
ber.   S. L. Smith and James S. King have signed some

portraits, including one of Theodore Roosevelt in each case.

The remarkable amount of work produced from the early seventies to the early nineties, naturally implied public support, but the cause of painter-etching suffered in the end. Commercial possibilities were exploited. As the "Sun" pointed out in 1894, the publishers of reproductive etchings killed the goose that laid the golden eggs. The story picture also did its work. We cannot get away entirely from the subject-matter. The artist cannot appeal by technique alone, if that technique be a mere parade of its self-sufficient perfection. But the cheap sentimentality usually most sure of general applause has as its almost inevitable concomitants a paucity of ideas, a slick manipulation that conceals its essential weakness. This sounds rather ungracious as an introduction to a paragraph on reproductive etching. For we had men of adaptative talent who rendered into black-and-white the canvases of celebrated artists—or such as would be sure to bring returns. The paintings were not always worthy of the talent exercised in their reproduction. There's the element of weakness through which this art lapsed, after its day of rich harvest for publisher and artist. Reproductive etching, employed on worthy work, was its own best justification. It is an unfortunate prejudice which rejects any reproductive work while accepting inferior productions because they are "painter-etchings." Robert W. Weir's plan to reproduce old pictures, as early as 1820, was not repeated until half-a-century later. In 1875 S. J. Ferris, a careful worker, who stippled and

rouletted to get tone and color, etched a head after Fortuny and two plates after Knaus. The success encour-
aged the publisher to order *The Chariot Race,* which was
etched by Ferris and Peter Moran. Wray records that
prepared copper being not easily procurable at that date,
these two artists "pounded out the bottom of a copper
boiler, and coated it with their home-made preparation."
A few years later, James S. King, then in Paris, produced
some heads after Rembrandt, sold to "L'Art" in 1882,
and Hals, executed with a knowledge of the process due
partly perhaps to discriminating study of the works of
Flameng and other French masters.

This newly opened field was cultivated by dealers with
such energy that a number of artists were enlisted in the
cause. Nearly all of these were won from the ranks of
painters and not from those of professional engravers
and etchers. Two of the latter who were particularly
well equipped for such work—James D. Smillie and
Stephen A. Schoff—were almost entirely passed over.
Smillie did some smaller plates after Bridgman, Homer,
Jacque, Pasini, for the "American Art Review" and a
large and effective one after Huntington's *Goldsmith's
Daughter.* Schoff's portrait of Mrs. C. F. Adams after
Wm. M. Hunt showed a formal, though not mechanical,
manner that well rendered the "quiet nobility of the
original." Koehler cites later work as examples of the
freer style which he developed,—portraits of Gen.
Devens after Vinton, of a young lady after Thayer, and
At the Piano after Fowler—each showing effective variation of treatment in accord with the original. Sidney L.

Smith did some small plates of remarkable delicacy, used as book illustrations,—Bastien-Lepage's *Jeanne d'Arc* and Makart's *Diana's Hunting Party*—as well as etchings of art objects for the defunct "Studio" of New York. In the list of names signed to reproductive etchings there will be recognized a number of painters, interpreting, with varying degrees of success, their own works as well as those of other painters. Thomas Moran showed a truly "phenomenal skill"; Hamilton Hamilton signed such ambitious plates as *The Communicants* after Breton (1886), *The Fisherman's Courtship* (1889), and Hovenden's *In the Hands of the Enemy;* Shirlaw translated E. Johnson's *The Reprimand.* Charles Walter Stetson's large plates after French artists, executed for a private gentleman in Providence, are characterized by Koehler as highly effective despite wild daring and deficient schooling. S. J. Guy, C. Y. Turner, F. Dielman, W. H. Lippincott, Leon Moran, C. R. Grant and others were similarly engaged in putting into black-and-white the works of various painters, principally Americans. Others were more completely identified with the etcher's art: James Fagan, H. Pruett Share, Miss Edith Penman, F. Raubichek (among whose plates was *Evening Shadows,* after Minor), Parrish, Charles A. Walker, who rendered French landscapists or Mauve with fine adaptation to the original, though perhaps too strong a tendency to reproduce brush-marks rather than spirit, and Aug. Barry, who copied Charles H. Miller's Long Island landscapes with somewhat untutored force, and reproduced also Haden's

Breaking up of the Agamemnon, and *Shere Mill Pond* (published by J. M. Huffington). G. W. H. Ritchie attempted to serve the timely interest in his "Etchings of notable Academy Pictures," a handbook issued in 1885.

One is struck by the quick conquest of technique, the very respectable degree of attainment. Yet one feels that in some cases the task was approached a little too light-heartedly. The qualities demanded of a reproductive etcher form a combination not too common: knowledge of form and color, ability to adapt himself with sympathy and understanding to the work which he is interpreting, and that most necessary factor, patience. It does not seem that all the men had the necessary equipment for the work which the publishers led them to undertake. The abuse of reproductive etching caused the New York Etching Club to close its exhibitions to most of these productions. Urgency of publishers caused overproduction, and turned legitimate interest into a fad. There came a demand for elaboration, which, as Hitchcock said, "injured etching by blurring its legitimate characteristics." Effects of tonality were aimed at, in which the distinguishing characteristic of the etching, the line, was lost sight of. The art was cheapened, commercial products found their place on the "bargain counter." Discredit was brought on the whole business.

Meanwhile, painter-etching languished. Koehler, as early as 1892, found that the various etching societies, organized with such enthusiasm, had been for years in a state of innocuous somnolence. When etching was on the wane, Koehler, Hitchcock, J. D. Smillie and Wray agreed that though commercially the fad was over, and production lessened, the average quality would be better. It would respond to a demand for, and understanding of, the personal force which makes a painter etching what it is, a thing apart, with characteristics based on its very nature and therefore different from those in any other graphic art.

To-day we find that etching as a means of direct expression for the artist has come to its own again.

CHAPTER II

ETCHING: THE PRESENT REVIVAL

IN recent years the fascination of this art as a means of original creation has been appreciated by those of the younger generation. Classes were organized at the National Academy and the Art Students' League, in New York City, under Smillie, Mielatz, Vojtech Preissig and Pennell. General exhibitions as well as single-artist shows have been arranged in increasing numbers by print departments of museums and libraries, and by print dealers. The Painter Gravers of America and the New York Etching Club have done their work and gone. Effort now crystallizes around the Chicago Society of Etchers and the Brooklyn Society of Etchers, both broadening into a national inclusiveness, and the California Society of Etchers. And the Academy has included the graphic arts in its shows. This renaissance is anything but startling or revolutionary. In the best of this newer work the true nature of the medium is respected and is adapted to each individuality—a necessity in the practice of any art.

Etching is with us to-day,—quite. The movement for painter-etching has persisted, in fact, ever since the impulse of the old Etching Club. Not always vigorously, but on the whole with increasing force. To-day the art flourishes in a manner heartening and in a measure also calling for caution, for fear of overdoing. It is so easy to make an etching. Passing flirtation will not disclose the finer nature of etching to the artist,—nor will a protracted dalliance without serious intentions. To strive, as did Weir for example, for expression in a medium with serious and sympathetic interest in its own peculiar qualities, its bounds and its opportunities, involves a fundamental attitude on which it may not be amiss to dwell in these days of facile practice of the art, an easy yielding to the temptation to print.

We have etchers of various minds, moods and degrees of ability. They illustrate the adaptability of the etched line to figure pieces, portraits, landscapes, city scenes, architecture and still life. They exemplify the interest of home scenes and the lure of old-world subjects. They offer the incisive line in pure etching, the velvety richness of dry-point, the quivering crayon-like stroke of soft ground etching. They give us the etched line in clean-wiped nakedness and clothed in the gauze of retroussage or the heavier garments of aquatint. They demonstrate the possibilities of color. They give the choice of technical dexterity or of a personal force that thrusts back technique into its proper place as a language.

Naturally, in some of the earlier productions by these recent arrivals the influence of certain vigorous personalities in the annals of the art makes itself felt,—Whistler, Meryon, Legros, Strang, Zorn or Helleu—in that gradation of variations lying between imitation and adaptation. The individual temperament may at first attach itself to the prior expression which strikes the chord most sympathetic to it, until the artist, passing through this

transitory stage, attains his natural mode of expression.
Some of the younger etchers have worked abroad mainly,
but not a few have found inspiration in their own land,
seeking subjects in city and country, from Gloucester to
San Francisco, and presenting them with more or less
clearly individual point of view. Often, indeed, have
they revealed to us new phases, different aspects, even the
very essence, of things which we had seen unseeing.

Joseph Pennell, long resident in England, has in recent
years come back to preach the gospel of beauty to be
found here, and has exercised the mastery of his art in
the delineation of the tall buildings of New York and
the industrial establishments of Pittsburgh and other
places. In his hymn to the "Wonders of Work" he has
been joined occasionally. Thus, by R. M. Pearson in
Structural Iron, by Thomas E. Tallmadge in *Steel Construction,* by F. K. Detwiller in *Framing Up* (an aquatint picture of the building of wooden ships, one of a
series done for the Government).

Charles Henry White again emphasized the old truth
that there is beauty to be found in every-day surroundings
and in our own land, and set before us the picturesque
qualities of street and alley, of waterfront and factory
district, in New York, Boston, New Orleans, Pittsburgh
and other American cities. Many of his etchings were
reproduced as illustrations for his humorous and
sprightly papers on various phases of city life, published
in "Harper's Magazine." B. J. Olsson-Nordfeldt has
offered individual impressions of New York and particularly of Chicago. The titles of his *Chicago series* are an

From "Harper's Magazine." Copyright, 1906, by Harper & Brothers
A BIT OF MOUNT VERNON ST., BOSTON
Etching by Charles Henry White

illuminating index to his preferences as to subject: *Grain Elevators, Smoke, Coal-chutes, Gas Tank Town, Bessemer Converters.* He has also rendered the spirit of Provincetown, whose whaling flavor likewise attracted John C. Vondrous, who, to quote Royal Cortissoz, has "an admirable pictorial faculty," and who has steadily improved. Henry Winslow, insisting less, perhaps, on the topography of the locality than some etchers of particular places, and more on a personal viewpoint, has also chosen scenes in New York. E. T. Hurley, pupil of Duveneck, vocationally identified with Rookwood Pottery, avocationally etches his tribute to his native city, Cincinnati. These unassuming, direct records of things that have meant much to him have at various times been reproduced and gathered into attractive little volumes.

In his *Norlands series* Cadwallader Washburn pictured the meadows, woods and streams of Maine in a spirit of loving intimacy with nature; and J. André Smith has sketched the shores of the Hudson, a bridge in Connecticut, bits of Central Park, New York, *trains and apartment houses* in New York City, a tree-lined brook in Long Island, in a straightforward, natural manner, always with a personal touch and viewpoint. Furthermore, New York City has offered picturesque nooks and corners to Henry Deville (who happily presents the unfamiliar, lovingly seen, without flourish), H. A. Webster, W. J. Quinlan, C. B. King, Vondrous, W. A. Sherwood, V. Trowbridge, John T. Arms, H. B. Shope (the two latter bringing their architectural training into play in the delineation of buildings), Hassam; Sears Gallagher (whose Brooklyn Bridge is one of his most effective plates), John Marin (whose sky-scrapers of his later period bend and sway like storm-swept trees), and Curt Szekessy; the Harlem River to H. H. Osgood; Chicago to Pearson, Philip Sawyer and Katherine Merrill; Long Branch to A. T. Millar; Philadelphia to Walter Hale.

The West, where Will Sparks,. Gottardo Piazzoni and Mrs. Marion Holden Pope are among those who have directed local interest to the charm of the art, has formed an alluring subject to some of our etchers. Edward Borein and Rose Santee (Southwestern country subjects) have been held by the picturesqueness of the Ranch. R. F. Seymour lingers over *Old Cypress Trees* at Del Monte.

Roi Partridge presents Mount Rainier as *The Marvelous Mountain*, with an energetic line, and R. B. Harshe, with similar linear boldness, shows *Ostrich Tree, Monterey* and other bits of California. Ralph M. Pearson, having joined the Taos group, has in his latest work aimed at an abstract esthetic and decorative expression, the facts, while not evaded, being remolded to fit design; "Splendid in space and in a sense of imagination," says the "N. Y. Times."

George Elbert Burr devotes himself to the presentation of the American Desert, with a realism that bears the restraint of dignified reserve, and what one has called a "subtle imagery." Aquatint and soft ground at times soften the asperity of line.

Landscape in its relation to mankind, and *vice versa*, is the theme of the Arizona scenes by Mahonri Young, who works with a lightness of suggestion that seems like

THE FIRST SNOW
Etching by Mahonri Young

a reaction from his sculptures. Yet his gesture is big, and gives a feeling of compact solidity. His *First Snow,* a jolly bit of observation, men and boys scurrying about in an ant-like activity, is a scene in New Jersey. In New Jersey his namesake, C. Jac Young, has found thankful subjects in the meadows, at Hook Mountain, and elsewhere. There are further specialties in the interpretation of the appeal of local interest. Earl H. Reed has made quite his own field the dune region along Lake Michigan, which moves him to a graceful expression of mood, and which he describes also with the pen in the volume "Sketches in Duneland" (1918). Frederick T. Weber has done a *Long Island Series,* unaffected bits of roadside views with accent of dry-point that does not lose the line in the mud of burr. Reticence in contrasts of accent appears in the soft, almost hesitant strokes that mark the intimate bits of midwestern country by W. G. Reindel. Gloucester has drawn Little, Lever and Nordell.

There are, too, artists who have pictured our life here and there, as choice or chance or the daily task led them about. R. M. Pearson has observed *Asphalters* in Chicago, or *Winter* at Elmerhol, or *High-Gate Bridge,* his industrial subjects sometimes having a slightly allegorical flavor born of the concept, not of the trappings of symbolical mummery. Earl Horter, whose ever-ready pencil traces his wanderings, has etched, with the quality of an engaging style, *Smelters in Pittsburgh,* an *Antique Shop* in Nantucket, or *Balconies* in New Orleans, the last-named of a crisp lightness of suggestion. Thomas

W. and Helen B. Stevens did a series of Universities and Colleges, Huc Mazelot Luquiens has devoted himself to Yale. And there is notably John W. Winkler, of the Pacific Coast, whose city views are set down with distinction and a pliant yet incisive line that somehow recalls Whistler of the early London period and yet remains individual.

In the process of de-specialization, there comes, for instance, H. B. Shope, drawn to architectural subjects naturally by profession, yet going off into the open country to enjoy his delight in tree and meadow and hill, of which he tells with delicacy and elegance, and the reticence of restraint of the well-bred. John Taylor Arms delineates architectural subjects (lingering lovingly and painstakingly over a chimera, for instance), landscapes, horses, ships and what not, with a growing feeling for tonal effect. The village street, Fifth Avenue, a boat-house, the lake-like pattern of low-tide water, bathers at the waterside, all comes easily within the scope of Childe Hassam's art. An impressionist interested in problems of color and light, he brings them with him to the copperplate, producing prints that quiver with live sunlight, that are, as the "Evening Post's" critic said in 1915, "the fresh expression . . . of a genuine artist's sense of the delightfulness of life."

An eager, searching experimenter in the processes of the graphic arts, Ernest Haskell has tried various subjects in various media and techniques, always bringing and inducing interest, with a "point of view invariably fresh and engaging," to quote A. E. Gallatin. He never bores you.

Sears Gallagher and F. G. Hall, who has been credited with "searching, discriminating vision," G. A. Hoffmann, W. H. W. Bicknell (*Cape Cod Dunes* and the like), Stanley W. Woodward bring further notes of interest and variety into the record of interpretation of our landscape. To that, Paul Dougherty has added a few plates,—*Wooded Landscape, Shipyard, Cedars by the Sea*—the unpretentious impressions of a painter, set down without hesitation, with knowledge, and with reserve.

The sea and its varying coast, subject ever engrossing, is pictured by Charles H. Woodbury with a certain big air of impatient gesture in the swirling lines of sky and wave, a line widely spaced and with an errant appearance but a definite effect. More calm, though emphatic, is Philip Little in plates such as *Herring Weirs, Maine,* and George E. Wales makes sober pictures of ships.

In plates such as those by these artists we find much honest, and frequently successful, endeavor to show that subjects are at our door and to seize and present the character of locality. Such art in its highest potentiality will be a reflection of American life and aims and progress, summarized by the artist's power of grasping and suggesting the prevailing spirit of time and place and people.

Figure etchers have increased in recent years, and with a growing range of subjects. George ("Pop") Hart, of whom the "N. Y. Times" said that he "works with the freedom and the bondage of a true classic," and that "the pattern of his etching of women bathing in mountain pools . . . is superb in its variety and restraint," achieves in his picture of a plowman (*The Toilers*) a suggestion of typical experience that makes you forget matters of technique. If recollection of Millet rises, it is but faintly, for there is no hint of similarity in treatment. Eugene Higgins also deals with types, skirting the domain of allegory almost, investing his figures and their setting of mysteriously shadowed buildings, or of racked landscapes, with an expression of theme nearly always set in a minor key. He does not preach, except by presentation of condition, any more than does John Sloan, who looks with kindly humor and tolerance on the life about him, viewing it, as W. B. McCormick puts it, neither from the clouds nor from the gutter, but from the sidewalk. What he sees he presents with a faint suggestion of John Leech, quietly pointing the moral of the scene, with no trace of the bitterness of the over-zealous reformer. W. J. Glackens, likewise a delineator of the tenement-house district, has done but a few plates. Jerome Myers is attracted by child life in New York City's East Side, and Therese Bernstein has made such notes of the life of that section as her soft-ground "The Organ Grinder." Edward Hopper has a sense of humor apparently based on observation that goes beyond the surface, as in *East Side Interior*. H. Devitt Welsh shows an imagination somewhat grim, perhaps even sardonic, in plates such as *John Barleycorn*.

In A. Allen Lewis one encounters a certain sternness of style, an acerbity almost, that moves him at times into the neighborhood of Legros. The synthetization in his work expresses not only essential fact but essential significance in a subject meeting his mood and viewpoint. In a different mood, delight in the subject *per se,* are the plates of Dwight C. Sturges, among them a character study of an old copper-plate printer, and Arthur W. Heintzelman, whose subjects vary from a genially straightforward presentation of old age such as his multi-prize-winning *Three Score and Ten* to his pictures of a child playing in the water, its nude little body in unconscious adjustment to the accompaniment of decorative pattern which branches fling across the scenes. In the matter of setting, Kerr Eby emphasizes the fact that it is often difficult to pigeon-hole an artist by specialty. The human interest, whether freely indicated or subtly implied, always enters into its proper relation with the surroundings. As a soldier in the World War he pictured his fellows-in-arms with human sympathy, an artist's sensitiveness to mode of presentation, and the emphasis of a thinking observer. But he notes also a little tragedy of animal life, a disconsolate horse *Left behind* in a driving rain. And he shows us a *Beggar* in Algiers, or camels (*Desert Freight*) or what not, with the same welding of man and his entourage into one. Then back to his own land for unexciting themes which yet, as in the simple *Hay Barrack,* palpitate with the homely and intimate feeling of the scene. Keen observation appears in plates such as *Fitting the Shoe—the Blacksmith Shop,* by Haydon Jones, the cartoonist. Margaret Ryerson and Mathilde de

Cordoba make a specialty of studies in the grace of childhood.

W. Auerbach-Levy has offered characteristic single-figure studies of grave and bearded old men of Israel. Emil Fuchs turns aside at times from sculpture and painting to etch portraits and other figure-pieces. And Kenneth Hayes Miller, too, has made excursions into this field. By way of contrast to all this, there is Troy Kinney, who weaves the motions of stage dancers into designs that twirl with life made into engaging swirl of pattern. Anne Goldthwaite, who has etched some dancers with a joyous vivacity and lightness, has brought the same gayety to other subjects, including some portraits marked by a deft, caressing line. Then there is the humor of Peggy Bacon. In the field of portraiture, Otto J. Schneider has produced suavely virile characterization of Lincoln, Emerson and Mark Twain, as well as graceful female portraits, with a suggestion of Helleu, but individual nevertheless. Dainty elegance marks the female portraits by A. G. Learned. Walter Tittle's portraits of men include the series of the delegates to the Washington Disarmament Conference; his bit of unposed femininity wearing a *Sun Hat* is done less incisively, with a noteworthy translucency of shadow on the face. And there are Jacques Reich's finished heads of prominent men.

Still with the figure etchers, we turn to the animal world, which Will Simmons presents in a vein of quaint humor with a basis of seriousness, as in his monkey subject, *Pursuit of the Impossible,* or with an unmixed

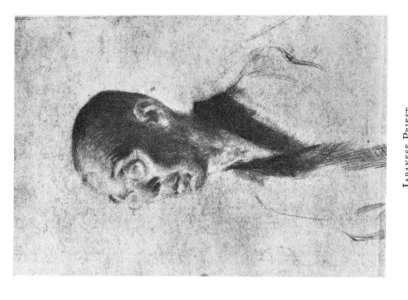

RALPH WALDO EMERSON
Etching by Otto J. Schneider

JAPANESE PRIEST
Dry-point by Cadwallader Washburn

preoccupation with form, giving a feeling of sculpturesque solidity in his *Two Condors* massed on a rock. Unassuming little bird pictures bear the signature of Charles E. Heil. Dog portraits by Robert Armistead have noteworthy landscape settings. Roland Clark shows a sportsman's delight in his etchings of game birds, a specialty that has been cultivated in a similar spirit and with notable success by Frank W. Benson, who to a strong love of animal life joins an accurate knowledge of the movements of birds, and an accurate draughtsmanship to interpret it. Often he shows his water birds in flight, with ever-renewed stress on the decorative pattern they made against the sky. Then again he takes us to a placid pool in which *Broadbills* are swimming, alert yet calmly sure, their bodies rendered with appropriate application of dry-point. Incidentally he has produced a new variety of sporting print, strangely different in its fine artistic vision from the sort of thing which once, in the Alken period, served the British sportsman.

Of the etchers of city views and landscape, some have worked abroad as well. Olsson-Nordfeldt has etched Italian, Spanish and African series. Osgood has been occupied by Paris and London, André Smith by rural England and Spain. C. W. Dahlgreen has similarly wandered in search of the picturesque. Winslow has gone to Paris, and Vondrous to Prague. Louis C. Rosenberg's Italian and Spanish scenes include *Isola Tiberina*, of a precise lightness.

A noteworthy group of men has lived mostly or altogether abroad, working much under foreign influence

(Meryon, for instance) and choosing foreign subjects.
Among them E. L. Warner, with a delicate sense of quaint
old-world beauties. The grocery, an old mill, at Mon-
treuil-sur-Mer, disclosed to him their hidden charm.
Donald Shaw MacLaughlan, a Canadian, interprets
locality in a personal manner which, as Wedmore has
pointed out, is neither eccentric nor commonplace. He
changed from the precision and elaboration of his earlier
plates to the freer manner of his Thames and Venetian
subjects, and *Lauterbrunnen,* "one of the few pictures
that realize the vastness of the mountains. . . . Space,
sweep, grandeur, rudeness and power are found in this
remarkable plate, which also is beautifully obedient to the
canons of the art."; Herman A. Webster, delighting in
out-of-the-way quarters of old French towns with sun-
baked walls and mysterious shadows in dark corners, has
felt the stern charm of Meryon, yet goes on his own way.
In some of his plates, definite sureness is linked with a
certain severity, in others there is a richness which in some
original drawings becomes a lusciousness that makes one
regret that he has not tried the lithographic crayon.
George C. Aid, attracted by the problem of sunlight sim-
mering on hot stones and on vibrating water, offered five
different impressions of the cool arches of the Pont Neuf
in Paris and the houses beyond, in the quivering light of a
summer day. His *Location de Voitures à Bras* contrasts
in its vigorous handling with the airy grace of the *Hotel
de Cluny,* with its vine-crowned wall and the slate-covered
sloping roofs beyond.

Louis Orr, brilliant, with a sweeping, even redundant

gesture, "loves the picturesque," as Clement Janin says, "and at need creates it," massing his lines with what W. H. Downes calls "a fine sense of monumental effect." Roi Partridge sees a Seine bridge from the standpoint of *Dancing Water,* dancing in broad bands of line that weave a pattern without losing limpidity. Alonzo E. Webb began to attract attention in Paris about 1921 with *Sainte Chapelle* and other plates. Robert F. Logan interprets French villages and French architecture, as the "N. Y. Times" finds, "with a flexible formality that accords with the spirit of France." Katherine Kimball draws without frills, with a dry soberness that has its subtleties of honest observation. Where shall one stop in recounting etched proof of the attraction of Paris? Thomas R. Congdon saw and placed *St. Etienne du Mont* with solidity of mass and richness of shadow. Frank M. and Caroline H. Armington and Adelaide Vose Congdon see the picturesque somewhat objectively and so present it in clear language.

Where these artists have shown the structural aspect of Paris, the life of the city has attracted Lester G. Hornby, seen as a picture in which houses and streets and people form a characteristic ensemble, recorded with gayety and a light yet precise indication. That gives us such a delightful bit of alley life as *Passage de la petite Boucherie,* full of rich shadows and bright sunlight.

All these artists have devoted themselves mainly to scenes in Paris and other parts of France, that apparently inexhaustible storehouse of attractive subjects. Others have satisfied their sense of the picturesque in Italy. G.

Walter Chandler found odd bits in Florence, Milan and Perugia,—a covered archway, a dimly lighted shop interior, women washing in the little stream flowing at the rear of their houses, dark arches of sunny bridges. John Marin, when he turned to etching in 1906, produced delicate views of Paris, Venice and Amsterdam.

Both Florence and Venice have been pictured by Ernest D. Roth, at first with a careful adherence to detailed fact and the use of the line to render tones. In his later work this painstaking observation has been subordinated to the tact of discrimination; having first learned what he might put in, he learned what he could leave out,—which is quite different from leaving out what you have not learned to express. His line, though yet definite, has become ingratiating rather than insistent. Earl Horter's excursion into Naples is also to be noted. And Mrs. Bertha E. Jaques, long secretary of the Chicago Society of Etchers, has done engaging bits of intimate waterside, such as *The Tangle, Chioggia, Near Venice.*

Whistler's influence is apparent in the earlier Venetian plates of more than one artist. One who so began is Cadwallader Washburn, who has found subjects in Venice, Japan, Mexico and Maine, and has presented them with feeling for the charm of every-day nature and for the picturesque qualities of buildings. In his Mexican series he shows buildings varying, in their aspect, with place, time and conditions of lighting, drawn with synthetic definiteness and direct sureness. Most recently he has haunted the bull-ring to make snapshots on copper with the eye and interest of a connoisseur of the Hispanic sport. Where Washburn was attracted by the gardens of Japan, or Chandler by the minarets of Benares,ᶜAddison T. Millar found food for his artistic leanings and his experimentative nature in Algiers, ever dear to artists. Yet he turned easily to the grayer skies of Holland, finding at Laren in a lane of birches, or a farmhouse or some other simple *motif,* a subject sufficient to disengage an expression of mood. Passing aspect or humor sometimes led him to print a day and a night effect from the same plate. That implies the well-understood manipulation of various rags, as well as other aids, in the process of wiping the plate after it has been inked and before the paper is laid upon it and run through the press. The use of "soft-ground etching" and other methods was for him a further means of attaining desired effects.

English scenes include Arthur Covey's *Victoria Station, London,* of a Brangwyn-like swing that gets its effect by its measured vigor more, perhaps, than by niceties of biting or line-work. In such plates as *The Pool Below London Bridge,* Henry Martin Hoyt (died 1920) showed a fine sense of composition and a generalization that expressed a feeling for tone with comparatively few lines. *Whistler's Funeral Service, Old Chelsea Church,* was observed and set down by Frank A. Nankivell. Kent and other places have yielded subjects to Katharine Kimball. J. Paul Verrées has brought from Belgium a natural interest in homeland scenes. Charles K. Gleeson, making transcripts here and there, in Venice, in Burgos, achieves in *Tavern of Seven Trees* a pleasing lightness of touch and an unconventional limpidity in the water.

The aid of color-printing has been invoked by several of our etchers. W. A. Sherwood has used color for his city views, Maud Hunt Squire for scenes of French life, cleverly done in few lines and flat tones of color, Mathilde de Cordoba for her amiable dry-points of child-life. Some of G. E. Burr's Colorado scenes are delicate color-printings from one plate, with soft-ground and aquatint as added aids. The use of color in pure etching is comparatively rare, because the bitten line is too tenuous a vehicle for this purpose. Generally, therefore, recourse is had to aquatint, the grain of which is better adapted to render flat tints, or even tints manipulated into variety of strength. Soft-ground etching is sometimes added. Such work is noted in the chapter on aquatint.

American etchers have increased greatly in recent years, and it is easy to grow enthusiastic over the vogue of etching. Closer study, and an elimination of leniency based on patriotic or local sympathy, may sweep away more than one temporary reputation. That will not hurt American art. There is enough in the general product of a sufficiently high order, there is a large enough proportion of etchers whose good intentions are backed up by an appreciable degree of ability, to make it possible to regard this recent movement with some degree of satisfaction.

There has been appreciation of some phases of this effort, as far as outward signs go. These younger men are being assiduously written up in magazine articles and in print-sellers catalogues, their works are frequently exhibited, and one hears of sales. "One-man shows" at the galleries of dealers, and in museums and clubs, have been devoted to various etchers. Widely differing individualities seek and find expression in this art, so intimate in character. There is no violent novelty in the various personal phases of this movement, no obstreperous shriek, no blatant blare of revolt. Individuality finds expression in accordance with the limits and possibilities of the medium. This attitude, the only proper one in any form of art, finds technical expression for a realization of the possibilities of a medium combined with a given individuality. Each medium, be it brush and canvas, chisel and stone, burin and wood-block, or needle and copper-plate, has its possibilities and its limits, both of which must be clearly understood to produce the best results, results to which the nature of the medium gives its characteristic flavor. That does not imply hampering of individuality, but simply its orderly expression. Submission to the necessities imposed by the tool is no more a curb on genius than the grammar of a language.

Etching is not an art of big effects, of striking appeal to the great mass. Etching is eminently a "painter art," reproducing a given design in a number of prints of which each is essentially the artist's work, particularly if the artist is his own printer, as Whistler was, as Pennell is, and many others. It forms an immediate, direct medium for the expression of the more intimate phases of artistic personality. It is based on precise delicacy, not on broad impressions, yet its strength lies in summariness, in compressed statement and not in abundant detail. It is an art of suggestion, of selection. An exhibition of etchings fills in art somewhat the function of chamber music concerts in the sister art.

Subjects are at our door. American subjects for the American artist, the American public, and the American collector. Our art can be of the soil and reflect our life and aims, our traditions and our progress, seen through the selecting and idealizing vision of the artist.

These facts make the present revival of interest in etching more than a passing fad, make it a hopeful sign, a factor of importance in the future development of American art.

CHAPTER III

ENGRAVING IN LINE AND STIPPLE: THE EIGHTEENTH CENTURY

THE history of graphic art in America, before the Revolution, is not extensive. A young people wresting its existence from nature and gradually growing into national life, had no time for the cultivation of the arts Any satisfaction of esthetic wants had to come mainly from Europe.

During the period of discovery and settlement, the illustrations by Jacques Le Moyne for his "Narratio" of the expedition sent to Florida in 1564 under Jean Ribaut and by John White for the account of Raleigh's Virginia venture of 1585-86 (both issued by DeBry), the plates in Champlain's "Voyages," John Smith's "General History of Virginia" (1624), and Du Creux's "Historiæ Canadensis" (1664) comprise practically all there was of contemporary illustrated books relating to this country and its aborigines.

As settlements grew up and expanded, views of the same were prepared in Europe, particularly in the case of larger communities such as Boston or New York. Of the latter, for example, there exists an interesting series of views. The earliest, published in "Beschrijvinghe van Virginia, Neuw Nederlandt [etc.]," by Joost Hartgers, in 1651, shows the city about 1630. Then come the Visscher (about 1652), Montanus (1671), and Allard (1673) views, the "South East" and "South West" views by Canot after Howdell (1768), and so on to 1800, duly listed and described by I. N. Phelps Stokes. Activity increased in this field and the nineteenth century saw a steady flow of such views of the metropolis even before the advent of the camera which records the rapidity of change caused by the rapid disappearance of old buildings,—and of newer ones, too,—and the erection of higher ones.

During the pre-Revolutionary period it was in the field of applied art that American art first effected accomplishment worthy of record. That is seen in our silverware; from those who produced it there came also our earliest engravings on metal. (The first engraving produced in the colonies, C. H. Walsh tells us, was a map, 1683, by R. Simpson.) From the first copper-plate engraver in the Colonies known to us by name, John Conny or Cony, who was working as early as 1700, it was the silversmiths who were among the earliest to supply such line-engravings as the needs of the hour justified. Not a few of these men advertised as engravers on gold, silver, copper, steel, brass and pewter, attacking various metals and problems with the assurance of necessity. Henry Pursell was ready (1775) to do "crests, . . . door-plates, dog collars, etc." Francis Dewing, who came from England in 1716, announced of himself: "he likewise cuts neatly in wood and printeth calicoes." And Rollinson is "credited with having ornamented the silver buttons on

The Rev.ᵈ JONATHAN MAYHEW. DD.
Paſtor of the Weſt Church. BOSTON. N.E.
OB.! JULY. 9ᵗʰ 1766. Æ.46

Line Engraving on Copper by Paul Revere
This portrait, supposed to exist, had not been seen by D. M. Stauffer and
other authorities, until an impression came to light in the New York Public
Library. Shortly after, another one was discovered by C. S. Brigham.

the coat worn by Washington at his inauguration as president."

"The scarcity of metallic money among the early Colonists, and the necessary issue of a paper currency to meet this condition," says Stauffer, "probably created the first serious demand for the work of a copper-plate engraver." John Conny, who did Massachusetts bills of credit in 1702–03, and possibly those of 1690, is our earliest known producer of plates for paper money Among eighteenth century engravers of money were also Thomas Sparrow, who did plates for Maryland issues in 1770–74, and Abner Reed.

Portraiture answered a natural want, and the first native production on copper in this specialty, as far as known, is a copy of an English engraving of the Rev. Increase Mather, "little more than scratched upon copper" in 1701 by Thomas Emmes of Boston, and published in Boston in the same year as a frontispiece to a sermon ("The Blessed Hope, etc.") by Mather. Later portraits such as that of Isaac Watts by James Turner (Boston, 1746), hard as a nail, are labored in helpless striving to gain effect without sufficient skill. Those characteristics one may find even much later,—say in the portrait of Washington, with snake and the motto "Don't tread on me," by Buxton, in "A poetical Epistle to His Excellency George Washington" (Providence, 1781). This plate was copied from the one by William Sharp, the English engraver, in the London (1780) edition of the book. Even at the very end of the century one finds, as in the work of Smither or James Allen (who did a primitive Bonaparte in 1792), a helplessness that is almost touching. The need of maps and the interest in views seem fairly natural. Francis Dewing's plan of Boston (1722), from a drawing by Capt. John Bonner, is presumably the earliest one on copper made in this country. In Cadwallader Colden's "Papers relating to the Indian trade" (New York: Bradford, 1724), there appears a map of the Five Indian Nations, which Mr. Wilberforce Eames thinks was undoubtedly done in New York, and is probably the first one executed in the middle colonies. Others who met the need for maps were Abel Buell, Thomas Johnston (plan of Boston, published by Burgis in 1729), James Turner, M. G. de Bruls (Niagara, 1759), Bernard Romans and William Barker.

Famous among early views is the *South Prospect of the City of New York* (1717) of William Burgis, probably, as W. L. Andrews says, the first view engraved in America. In the New York Historical Society's impression, the engraver's name is torn off; a second one, recently found, is complete, signed *I. Harris Sc.,* as is Bakewell's re-issue (1746). Stauffer believed that Burgis simply published this and other plates (some signed by known engravers), his mezzotint view of Boston Light House being the only engraving signed by Burgis which he had seen. The Burgis view of New York was often copied or adapted, wholly or in part, by various engravers, particularly that portion showing the site of the later Fulton Ferry in Brooklyn. The name of Burgis as publisher appears also on a picture of Harvard College (*A Prospect of the*

Colledges in Cambridge in New England), and on one of the New Dutch Church in New York City.   Still other views serve to indicate gradual increase of home production   There were the *South East View of Boston* (1743), published by William Price; James Turner's view of Boston, with some Indian scenes below ("American Magazine," Boston, 1744) ; *Perspective View of the Pennsylvania Hospital* (1761),—selling for "1 shilling plain and 2 colored,"—by James Claypoole, Jr.; *A South East Prospect of Pennsylvania Hospital*, by J. Steeper and H. Dawkins, after Montgomery and Winters (1775); *North West Prospect of Nassau Hall . . ., N. J.*, by H. Dawkins after W. Tennant; and others, coarse work and thin.

There was other opportunity also for the engravers, book-plates to be done, and business cards (that by Henry Dawkins for Benj. Harbeson quite brave in elaboration of the Chippendale style), billheads, certificates of membership (e.g., Revere's certificate of enlistment in His Majesty's North Battery, Boston).   Also printers' ornaments, such as the coat of arms of William Penn engraved by James Turner, presumably on type-metal, for the title of the "Philadelphia Gazette" (1767), or the type-metal vignette for the "Pennsylvania Magazine" (1775), by J. Smither.   Sheet music, too; by Thomas Johnston, Henry Dawkins ("Urania," a music book, 1761), John Norman (1781), or Isaac Sanford (1783), both title and music being usually engraved by the same hand.

Such incidental productions were executed by Nathaniel

Morse, Thomas Johnston, James Turner, Elisha Gallaudet, James Claypoole, Jr., Henry Dawkins, Nathaniel Hurd, Robert Aitken. Likewise by those who take us more definitely into Revolutionary and post-Revolution days: Abraham Godwin, Bernard Romans, James Smither, John Norman, Benjamin Jones, Paul Revere, N. Dearborn, Joseph Callender, Amos Doolittle, Joseph Bowes, N. Hurd, Robert Scot. And by those whose activity reached well into the following century (in which even A. B. Durand did not disdain to engrave tickets of admission to balls, and like things): William Hamlin, James Poupard, Ralph Rawdon, John Vallance, Peter Rushton Maverick and his son Peter, the latter's card significantly advertising "a general graphic business."

The crudeness of the early prints is more apparent, perhaps, in portraits than elsewhere, but it characterizes eighteenth century work generally. Well into the nineteenth century, in fact, our art was essentially provincial, much of it a reflection, often quite weak, of European models. The many names recorded by Stauffer and others are not infrequently offered in a tone of kindly indulgence or frank apology. "Many of the early portraits which illustrate this crucial period of our history," says W. L. Andrews, "are so coarse and crude in design and execution that by means of their very grotesqueness they exercise a certain weird fascination on the collector." Occasionally one comes across contemporary acknowledgment of insufficiency. Publishers or editors, even as late as the second decade of the nineteenth century, ask the indulgence of their readers on the plea that the illustrations are by native talent,—appealing for aid to an infant industry, as it were. The advertisement of a Bible published by Isaiah Thomas at Worcester in 1791, and for which Joseph H. Seymour did thirty-two engravings, reads: "These plates were engraved . . . in this town in 1791 . . . and the Editor doubts not but a proper allowance will be made for work engraved by an Artist who obtained his knowledge in this country, compared with that done by European engravers who have settled in the United States." The work of our native engravers was not invariably accepted uncritically. Norman's plates in the "Impartial History" (Boston, 1781–82) met with a scathing criticism from the "Freeman's Journal" (Philadelphia), January 26, 1795. The portraits of Knox, Samuel Adams and Green were named as particularly bad, with the comment, "Surely such extraordinary figures are not intended to give the rising generation an improved taste in the arts of design and sculpture." The prints in this American edition of this book are not, apparently, always copied from those in the English one, and even when so copied, there may be changes in detail, as in the full-length Washington, on which Norman has put a different head in a different position. W. L. Andrews adds his testimony to the effect that Norman's portraits of General and Mrs. Washington (Boston, 1782), rare prints by the way, are "atrociously bad" and rival the Doolittle battle-pieces in that respect. As a collector, however, Mr. Andrews did not reject that of which he disapproved from the artistic standpoint. We may join him in open-eyed realization of the faults of much of this early work without either lessening our patriotico-sentimental affection for it or having any fear of lowering its price in the collector's market. These early attempts on copper appeal to us because they bear the very imprint of those days. Human activity, more than art, speaks to us from these weak efforts.

Through the Revolution and its after results the American colonists were naturally thrown more on their own resources. Furthermore, they did things that made history and that called for illustration of events and portraits of chief actors. In the first place, to carry on the war, money was needed, and examination of examples of the paper currency of that time is interesting occupation. Some of it is partly engraved and partly printed; or, again, the border may be a composite affair of type-metal ornaments and symbols strung together. A piece of Massachusetts Bay currency of 1779, showing the pine tree in the upper left corner, and with the date put on with a stamp printing white on black (!), is lettered at the bottom: "death to counterfeit," recalling the severe English law. We had counterfeiters in Colonial days. Abel Buell (who subsequently worked for the government), Joseph Billings, Henry Dawkins and Richard Brunton are among the engravers credited with taking advantage of the ease with which our early notes could be forged. The Revolution brought us our first historical prints. The *Boston Massacre* (1770), a hand-colored engraving by Revere, is a famous and rare old print, seldom enough seen but known through reproductions and the engraved copy by Sidney L. Smith. About 1880,

BOSTON MASSACRE
Engraving by Paul Revere

Mr. Stauffer told me, the Revere family had Daniels of Boston strike off a few impressions without the inscription. And W. L. Andrews notes several contemporary copies of the print, in England and America. In a letter from Henry Pelham (see "Bibliographer" for March, 1902), Revere is charged with having copied Pelham's engraving of the massacre. For a long time no such print was known to exist, but a few years ago an impression came into the hands of C. S. Brigham, of the American Antiquarian Society. Previously, in 1768, Revere had done two views of Boston, one on copper (existing in colored impressions and in restrikes, without inscription), the other on wood or type-metal, showing the landing of British troops. In the "Royal American Magazine" for January, 1774, there appeared a small copy of this view, with the title *View of the Town of Boston with several Ships of War in the Harbour.*

Though crude enough, the *Massacre* seems rather better in execution than the set of four plates by Amos Doolittle (re-engraved in our day by S. L. Smith) from drawings by Ralph Earle, picturing the engagements at Concord and Lexington, also colored by hand. One of the four, the *Battle of Lexington,* was re-engraved on a smaller scale by A. Doolittle and J. W. Barber in 1832. The Battle of Lexington was illustrated much later (1798), by Tiebout in an engraving after Tisdale, also to be seen in color. And Trumbull executed a painting of the affair at Bunker Hill, reproduced on two plates in John Norman's largest engraving, and more than once in the nineteenth century. A few months before the Doolittle prints there had appeared Romans's *Exact View of the late Battle at Charlestown* (Philadelphia, 1775). This print of the Battle of Bunker Hill was copied on a smaller scale by Robert Aitken in a fearful and wonderful engraving (*Correct View, etc.*) with cannon drawn on the school-boy principle of two parallel lines with an oval at each end. Two further interesting illustrations of events in the war, both *N. G. Inv.* and engraved by John Norman, appeared as frontispieces to two books published soon after the occurrences to which they related. The first, in "The Battle of Bunker's Hill. By a gentleman of Maryland" (Philadelphia, 1776), depicts *The Death of Gen. Warren,* crudely, yet with rough dramatic vigor. The other, *Death of Montgomery,* in the pamphlet of the same name (Philadelphia, 1777), is a bit more theatrical, perhaps, in its strong contrasts of light and shade, but looks surer in drawing.

Edward Savage's large *Signing the Declaration of Independence,* in line and stipple, remained unfinished. It opened the drama which had its last act in the event pictured in Tanner's engraving of *The Surrender of Cornwallis at Yorktown,* from a drawing by J. F. Renault. J. F. Renault did also a *Triumph of Liberty, Engraved by P. C. Verger* (1796), issued in France, with about as much truth to facts as in the Yorktown design. Amos Doolittle's *Federal Hall* (1790), from a drawing by Peter Lacour ("the only contemporary view of the inauguration of Washington"), and *View of the Triumphal Arch and Colonnade, erected in Boston, in Honor of the President,* 1789, mark the inauguration of a new era.

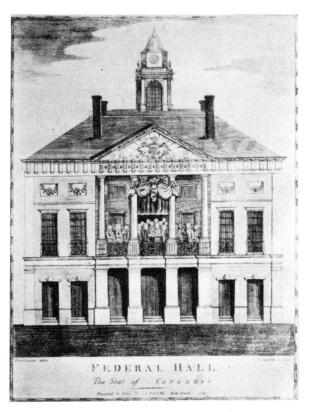

FEDERAL HALL.
The Seat of Congress

WASHINGTON'S INAUGURATION
Engraving by Doolittle

War maps and plans were furnished during the conflict by Bernard Romans, Robert Aitken (who copied Romans's "Map of the Seat of War"), John Norman, Abernethie, and J. Smither. Portraiture was bound to develop. Revolutionary heroes were depicted for public edification with despatch, if not always with neatness. Revere, Dearborn, Doolittle and others supplied pictures which have already been sufficiently characterized. These old prints were listed by Stauffer, and to him the reader may go for details.

As affairs became more settled, there came about increasing proficiency in the handling of the engraver's tools. There resulted also revision of early impressions; prominent Americans roughly portrayed were again presented, with more art. They were repeatedly pictured in certain cases, particularly Franklin, Jefferson and Lafayette, but none to anything like the same extent as Washington. It seemed to be the ambition of almost every portrait engraver of those and later days to produce at least one counterfeit presentment of the Father of his Country; more than one engraver had several to his credit. Washington portraiture has a little literature of its own.

The foreign element in this country had its part in preserving for future generations the features of those who were prominent in directing the fortunes of the young nation. Du Simitière (whose portraits, says W. L. Andrews, are poor, though "taken from life,"—they were engraved by B. L. Prevost, Paris) and St. Memin left particularly many records of the lineaments of those on whom the light of publicity fell in those days. St. Memin, from a crayon drawing in profile, made with the aid of the "physionotrace," which he reduced with a pantograph to a circle about two inches in diameter, scratched a light outline on copper, finishing with the roulette.

Abroad, events in our land attracted attention, and portraits were produced that bore more or less—often less—resemblance to the originals. Franklin could at least be drawn from the life by the French—*vide* Duplessis and Cochin. But by the time Cochin's impression of him had reached Germany, it could hardly be recognized in the traduction of J. C. Haid's mezzotint, with a rather Teutonic aspect, as we may find it also in some portraits of Washington. The demand for portraiture occasionally resulted in "truly exhaustive efforts of the artist's imagination," as W. L. Andrews characterized John Michael Probst's conceptions of Charles Lee and Putnam. Other such fabrications are the sober, Hollandish, bearded "W. Pen," in a book of travels in the United States, published in Utrecht in the seventeenth century, and Chapman's bust, in stipple, of Washington, with side whiskers, signed *R. K. Porter, R. N. del.*

The imaginary portrait—call it "fake," if you will— was not unknown then and later. Revere's "Col. Benjamin Church" (1772) was worked up from the portrait of C. Churchill in Smollett's "History of England" (1758–65). His full-length of King Philip, as Andrews points out, is "evolved entirely from his own consciousness." The full-length Washington (possibly by John

Norman, thinks C. H. Hart), "in Roman dress as ordered by Congress for the monument to be erected in Philadelphia," was transformed from Sir William de la More, in full coat of mail. One can continue this paragraph on un-authenticity to much later dates, to include, for instance, the Franklin bust portrait, of the Wilson type, engraved by F. Halpin, which, despite its eighteenth century garb, did duty as a picture of Roger Williams. Necessity of quick production gave rise to the expedient of taking out the head on an already engraved plate and· substituting another. The James Madison signed *Bona del Parte sculp* is Akin's portrait of Benjamin Rush, with head and signature changed. A. H. Ritchie's full-length portrait of Abraham Lincoln was originally one of Calhoun. H. B. Hall substituted a line-engraved bust portrait of Lincoln in an oval frame in an old stipple engraving, representing Diogenes leaning over the frame:

"Diogenes his lantern needs no more,
    An honest man is found!—the search is o'er."

Still quicker results could be attained by changing only the name of the personage; Michele Pekenino, an engraver reconstructed by Stauffer, produced a portrait of Bolivar by changing the lettering on his head of A. B. Durand. The portrait of *James Arlington Bennet, LL.D., at 30,* by Story and Atwood after J. Neagle, appears also with Bennet's name replaced by that of *Aesop.*

Possibly the greater facility with which stipple could be executed had something to do with the fact that it is in stipple that some of the first portraits of technical merit were produced here. The first one of real account by an American-born engraver was the work of Cornelius Tiebout, as is pointed out by Stauffer, who adds that Peale and Savage, though they had issued earlier portraits, were painters who did some occasional portraits rather than engravers by profession. The portrait by Tiebout referred to was that of Jay, published in 1795 in London, where Tiebout had gone to study. One of his best is the large half-length of William White, D.D., after Stuart, the face well modeled though pale. In the one of Simon Snyder this paleness becomes colorlessness, a characterization which will apply to much of the stipple work of this and of later times. Tiebout did sufficient work of this thin quality. His memorial design of Washington on a pedestal, with Bowling-Green, New York City, in the background, after Buxton (1798), which exists in an impression on satin, was done in line, in which manner he had worked before taking up stipple, and had executed a plan of New York for the directory of that city for 1787.

Edward Savage, painter, engraver, publisher, used stipple with a certain vigor. His portrait of Franklin (bespectacled and reading), after Martin, seems better in drawing and modeling—perhaps because not designed by himself—than his bourgeois-like Washington or the well-known *Washington and His Family*. His small bust portrait of Washington (1792) after his own painting, shows remarkably minute stippling in the face. It is almost entirely dotted, with a modicum of line work on coat and wig; an honest, careful job. His paintings were occasionally engraved by others; Tanner did a Washington in stipple, and David Edwin his *Landing of Columbus,* published by Savage in 1800. J. W. Jarvis began as an engraver with Savage, and in a bitter attack denied his master's authorship of the engravings issued under his name. But Dunlap's similar statement that Savage could not engrave and that his apprentice David Edwin really did the work, was emphatically denied by W. S. Baker and C. H. Hart.

Edwin, who when he came to Philadelphia in 1797 found difficulty from the want of the necessary tools and a proper press, became "one of the most prolific and popular portrait engravers of the period." Hart places him above Bartolozzi, as "superior in manner," and contemporary criticism ("Port Folio," October, 1810, p. 329) said of his quite indifferent *Maternal Affection,* a little mother-and-child *genre,* "his copy, both for spirit and elegance, unquestionably transcends the British original." His plates show marked ability and facility. Exigencies of production may have resulted in not a few portraits which do not rise much above the average of, say, Chapman in England. But his work includes such able performances as the large portraits of James Madison and Thomas McKean (1803, particularly good), after Stuart, or the Alexander I, of the smaller size of the majority of his portraits, and with the delicacy of a miniature. He did a number of plates after Stuart, of whose friendship, we are told, he was exceedingly proud.

Use of stipple increased; free effect, and softness appropriate especially in the treatment of the face, were elements to commend it. A number of engravers, some of them better known by their line work, practised the dotting art more or less: Doolittle (whose Alexander I is perhaps the best portrait he ever did), Thomas Clarke (who did an indifferent Lafayette), John Galland, John James Barralet (whose designs were often engraved by others), W. S. Leney, Alexander Anderson (executed a thin but not bad military portrait after Jarvis), Rollinson, Abner Reed, Benjamin Tanner, the Mavericks, Elkanah Tisdale and John Scoles. Two Englishmen who worked here for a while were H. Houston and Robert Field. Houston drew and engraved a rather stiff half-length of John Adams, and engraved a bust of J. P. Kemble (1796), after "Steward," quite juicy in effect.

There was some little use of stipple also in landscape work. Examples of this are Tiebout's *The Cascade, Luzerne County, Pa.*, poor enough, and his *Cottage Scene*, a good-sized plate after W. Bigg.

Stipple was to be much used for magazine illustration, a field in which line-engraving had already been employed to some extent. Among the periodicals which offered some opportunity to our line-engravers were: "Royal American Magazine" (Boston: Revere, Callender); "Pennsylvania Magazine" (Robert Aitken, Poupard); "Boston Magazine" (J. Norman); "Columbian Magazine" (Philadelphia: J. Trenchard); "Massachusetts Magazine" (Boston: Samuel Hill); "New York Magazine" (Scoles); "American Universal Magazine" (Philadelphia: Houston, Smither, Bowes, Harrison, Thomas Clarke). During the war, a considerable proportion of the plates in these magazines naturally related to the conflict: plans, views, battle scenes, portraits of commanders predominated. With the advent of peace there came increasing production of books with illustrations. There had been the occasional portrait or map in a volume. Book-illustration with copper-plate engravings had begun, not always with happiest results, as we have seen in the case of Norman, who did also a frontispiece and fifteen plates for the Fables of Æsop by Robert Dodsley (Philadelphia: Robert Bell, 1777). Now, more systematic and extended illustration was attempted. David Longworth of New York brought out an edition of Telemachus with plates by Thomas Clarke, Scoles engraved a frontispiece, sufficiently hard, after Tisdale, and there were other evidences of this increased activity. This found an outlet especially in editions of the Bible, by Isaiah Thomas (1791), with thirty-two plates by J. H. Seymour, Brown's Bible (1792), with engravings by Tiebout, Maverick, Doolittle, Rollinson, A. Godwin, Collins's Quarto Bible (second edition, 1807), the Carey Bibles, and Paul Wright's "Life of Christ" (Philadelphia, 1795), giving about the worst of which the engravers were capable. The publication of cyclopedias began, too, calling for much illustration,—Dobson's edition of Rees' Encyclopædia (1794–1803), and the Philadelphia (1806–13) edition of the Edinburgh Encyclopædia. While these offered little opportunity for the display of artistic qualities—the plates were mostly illustrations in science, natural history, and useful arts—they enlisted the service of practically all engravers of any note. With such under-takings, extending by date of issue into the nineteenth century, we pass out of the eighteenth into the hopes and aims and achievements of a new period.

CHAPTER IV

LINE AND STIPPLE IN THE NINETEENTH CENTURY

In the new century there came a marked increase in engravers and a noteworthy advance in technical ability. Two important factors in the development of engraving were the demand for magazine and book illustration and the need of well-executed bank-notes. Periodicals such as the "Polyanthos" (Boston), "Port Folio," "The Analectic," Delaplaine's "Emporium of Arts and Sciences" (Philadelphia) and the "Rhode Island Literary Repository," issued between 1800 and 1820, laid some stress on the portraits and views by Edwin, Hamlin, T. Gimbrede, S. Harris, Snyder and others, which they offered their readers. One may run with some satisfaction through the files of the "Port Folio," for example, and note the increased assurance and skill with which the artists handled their tools, particularly in the production of portraits after Stuart, Wood and others. Stipple was the medium usually chosen for the latter. Previously, such dotted portraits had a pale gray, somewhat washed-out effect; now there came more vigorous and varied handling, giving richer effect without loss of delicacy. See, for example, the stipple portraits in Delaplaine's "Repository of the Lives and Portraits of distinguished American

Characters" (Philadelphia, 1815), by Edwin, Boyd, Longacre, W. S. Leney (a smooth, dexterous worker), W. R. Jones, Goodman & Piggot and J. Heath. In not a few cases during this period this new force runs to a heavy black, almost as colorless as the washed-out gray of the preceding period. But this tendency to black, again, may rise to a richness that is of a resounding sonority in J. B. Longacre's large portrait of Andrew Jackson, after Sully, executed with a force and breadth in accord with the size of the plate. Longacre, who later became engraver to the U. S. Mint, managed to get some color and life into even his least important portraits; his small *Alexander Macomb* after Sully is quite delightful in its easy flow and succulence. He had a noteworthy part in raising the standard of engraving in this country. With James Herring he published "The National Portrait Gallery of distinguished Americans" (New York, 1834–39). It is said that the standard of excellence for the engravings was set so high that after employing the best engravers in the country, others had to be brought over from Europe. It was good stipple work that this venture brought forth, showing practical craftsmanship, and characterized by a certain vigor. A number of the plates were by Longacre himself (some after his own drawings from life), others by T. B. Welch, George Parker, Prud'homme, E. Wellmore, W. A. Wilmer, I. B. Forrest, J. Gross, etc. Other engravers, including not a few workers in line, were identified with this art of the dot during 1800–1840: W. Haines, Abel Bowen, C. Gobrecht, Thomas Gimbredge and his son J. N. Gim-

ANDREW JACKSON
After Sully.   Stipple engraving by J. B. Longacre

brede, J. R. Smith, George Graham, Joseph Cone, John Vallance, John Boyd, Bridport and W. R. Jones.

Not all the work was good; as late as 1812 one comes across portraits such as those by John Eckstein in which to helplessness is added the provincial assurance of the insufficiently equipped designer (Eckstein himself). But on the whole the engravers worked with increased ability and discrimination, and in certain instances were apparently spurred on to better efforts by the merits of the original which they copied. Hence their work varied, and from the mass of smoothly executed stipple plates there stand out various portraits. Thomas Gimbrede's *James Monroe* after I. Van Der Lyn, Vallance's *Hugh Blair,* Bridport's luscious *Conwell* and Boyd's strong and broad *John Fennell* after Wood are in each case probably the best portrait by the respective engraver. Smith's *James Bowdoin* has both delicacy and swing, and his portraits of Commodores Rodgers and Bainbridge show grasp of character. There is a certain delicacy in Cone's miniature *A. H. Judson,* and color and *verve* in *Philip Tidyman* after Sully by T. B. Welch and A. B. Walter. The last-named painter's *D. D. Tompkins* is well caught, in the suave sweep of the modeling in the face, by Jones.

There was some use of stipple for views and historical pieces, say G. G. Smith's *U. S. Squadron under Commodore Bainbridge returning triumphant from the Mediterranean in 1815,* designed by J. B. Fanning, or William Birch's small views of *The Country Seats of the United States.* In the last, stipple and line are combined, and hand-coloring further serves to smooth over things

Usually, in landscapes and figure-pieces, the line entered more or less to re-enforce the dots. In portraiture, stipple undefiled was nearly always used for faces and backgrounds, and sometimes even for the whole plate, as in some by Longacre, Welch (*Franklin*), W. A. Wilmer, or Prud'homme (*Henry Lee*) in the Longacre-Herring "Portrait Gallery." Even the use of the line, particularly for the clothes, in the hands of certain men lost some of the insistence which others gave it.

John Norman had begun to apply a mixture of graverwork and stipple in his portraits of Revolutionary heroes. With Revere (in the rare portrait of Jonathan Mayhew), Poupard and others, he foreshadowed the "mixed manner" which in the middle of the nineteenth century degenerated into the production of a characterless, machine-made sauce, in which certain engravers served all their portraits in the same spice-less manner. One may study this as early as 1853–54 in John Livingston's "Portraits of Eminent Americans" with plates by various engravers. There is one by Frederick Halpin, for instance, with the face in stipple, the hair in line, the coat rouletted and the background ruled. Yet Halpin could do portraits as good as that of J. F. Kensett after George H. Baker.

Meanwhile, the art of line-engraving had likewise been developed. There was still some of the occasional work —cards, certificates and what not—at which we found the eighteenth century engravers busy. William Main, a pupil of Morghen (whose *Last Supper* after Da Vinci inspired Kearny, J. B. Neagle, Pease and Burt each to attempt the same subject), said in a letter to Dunlap that most of his early engraving was of "visiting cards, door plates and dog collars." One may come across such pieces as an advertising view of a hotel in Augusta (1822) by Neagle after Shaw, or a card for Clark & Raymond's "fashionable hat store," New York, after J. R. Smith by P. Maverick, who applied cupids to commercial needs in his cards for A. Maverick and for Boureau & Co.'s jewelry and hardware store. Thackara, Hamlin and others found similar employment. Here, too, may be noted P. Maverick's card for Columbia College Commencement, 1822. Maverick's own announcement, issued from 149 Broadway, includes engraving, copper-plate printing, lithography; and *bank-notes engraved on copper or steel, with all the variety of die work and machine facilities now in use.*

Book-illustration in line increased. Activity in Bible and encyclopedia publication was mentioned in the preceding chapter. More latitude would naturally be offered in illustrations for works of *belles-lettres,* and these, too, increased and improved,—relatively. When designer and engraver were both of native origin one might look for results such as those in a scene from "The Contrast," by P. Maverick, *W. Dunlap inv. et del.,* fearful to behold, in design and execution. E. Tisdale's drawings for the poetical works of John Trumbull (Hartford, 1820), engraved by W. H. Bassett and Tisdale himself, though not remarkable productions, show at least more ease. Designers and engravers improved in time. In the early decades of the century, line-plates in books were engraved,

frequently after English originals for American re-
prints, by Joseph H. Seymour (Hayley's "Triumph of
Temper"), Scot and Allardice (Campbell's edition of
Hume's History of England), Rollinson (a quite graceful title-page for a Horace of 1830), Gideon Fairman
(vignettes for title-pages; he designed also for other
engravers), C. G. Childs (plates after Inman for "The
Spy," Philadelphia, 1822–24; after Stothard for "Heart
of Midlothian"), J. B. Neagle after W. M. Craig and
English designers, Tiebout (illustrations in stipple, for
the works of Cowper and others, after Smirke *et al*),
Tanner after Corbould. P. Maverick did illustrations
after Thurston, Stothard, Corbould, Burney and Westall,
for "Lalla Rookh," "Sentimental Journey," "Tristram
Shandy," and Hayley's "Triumphs of Temper," New
York, 1809. In the last, the little engravings are scattered through the text, an unusual matter. Alexander
Lawson engraved illustrations after J. J. Barralet, and
did plates for Alexander Wilson's work of ornithology; a
collection of his engravings is in the Academy of Natural
Sciences, Philadelphia.

In the twenties and thirties, there were the neatly en-
graved little views of New York City (published by
Bourne, 1831) after C. Burton, by Fenner & Sears, W.
D. Smith, Gimber, Hatch & Smillie and H. Fossette (who
also engraved after his own designs) : after A. I. Stans-
bury by Rawdon, Clark & Co. (1828) or Danforth; after
J. H. Dakin by Barnard & Dick. Later came Hinton's
"History and Topography of the United States" (Boston,

1834) with illustrations, generally drawn by American artists, most of them engraved by John Archer.

In the early days of the century, there fell to the engraver also the illustration of important current events. In our age of the camera, daily happenings are chronicled pictorially with an easy copiousness that gives a momentary importance to innumerable persons, things or occurrences with which the old-time engravers could not have occupied their burins. They recorded such matters of moment as particularly interested, or deeply stirred, their contemporaries. For instance, the landing of Lafayette, pictured by Samuel Maverick (1824, published by Imbert), or the launch of the steam frigate Fulton, by Tanner (1815) after a drawing by Barralet. The War of 1812 naturally called forth graven records of victories on land and sea. Tanner was particularly busy in depicting naval actions. He glorified Perry's victory on Lake Erie, 1813, *J. J. Barralet delt.* (1815), and Macdonough's on Lake Champlain, 1814, *H. Reinagle pinxt* (1816), and pictured United States and Macedonia, *T. Birch pinxt* (1813). Two views of the Battle of Lake Erie, by Sully and Kearny, were engraved by Murray, Draper, Fairman & Co., and Thomas Birch's painting of Perry's victory was reproduced by A. Lawson.

The growing country was to be pictured in its urban aspects and its natural beauties and wonders. In the last dozen years of the eighteenth century, the production of views had already begun to increase. S. Hill, for instance, drew and engraved a view of Cambridge and one of the seat of John Hancock (1789) for the "Massachusetts

Magazine." In the "New York Magazine" we find views by Tiebout: Trinity Church, after I. Anderson (1790), Columbia College after I. Anderson, and Richmond Hill (1790). The Mavericks and Birch were also working before 1800, and after that date the younger Maverick did some creditable little views after W. G. Wall (*New York City, from New Jersey* existing in at least ,three states), Alexander Robertson and Inman. Like Birch, Cephas G. Childs published a set of views of Philadelphia, most of them engraved by himself, and John Exilious had engraved from his own drawing a large view of the Pennsylvania Hospital. Just a few instances these, representing a respectable amount of production.

The Philadelphia "Port Folio," edited by "Oliver Oldschool," occasionally published line-engraved views, and one notes with amusement that when the picture of the Catskills, with a steamboat in the foreground (by Hewitt after J. Glennie), was changed by taking the sail off the boat, the engraver omitted to remove the reflection of the sail in the water. In the forties and fifties came large views such as the one of New York City from the Latting Observatory (1855) by W. Wellstood after B. E. Smith.

Such views met the demands of an interest in locality; others mirror the growing attention paid by American painters to landscape. This is felt in such an early production as *The American Landscape,* engraved by A. B. Durand, which did not live beyond the six plates of No. 1 (1830). It appears notably in the large plates after Thomas Cole's series of paintings, *The Voyage of Life,*

by James Smillie, our most able landscape engraver. This
growing appreciation of the landscape *per se* is reflected
also in smaller plates by Hinshelwood and others after
Huntington, J. W. Casilear (himself, like the painters
Durand, Kensett, Nathaniel Jocelyn, J. A. Oertel and
Shirlaw, originally an engraver), James M. and W.
Hart, Jervis McEntee, W. L. Sonntag, D. Johnson, S.
R. Gifford, A. D. Shattuck and A. Bierstadt. However,
the topographical feeling was naturally still strong, the
exact reproduction of the definite locality. It is very easy
to have a fling at the "Hudson River School." The time
was not ripe then for the painting of the landscape for
the sake of the mood it inspires. Yet one gets the impression that in many cases the painters honestly loved
their subjects. Durand painted his tree-trunks, for instance, with understanding and sympathy. And it was
not only the large and pretentiously impressive scenes *à la*
Church or Cole that were painted. The same Durand
who depicted the "White Mountain Scenery: Franconia
Notch," panoramic in its comprehensiveness, did also the
cool, restful wood interior, of intimate charm, which for
years hung opposite to it in the old Lenox Library Building in New York City. These painters found beauty in
their home land, and told their compatriots of it, and the
message was spread farther by the engravers who reproduced their works.

Some of the latest products of this spirit are found in
the not remarkable plates in "The National Gallery of
American Landscape" (New York: W. Pate & Co.) by
J. D. Smillie, Pease, Henry Beckwith, Wellstood, Hin-

shelwood and others, the last two mentioned, together with S. V. Hunt and others, being engaged also in yet thinner work for "Picturesque America" (New York, 1874) after Bierstadt, Church, Bellows and Kensett.

But the last was a chronological divagation, and returning to mid-century there are found freshness and immediateness of view also in the figure paintings of the time, by W. S. Mount, F. W. Edmonds, R. Caton Woodville, W. Ranney *et al.* These were done with a healthy interest in the daily life and home doings of the small man of the street and the country in the East, the flatboatman of the Ohio, the pioneers and trappers of the West. The line-engravings in which these works were reproduced served a distinct and educational purpose in bringing before a larger public a knowledge of paintings, of the progress of American art, and of the spirit that actuated it.

The beauties of our land,—both in its wilder aspects and in the calmer beauty of rural scenery in the more closely inhabited East;—scenes in our national history; the life of the Indian and the trapper; the farmer at work and at play, driving a horse trade, whittling a stick, or listening to "Old Dan Tucker" or some other popular air of the day scraped by a fiddler of local reputation, such aspects of our life and surroundings were brought before our public both in smaller engravings and in the large framing prints so popular then. There were reproduced, in small and large plates, such paintings as W. S. Mount's *Swapping Horses* (engraved by Joseph Andrews, 1839), *The Raffle, The Painter's Study* (engraved by A. Lawson), *Long Island Farmer* (engraved by Hinshelwood), *The Tough Story*, *The Rabbit Trap* and *The Disagreeable Surprise* (the last three engraved by J. I. Pease); H. Inman's *Mumble the Peg;* J. G. Clonney's *Militia Training* (engraved by J. I. Pease); J. L. Krimmel's *Election Day in Philadelphia,* by Lawson; and W. Ranney's *The Trapper's last Shot* (engraved by T. D. Booth, of Cincinnati). The very titles indicate the assiduous cultivation of an American *genre,* in place of the sweetly sentimental variety once fostered in engravings such as those by E. Gallaudet. When arguments against the "anecdotal *genre*" are exhausted, the question remains: was not this home product preferable to the weak sentimentality of certain souls expatriated in fact or in mood, whose foreign scenery or Italian shepherd boys are weak reconstructions on old recipes?

Good work was done in the large framing prints. Alfred Jones engraved *Farmer's Nooning* ("Apollo Association," 1843) after W. S. Mount, *Sparking* (1844) and *The New Scholar* (1850), both after F. W. Edmonds, and *Mexican News* (1851) after R. C. Woodville. Woodville's *Old '76 and young '48* was put into black-and-white by J. I. Pease. Ranney's *Duck Shooting,* R. C. Woodville's *Card Players* (1850) and Mount's *Bargaining for a Horse* (1851) were reproduced by Charles Burt. All of these were issued as premiums by the American Art Union, which flourished particularly in the forties and fifties. Similar associations were the Art Union of Philadelphia and the Western Art Union. It is recorded also that the Western Methodist Book Concern, "by its publication of good engravings, exercised a decided influence on public taste in that section of the country." This Western firm employed William Wellstood, who also reproduced American paintings. Inevitably, weak and colorless paintings were also engraved, illustrating no national spirit or characteristics, examples of fatuous story-telling art.

In plates of the character of those which have been mentioned, what there was of dignity or raciness or humor in the appeal of American painters on the ground of such national beauty or interest as it was given to them to see, was transmitted to wider circles than the paintings alone would have reached. These plates are interesting records of the costume and customs, the mental and moral viewpoint of our people at that time.

Furthermore, striking scenes in our history were seized by painters and re-told by the graver: *Plymouth Rock* (1869) by Joseph Andrews and *Patrick Henry delivering his celebrated Speech in the House of Burgesses, Virginia, 1765,* by Alfred Jones (1852), both after P. F. Rothermel; *Capture of André* after Durand, *figures engraved by Jones, landscape by Smillie and Hinshelwood* (1845); *Marion crossing the Pedee* after W. Ranney (1851), by Burt; *Washington at Valley Forge* by E. S. Best, and *Franklin before the Lords in Council* by Robert Whitechurch, both after Schussele. *Lady Washington's Reception Day* after Huntington and *On the March to the Sea* after Darley (an interesting "touched" copy is owned by the New York Public Library) were both engraved by A. H. Ritchie. These examples are not all cited as par-

ARIADNE
Line-engraving, from a Painting by John Vanderlyn, by A. B. Durand

ticularly remarkable engravings, but rather as indications of the taste of the time.

The artists of those days did not limit their activities to American subjects. The historical *genre* was cultivated. Leutze painted *The Image Breakers*, engraved by Jones (1850), and *Sir Walter Raleigh parting with his Wife* by Burt (1846). Among the paintings of J. W. Glass is the *Standard Bearer*, and among those of Daniel Huntington *The Signing of the Death Warrant of Lady Jane Grey* by Burt (1848). Shakespeare inspired effort (*Anne Page, Slender and Shallow* by Burt, 1850, after Leslie). The gorgeousness of tropical scenery was depicted by F. E. Church. The Bible story was told and the moral lesson inculcated (D. Huntington), the pictorial allegory was represented by Thomas Cole's two series, *Voyage of Life* engraved by Smillie, and "Course of Empire." And in the realm of the ideal there is to be recorded, primarily, the noble translation of John Vanderlyn's *Ariadne*, done in 1835 by A. B. Durand, particularly successful in rendering flesh. Koehler described this *Ariadne* as "the largest plate of such high, artistic achievement that ever appeared in America, of a purity and grace of graver-work in the figure of Ariadne—the landscape is mainly in etching—that need fear no comparison." This was Durand's last plate; he laid down the graver to take up the brush after fifteen years' work as an engraver—his first important production having been the *Declaration of Independence* (1820) after Trumbull.

Our engravers cut a figure in the art world in the first

half of the last century, if we may judge from the records of the National Academy of Design. A number of them were members of that body: P. Maverick, M. I. Danforth, Durand, W. J. Bennett, W. Main, C. C. Wright, J. A. Adams, J. W. Paradise, Prud'homme, S. W. Cheney, Alfred Jones, James Smillie, A. H. Ritchie, dates of election running from 1826 to 1871.

Meanwhile the supply of portraits increased enormously, and the field was soon left mainly to line-engraving. Stipple appeared at most in the machine-made effect of the "mixed manner" in the sixties and seventies, in which etching, graver-work, machine-ruling, stipple, rouletting, mezzotint were pressed into service to get quick and smooth results.

Delaplaine's "Repository" (1815), beside its stipple portraits, had had others in line by G. Fairman, Maverick and Neagle. Longacre and Herring's "Portrait Gallery" was also varied by the inclusion of line portraits, by A. B. Durand, R. W. Dodson (his *Simon Kenton* to be noted), T. Kelly, and J. W. Paradise. The younger Maverick, Peter, did not a little indifferent portrait work, without color or life. However, he could do as good a job as his *Cervantes* in line, or his comparatively rich little stipple portrait of *Oliver Ellsworth* after Trumbull. Kelly did much "shopwork," but could rise to the delicacy of his *J. R. Drake* after Rodgers (1820) and the force of his *N. Chapman, M. D.,* after Neagle. W. Hoogland was perhaps at his best in his *W. E. Channing.* R. W. Dodson did indeed produce for "Graham's Magazine" a group of female contributors which merited the sarcasm

of Frances Sargent Osgood's "Lines to Mr. Dodson."
But he has a number of good and quite rich plates to his
credit, *Richard Dale, Gen. Jonathan Williams* and *Alex.
V. Griswold.* Like Kelly he used long sweeping curves of
line as we see them in Durand's plates. M. I. Danforth
is an example of a trifle more conventional craftsmanship
and less art, although before his Irving after Leslie (the
portrait with the fur collar, so often engraved) one
almost forgets that. J. W. Steel similarly emulated the
fluency of lines of a Durand. In his *Commodore James
Barron,* the linear curves accent the rotund and genial
robustness of the subject; the delicate *John Vaughan*
after Sully is one of his best. Joseph Andrews was best
known by his portraits,—S. R. Koehler spoke of the
"tenderness" of the one of Amos Lawrence after Harding; his fur-collar *Franklin,* after Duplessis, which he
engraved in France, is familiar, and *J. Q. Adams,* after
Healy, is a good example. Alfred Jones executed a number of portraits, those of Washington, A. B. Durand, and
Carlyle having been pronounced "admirable examples of
a combination of line work with etching."

A striking characteristic of the nineteenth century work
is the attainment of a comparatively high general level of
technical proficiency, of mechanical dexterity.

A number of our engravers were either self-educated,
like James Smillie, or at least began their careers without
instruction or tools, even if they were regularly appren-
ticed afterward. William Rollinson, a "chaser of fancy
buttons," did a small stipple portrait of Washington in
1791 without previous knowledge. Joseph Ives Pease

made his first attempts with an old awl on a bit of thermometer brass, the printing being done on a roll press invented by himself. Alexander Anderson, who engraved first in copper, and did a good if conventional *St. John* after Domenichino, and a quite delicate portrait of John Carroll of Baltimore in line and stipple, learned the process, as a boy, from an encyclopedia. He had a silversmith roll out some copper pennies and experimented with a "graver made of the back-spring of a pocket-knife," printing on a rude rolling press which he constructed; later, he got a blacksmith to make him some tools. A. B. Durand's first efforts were made with tools of his own manufacture, on plates hammered out from copper coins. Gideon Fairman also began with tools of his own construction. John Cheney attempted engraving "without other instruction than that offered by books and the examination of such prints as came under his notice," making his own tools and hammering plates from the pieces of an old copper boiler.

A potent factor in the technical development of our line-engravers on copper appears in the demand for banknote work. Increased production brought systematization of work, labor-saving devices and contrivances intended to make counterfeiting more difficult. The traditional inventive genius of the American came into play, personified in Wm. Rollinson, John James Barralet, Jacob Perkins, Henry Tanner, J. G. Wellstood (founded the Columbia Bank Note Co. in 1871), James Bogardus, Cyrus Durand (not an engraver), W. L. Ormsby (author of "Description of the present System of Bank Note En-

graving," New York, 1852). They fathered ingenious
inventions or improvements,—lathes, ruling machines,
transfer machines tending to make the work more mechanical. Jacob Perkins not only in 1810 devised means
for substituting steel plates for copper, thus prolonging
the life of the plate, but introduced the use of die plates.
By this method, instead of engraving the whole note on
one plate, various portions of the design were engraved
on separate plates. From these they were transferred to
a decarbonized steel cylinder by means of the transfer
press. The cylinder, with the design thus appearing on
it in relief, was then hardened again, and could be used
any number of times for transferring the designs to plates
to be used for various bank-notes. In 1818, Perkins and
others went to England; subsequently, with Charles
Heath, the firm of Perkins and Heath was formed to
exploit the "Patent Hardened Steel Process."

In those days of State paper money, bank-note establishments arose in various parts of the country, and furnished employment to our line-engravers during the first
half of the nineteenth century. The connection of engravers with the management of such companies is indicated by firm names such as Durand & Co.; Durand,
Perkins & Co.; Tanner, Vallance, Kearny & Co.; Danforth, Perkins & Co.; Murray, Draper, Fairman &
Co.; Casilear, Durand, Burton and Edmunds; Rawdon,
Wright, Hatch & Smillie, and many more. Absorption
of firms resulted in 1858 in the formation of the American Bank Note Co., and there were later ones, such as
the Homer-Lee Bank-Note Co.

"By the middle of the century," says Stauffer, "American bank-note engraving had become deservedly famous throughout the world; much work was done for foreign governments, and in this class of work our engravers are still pre-eminent." While the exigencies of this work helped to develop craftsmanship, its influence on the whole promoted smooth dexterity and finesse rather than richness or delicacy. The Declaration of Independence, with a pictorial border, engraved in 1840, in a space of ¾ x 1½ inches, issued by the American Bank Note Co., is typical, in a measure. The use of mechanical devices such as the ruling machine (to which, the late J. D. Smillie once told me, he attached a clock-work to rule certain portions of the plate during the night, while he slept), would not have a tendency to promote freedom of handling, especially on the part of less vigorous and capable artistic personalities.

But on the other hand one must recognize the fact that the public was at least served with good drawing and clean engraving in the vignettes on its bank-notes. Among the designers of these there were capable artists. Durand, for instance, William Croome, F. O. C. Darley, and Walter Shirlaw. These vignettes were engraved with a certain boldness and richness of line,—as in the work of Alfred Jones. This free handling of the tool was often in refreshing contrast to the lathework or other machine-made production of the rest of the bill. If the deadening effect of bank-note engraving is deplored, it must be remembered that it gave employment to the best of our engravers. Durand, Smillie, Jones, Smillie's son, James

D., J. W. Casilear, whose *Sibyl* after Huntington was quite Durand-like in its beauty of line, Burt, Hinshelwood, and William Edgar Maishall, whose large portraits of Washington, Lincoln (at whose features probably every later nineteenth century engraver of any note had his try), Grant, Longfellow, Cooper, usually from his own paintings, were famous in their time.

Worthy of special note is Stephen A. Schoff, who could engrave in the regulation, formal style, as he showed in *Marius on the Ruins of Carthage* (Apollo Association, 1842) after Vanderlyn. But in a moonlight marine after M. F. H. De Haas, a portrait of Emerson after S. W. Rowse, and particularly in *Bathing Boys* after W. M. Hunt, he varies the line with a freedom and spirit akin to that of the "new school" of wood-engravers in this country. In the plate after Hunt, especially, the craftsman's delight in clean-cut curves, or in the employment of recognized conventions to express various textures, did not find expression. The line was broken and twisted to translate tones and color-values and even brush-marks. Yet the hand that produced this plate, almost a tour de force, could also rival the Turner engravers of Rogers' *Italy* in the delicate minuteness of *Bay of New York* after George Loring Brown, engraved for the "Ladies' Repository."

Line-engraving had its days as a medium for book-illustration. The results arouse rather mixed feelings. Such plates as had appeared in eighteenth century magazines, poor as they were, had at least a certain rough energy, and for us they have the antiquarian interest and the glamor of sentiment which age adds to such productions. And some of the earlier nineteenth century plates by the younger Maverick and others, or those after Burton, have been noted earlier in this chapter.

Magazine illustrations had shared in the general improvement. The "New York Mirror," in the thirties and forties, published a number of creditable views in the metropolis and elsewhere, from drawings by A. J. Davis, R. W. Weir and others, of interest also to the student of life in those days. A little later, "Ladies' Companion," "Ladies' Repository" (Cincinnati), "Columbian Magazine," "Graham's Magazine," "Evergreen," "Ladies' National Magazine" are among the names met with on engravings. The illustrations vary in merit. There is little that is worse, in the forties and fifties of this century, than the plates in certain magazines of the "Graham's" and "Godey's Lady's Book" type. One may instance, in "Godey's," title designs by W. E. Tucker, and illustrations engraved by the Illmans and others, weak and inane. W. S. Baker strained amiable tolerance when he asserted that Tucker's "plates are well engraved, and in fine taste, particularly the border and flower work furnished for magazines." From such disheartening work, even the insipid, becurled beauties of the annuals, the "keepsakes" and "gift books" stand out favorably by very contrast. There is a fascination about these old favorites, "elegant ornaments of the drawing-room table" (as one advertisement puts it), in their bindings with blind and gilt tooling of a style quite their own. You almost forget the artistic shortcomings of many of their illustrations as you handle them. They are so evidently born of the time, a time that offered such incongruities as these sentimental offerings and an uncouth vigor which, despite all caricaturing, surely must have been, if ever so vaguely, mirrored by Mrs. Trollope and Dickens.

During about 1830–60 "Affection's Gift," "Amaranth," "Baltimore Book," "Atlantic Souvenir," "The Talisman," "The Gift," "The Hyacinth," "Moss Rose," "Opal," "Token," "Lady's Cabinet Album," and numerous other annuals published, beside much poor stuff, some most pleasing examples of pure line work. These came from the gravers of Durand, Cheney, Andrews, Smillie, or such lesser lights as Danforth, Prud'homme, Balch, J. B. Neagle, Edward Gallaudet, G. B. Ellis, after paintings or drawings by Allston, Cole, Leslie, Doughty, G. L. Brown, Chapman,—all American artists. Repeatedly does Stauffer note that some given engraver's best work is to be found in these annuals. John Cheney's female heads speak to us of a refined taste. Dignity there is in his work, restraint, gentility, some conventionality, but also delicacy, and in *Guardian Angels,* after Reynolds, for instance, even a certain richness. "The best engraver of the female head in America," Baker called him.

The vogue of the gift book extended to descriptions of locality, such as W. C. Richards' "Georgia illustrated in a Series of Views, engraved on Steel by Rawdon, Wright, Hatch & Smillie, from Sketches made expressly for this work by T. A. Richards" (1842). It produced even a quarto apiece, in 1847, devoted to Mount Auburn and Greenwood cemeteries, respectively, with good landscapes, drawn by James Smillie and in part engraved by him, "in highly finished line engraving." "After 1861," wrote his son James D. to me in 1888, "he gave all his time to bank-note vignettes, excepting 1864, when he engraved his magnum opus 'The Rocky Mountains' after A. Bierstadt."

Less distinguished, often very much less, are the numerous plates published in books of travel in the forties. The name of William Henry Bartlett, the English illustrator, is a familiar one in this field. His drawings, reproduced in plates by English engravers, were copied by Americans, in some cases more than once.

Interesting, as home productions, are the illustrations of T. H. Matteson (painter of *The First Prayer in Congress,* engraved by H. S. Sadd) engraved by Milo Osborne and others. James Hamilton, the Philadelphia marine painter, also did some book designs. Matteson had a certain facility which to a greater degree characterized Darley. The latter's vignette illustrations for Cooper and Dickens were cleanly and understandingly reproduced by J. D. Smillie, Hinshelwood, Hollyer, A. V. Baulch, Schoff, and others. They remain the most pleasing and satisfactory examples of the employment of steel-engraving for book-illustration.

About 1860 there set in the beginning of the period of rank commercialism. Craftsmen such as Henry Bryan Hall, J. C. Buttre, H. Wright Smith, nimble manipulators of the tools of their art, flooded the land with portraits of the great and the less great, demand for likenesses of Civil War heroes increasing the number. Line plates such as those in Duyckinck's "National Portrait Gallery of Eminent Americans" (1862), executed after full-length paintings by Alonzo Chappel, make the stipple work in the Herring and Longacre "Portrait Gallery" appear even richer by contrast. There is nothing in the general run of this work of 1860–80 beyond a superficial technical slickness. In the case of Hall, extensive use of etching gave an appearance of free handling to his numerous portraits of men prominent in the American Revolution. A number of these were private plates, a selection of which, collected into a volume by Dr. T. A. Emmet, show the plates in various states. There are several of Washington, for example, in trial proofs not listed in C. H. Hart's monumental catalogue (Nos. 120, 268, 704). The volume is in the New York Public Library, where are also impressions of plates by Hall, corrected in wash, so-called "touched" proofs.

Others had not even the facility of these men, others whose work, thin, colorless, anemic, of a machine-made character, graces a certain type of town or county history or collective biography, a cheap decoy for the local magnate of plethoric pocketbook or for the wealthy relative to launch the genealogy. As a study of the wide difference even in mere craftsmanship, one has but to compare the best work of this period with the ordinary run of portraits by Durand or with the bold curves of the head of Cadwalader D. Colden, after Waldo and Jewett, by Peter Maverick and Durand & Co.

Commercialism is indicated in a measure also by the

publishing activity of certain engravers,—J. C. Buttre, and others. Conditions probably made such dual activity necessary in earlier days; Hurd, James Claypoole, Jr., Joseph Cone, W. Rollinson not only engraved prints but sold them.

Line-engravings by Americans—after paintings by Americans—figured in the lists of dealers as late as 1888: Hinshelwood, J. A. J. Wilcox, Henry Beckwith, F. Girsch and C. Schlecht being among the engravers so employed.

Line-engraving is anything but a dead art to-day. We handle its products daily in paper money, postage stamp, and government bonds. Line-engraving appears also on state occasions—say in the form of a vignette on a menu of a dinner to some notability, usually signed by the firm name of an engraving company or a silverware house or fashionable stationer. Commercial production, clean, smooth, thin, of an inconspicuous mediocrity. Occasionally there is an opportunity for the engraver of artistic ambition, as in the diploma of the Chicago World's Fair of 1893, by Charles Schlecht from a design by Will H. Low.

A use to which line-engraving is still put, and with signal success, is the reproduction of designs for book-plates, dealt with in the chapter on book-plates. The engravers of these have also been employed, as were their predecessors in the eighteenth century and the early nineteenth, to execute elaborate cards of invitation, diplomas, certificates and the like, such as those done for the Metropolitan Museum or the New York Historical

Society. It is a satisfaction that we possess these examples of an artistic solution of problems usually left to pure commercialism to solve. S. L. Smith and E. D. French and the other book-plate artists here mentioned, as well as the former wood-engravers F. S. King and W. M. Aikman, were engaged by the Society of Iconophiles of New York and the Iconographic Society of Boston to copy old engravings or photographs of architectural landmarks in those cities, or portraits of notable citizens. The Bibliophile Society of Boston has similarly engaged French, Hopson and the etcher W. H. H. Bicknell to engrave title-pages and illustrations for the books issued by it. And W. L. Andrews had engravings executed by French and Smith for several of his "limited edition" books.

Often, these modern line-engravers of book-plates work after their own designs. That brings us to a consideration of line-engraving as a painter art. J. Alden Weir once tried the graver in producing a nude figure, "Arcturus," which added an interesting document to the record of that masterful and sensitive experimenter. The greater difficulty in handling the graver keeps artists from adopting it as a means of original expression.

As a means of direct response to a need of reproduction of famous works of art, line-engraving is doomed here, as elsewhere. The glory of the large plate as a translation of painted masterpieces into the "framing print," once the pride of the parlor, has departed. The plates produced by Smillie, Burt, Durand, Jones, may be studied as examples of reproductive art in print rooms and private collections. The camera has taken their place in the work of introducing the art masterpieces of the ages to a wider public through translations into black-and-white.

COTTON MATHER
Mezzotint by Peter Pelham

CHAPTER V

MEZZOTINT (THE ART OF ROCKER AND SCRAPER)

DURING the period of the American Revolution there was witnessed in England a remarkable development of the art of mezzotint. This method of engraving has qualities peculiarly its own: a rich depth of velvety soft black, mellow lights, soft transitions and juicy, translucent shadows. It was peculiarly fitted for the reproduction of the air of distinction and stately grace that marked both the method and the subjects of the canvases in which the great portrait painters of the day—Reynolds, Gainsborough, Hoppner, Romney—perpetuated the noble lords and ladies of their land and time. In the American colonies, and subsequently in the young republic, circumstances necessary to bring about such a condition were missing to a great extent. Still, as early as 1727, Peter Pelham,—"the first man," says Stauffer, "who produced a really meritorious portrait plate in this country," painted and mezzotinted his very creditable portrait of Cotton Mather. Here, as in wood-engraving, the first recorded American product is a portrait of a Mather. But it is only one of fourteen which Pelham executed after he came to this country and after he had placed twenty to his credit in England. Another Mather —Increase—was pictured in a small mezzotint, *T. John-*

son fecit; probably Thomas Johnston, think Whitmore and Green, but Stauffer believes that this was the London engraver, Thomas Johnson. Other artists in the colonies made some attempts with "rocker" and "scraper." William Burgis, publisher of maps and prints, did a coarsely executed view of the lighthouse at the entrance to Boston Harbor, the only plate signed by him seen by Stauffer. Pelham's stepson, John Singleton Copley, who apparently had instruction from his stepfather in painting and engraving, has a small portrait of Rev. William Wellsteed of Boston (about 1753) to his credit. His painting of Nathaniel Hurd was scraped probably by Richard Jennys, who was working here about the beginning of the Revolution. Another portrait by Jennys is that of Rev. Jonathan Mayhew (about 1774), "printed and sold by Nat. Hurd." At about the same time Samuel Okey, an Englishman, was engraving and publishing mezzotints in Newport, R. I. His portraits included those of Rev. Thomas Hiscox (1773), Rev. James Honyman (1774) and Samuel Adams after J. Mitchell (1775), which last was copied in our day by J. Percy Sabin. Okey's *The Burgomaster,* after *Halls* [sic!] is the earliest attempt in the colonies to reproduce in mezzotint a painting by an old master. Benjamin Blyth did an allegorical composition, showing a tree, supporting an escutcheon with thirteen stars, growing out of the southern coast (at Portsmouth) of a map of England. The title is *Sacred to Liberty* and the designer is Cole. And some prominent actors in the conflict thus symbolically pictured were portrayed by Charles Willson Peale. That universal genius, interested in many things, was attracted by mezzotint and studied it in London. His plates include portraits of Washington, Franklin and Lafayette, all from his own designs. John Greenwood, born in Boston (1727), learned mezzotint in Holland and died in England (1792); it does not appear that he ever practised the art in the land of his birth.

An interesting figure in this list is Edward Savage, painter and stipple engraver. Noteworthy are the "soft and beautiful" reproduction of his own portrait of Washington, seated, and the portrait of Franklin, after Martin (London; 2d state: Boston), the latter good though perhaps lacking in subtlety and suavity. Two other mezzotints by him are of particular interest: *Muscipula* after Reynolds, as an echo of British achievement in this rich medium; *Eruption of Mount Etna in 1787* (published 1799), as an example of the not common use of the process in landscape work, and as an early specimen of American color printing. Savage's Washington portraits were reproduced in mezzotint—with emphasis on any stiffness in the originals—in 1799–1800, by William Hamlin (1772–1869) of Providence. Hamlin signed also a portrait of *Washington from Howdan's bust, Richmond, Va.,*—Houdon being meant, of course,—*Wm. Hamlin sc. at 91 years of age.* He put mezzotint to some unusual purposes, in *The Burning of the Frigate Philadelphia, in Tripoli Harbor, Feb. 1804,* and in a reversible picture, illustrating the pleasure of *Courtship* and the disillusionment of *Matrimony.* The last print may perhaps be regarded as an American contribution to the considerable output of mezzotinted humor in the last quarter of the eighteenth century in England. Hamlin was a manufacturer of nautical instruments, of whom Stauffer says: "As an engraver Mr. Hamlin made his own tools and worked practically without instruction." The result was bad enough,—a weak mixture of mezzotint and stipple, frequently worked over with the roulette.

These old engravers turned, with Yankee ease of adaptation, from one process to the other, working in etching, line-engraving, stipple, aquatint and mezzotint. They may have been actuated partly by an awakening interest in the media and partly by the desire to find new ways of arousing their public to a more liberal bestowal of the "honest penny" which they were trying to earn.

A number of the actors in the Revolution were pictured by mezzotinters in England. Thomas·Hart and others issued a number of anonymous plates, portraits of Putnam, Charles Lee, John Sullivan, David Wooster, Hancock, John Paul Jones, and Washington of course. Washington was notably portrayed also by Valentine Green. Simon's four Indian kings, much earlier in date, likewise come to mind as interesting foreign contributions to the iconography of Colonial history.

Entering the nineteenth century, one finds still occasional native efforts in this field, experiments or side-steppings rather than continued practice. For example, Bass Otis tried his hand at various processes, which has led Stauffer to suggest that the scraped reproductions of his portraits of William White and Rev. Joseph Eastburn, though unsigned, "may be experiments by Otis himself."

Another painter, John Wesley Jarvis, who engraved under Savage, produced portraits of David Rittenhouse and John H. Livington, both published by himself. John Rubens Smith, an industrious teacher of drawing, who showed a certain ability in various branches of graphic art, is credited with some mezzotint work, such as the portraits of Gen. Benjamin Lincoln (1811) from a picture by *Coll. H. Sargent*, James Patterson after Otis (1837), and Rev. Thomas Brainerd (published by Smith as late as 1840). There was another universal genius, John Roberts (1768–1803), erratic and unable to turn his inventiveness to practical advantage. Dunlap states that he devised "a new mode of stippling, produced by instruments executed by himself" and "made a printing-press for proving his work." By him, says Stauffer, "a small mezzotint portrait of Washington exists (1799) which is extremely rich in effect and shows fine execution." Alexander Lawson tried mezzotint as he tried etching. George Graham worked in mezzotint as well as in stipple, but with more application and success, apparently. His portrait of John Mason (1804), after Archibald Robertson, shows delicacy in handling and modeling, and feeling for tone and color. And A. B. Durand, the famous line-engraver, attempted mezzotint at least once, in a portrait of his friend Sylvester Graham (of bran bread fame), but did not finish the plate.

But the purposeful and extensive exploitation of mezzotint occurred in the days of John Sartain, who came to this country in 1830. He has spoken of conditions when he began work here, of the "inferior quality of plate printing; Frankfort black was an article unknown." The first mezzotint executed by him here was *Patriotism and Age* after Neagle. Of strongly artistic temperament, versatile and adaptative, and of decided business instincts, he was quick to see the advantages of mezzotint as an expeditious method for magazine illustration in that period (approximately 1835–55). Portraiture was called for, mostly, and plates to grace the "keepsakes" and like annuals. There were "Christmas Blossoms" (1847), "The Irving Offering" (1851), "Dew Drops" (1853), "Affection's Gift" (1854) and what not besides, which had such adornments in mezzotint,—becurled females of most "ladylike" aspect and story-telling pictures of a sometimes inane order. The portraits, the best part of this work on a smaller scale, were turned out by Sartain with smooth facility, and quick if not always profound seizure of general effect and character. A certain individual note predominates in his plates, a freedom and lightness of touch which softened the ill effects of rapid, commercial creation.

The possibilities of mezzotint as a medium for illustration led Sartain into alliance with publishing interests. "Graham's Magazine" was begun in 1841; before that, as Sartain himself wrote, magazines, when illustrated at all, used worn-out plates, but "Graham's" had a new plate engraved for each number. The success of the undertaking was immense, a circulation of 40,000 was reached, and Sartain said that he had to engrave "four steel plates of each subject in order to keep pace in the printing of them with the increased demand." He issued and edited the

SIR THOMAS LAWRENCE
After a painting by himself.   Mezzotint by John Sartain

"Foreign Semi-Monthly" and in 1847 owned and edited
"The American Gallery of Art." He did an enormous
amount of work beside that which he furnished regularly
to his own periodicals; so, in one summer, forty-five plates
for annuals. Even such spurts of speed were accomplished as the scraping of the portrait of Espartero, on a
"rush order," in one night. Unfortunately, comparatively large editions meant rapidly wearing plates, the
later impressions frequently ghostly shadows, perhaps
touched up by roulette and graver into a fictitious semblance of pristine freshness. Sartain used roulette and
line particularly in his smaller portraits; a full-length of
William Maginn (1842) is quite in roulette. He did
several portraits after Sully, the Horace Binney being
possibly his best portrait plate. "Now I am to be sullied
for sartain," is the remark attributed to some one whose
portrait by Sully was to be "scraped" by Sartain. In
such portraits as the large ones of Robert Gilmor and
Sir Thomas Lawrence, both after Lawrence, Sartain
showed what he could do when opportunity offered. In
them he reflected somewhat the achievements of Charles
Turner and Samuel Cousins, the epigones of the great
eighteenth century mezzotinters in England, who proved
once again that extreme development of technical ability
in an art is quite apt to precede decay.

This decadence was shown here, as in England, in the
commercialization of technique into the so-called "mixed
method," in which scraper, burin, roulette, ruling machine
and stippling were combined in a monotonous hodge-
podge to produce superficial results easily. The pre-

dominance of weak sentimentality and fictitious grace in the "annual" plates was a general characteristic of this period of Victorian art. The softer effects of mezzotint were more easily perverted into an invertebrate mushiness than the insistent graver work of the line-engraving. Rarely were large portraits done here which recalled in a measure the thoroughness and richness of the earlier British work, or even the ease of that of the nineteenth century. Sartain's have been noted. There is one of Sir Charles T. Metcalfe, after A. Bradish (Montreal, 1844), by William Warner, executed in a vigorous and broad manner. Warner's *John Swift,* after Sully, is rich in effect; the grace of this painter seems to have spurred engravers to emulation.

William Page, the painter, was mezzotinting as early as 1834. A portrait of Rev. James Milnor, with decided feeling for tones and color and chiaroscuro, and one of Edwin Forrest, are by him.

For a short period the mezzotint shared with the line-engraving the field of the large framing print. Here, also, Sartain's name is prominent. He signed, among others, *King Solomon and the Iron Worker* and *Men of Progress: American Inventors* (1862), both after Christian Schussele, Leutze's *John Knox and Mary Queen of Scots* (Art Union of Philadelphia), Rothermel's *Battle of Gettysburg,* West's *Christ rejected,* and John Blake White's *Gen. Marion . . . inviting a British Officer to Dinner* (Apollo Association, 1840). T. Doney engraved *The Jolly Flat Boat Men* after G. C. Bingham (American Art Union, 1845); A. H. Ritchie *Mercy's Dream* after Huntington, and Whitechurch *Clay addressing the Senate* after P. F. Rothermel.

Among Sartain's contemporaries who scraped portraits for the "American Whig Review" and other publications in the forties, were Thomas Doney and P. M. Whelpley. They were good craftsmen, with a somewhat heavier touch than Sartain's, a tendency to work more on the plate and to produce a darker, more somber tone (accentuated by blacker, colder ink), recalling the daguerreotype original a little more mechanically, perhaps. Doney's *Distinguished Americans at a Meeting of the New York Historical Society* (1854) contains over fifty portraits.

There were others: H. S. Sadd, Sartain's son Samuel, S. H. Gimber, Thomas B. Welch and his one-time (about 1840–48) partner Adam B. Walter. The "mixed method" was employed with light-hearted industry by H. Wright Smith (a pupil of Doney), George E. Perine, J. C. Buttre and others. Further names which illustrate the use of mezzotint by engravers identified rather with work on copper in line and stipple are those of J. C. McRae (*Bishop J. M. Wainwright,* after Thomas Hicks, 1854), Illman & Sons (Washington Family, after Savage), and Illman & Pilbrow (portrait of Washington), all cited solely as examples of the commercialization of mezzotint.

The tendency in "mixed method" portraits was, on the whole, toward burin-engraving. Line-engraving held its own to the final exclusion of mezzotint, and was in its turn supplanted, to a very great extent, by wood-engraving.

The peculiar qualities of mezzotint to invest portraiture with its richness and sonority were utilized by William Sartain, the painter (son of John Sartain), who did various portraits, Washington after Schuessele (1864), John Brown, Gen. Braddock (1899), Byron and Irving, the last two printed in brown, a color that has been found more satisfactory to many than an absolute black. Max Rosenthal used mezzotint creditably, and in its pure form, in portraits of William Dunlap, Benjamin Harrison and Washington, after Stuart.

The most recent use of the mezzotint tools has placed them at the service of the color print, a field in which American artists of to-day do not stand second to their British contemporaries. S. Arlent Edwards has achieved noteworthy and international prominence in this field. Catalogues of his work include plates after artists of quite different periods, styles and points of view,—Gainsborough, Hals, Greuze, Da Vinci, Lancret, Ghirlandaio, Rembrandt, Vigée Le Brun, Morland, Holbein, Van Dyck, Luini, Botticelli. The great variety in method and subjects indicated by this list, taking us away from the former almost uniform choice of British paintings, he has reproduced with a soft richness of color. In the latter he has not hesitated to vary occasionally from the originals. Such emphasis on the personal element in these translations from canvas to paper makes the product something to be collected for the sake of the engraver quite apart from consideration of the original artist. His

Courtesy of Charles Scribner's Sons

EVENING, RACQUETTE LAKE
Mezzotint by J. D. Smillie

plates are produced in one printing, without retouching by hand on the print. His *Visit to the Boarding School,* after Morland, was considered by Frederick R. Halsey "His best, certainly technically." Charles Bird and J. S. King have also been enlisted in the service of this specialty, which has its circle of discriminating and admiring collectors. In recent years Frederick Reynolds, coming to us from England, has used mezzotint not only in reproductions of paintings by the old masters, but also in the production of portraits of noted Americans, past and present—Clay, Lincoln, Woodrow Wilson, Chief Justice F. D. White.

Original production in mezzotint is rare enough abroad and more so with us. One of our artists, at least, used this medium, with a freedom of manner and a richness of effect that open up interesting possibilities in its use as a painter art. That was James D. Smillie, a master craftsman, whose *Hollyhocks,* a plate of quiet charm, is said to have been scraped direct from nature. At the American Water Color Society's exhibition of 1911 there were shown his *Evening, Raquette Lake; Double Hollyhocks; A Piece of Jade* and *A Shoreless Sea,* the last an unfinished plate, free in feeling, "the best he ever did," said Mr. Mielatz. And John Henry Hill, painter and etcher, was led by his admiration for Turner to copy in mezzotint a plate in the *Liber Studiorum,* while Otis Weber reproduced his painting, *A rockbound Coast,* in etching-and mezzotint..

It seems useless to hope that any painters may turn

occasionally to the medium which offers them such interesting and profitable by-roads to explore by way of mental diversion. Perhaps some of the specialists who have in recent years labored so well to revive the appreciation of painter-etching may be led to give attention to mezzotint.

CHAPTER VI

AQUATINT AND SOME OTHER TINTS

AQUATINT is a response to the demand for tone, for a certain completeness of effect instead of the suggestion of the etching, for a fuller rendition of light and shade in place of the line of the line-engraving on copper. The process was used in France, for the color prints of Debucourt, Descourtis *et al.*, with complexity of manipulation and a superimposition of printings. These quite obliterated the traces of its characteristic features, the peculiarly reticulated grain caused by the powdered resin (dusted on to the plate or applied suspended in alcohol), which formed an etching ground when the plate was put in the acid bath. This feature was prominent in English work, in which the evident prime *raison d'être* of the process, the imitation of wash drawings in water color or sepia, is quite apparent. Aquatinting was much used for the illustration of books of travel after drawings executed in light outlines and flat washes of color or monotone. Such an extensive use was not to be expected in the United States, but the possibilities of the process evidently appealed to some experimentative spirits here. In 1799 Edward Savage painted and engraved two pictures of *The Constellation and L'Insurgent*, one of the fight and another of *the chace*. In May, 1811, some landscape plates (views of Fort Putnam and Fort Clinton) appeared in the Philadelphia "Port Folio," very crude, accompanied by high-sounding and hopeful letter-press comments. Bass Otis, the portrait painter, tried his hand also at aquatinting, in *Playing at Draughts,* after Burnet, and in portraits of Philip S. Physick, M.D., and the Rev. Abner Kneeland. An earlier *View of the Old Brick Meeting House in Boston,* 1808, drawn by John Rubens Smith and engraved by J. Kidder, is much better than the "Port Folio" plates mentioned, showing good contrasts of light and shade, with rolling clouds to counteract the straight lines of the buildings. Kidder's plates include several other Boston views, one (*Court House*) after his own design. *His View on Boston Common,* published in "The Polyanthos" (Boston, June, 1813), was referred to editorially as the work of "Master J. Kidder," and "his first essay in aquatinta." J. R. Smith himself did Pennsylvania, New York, and Rhode Island views, all large (*Catskill Mountain House* as late as 1830), some after his own designs, as was also a fireman's certificate. Two *Hudson River Portfolio* plates—No. 2: *Junction of the Sacandaga and Hudson Rivers* and No. 3: *Hadley's Falls*—appeared over his name. Wm. Hamlin of Providence, mezzotint engraver, did in aquatint *Peacock and L'Epervoir* (naval combat) and *U. S. Ship Philadelphia at Tripoli* (ship on fire). Francis Kearny, like Smith, tried his hand at various media; he studied aquatint and other processes "principally by the aid of books." Still another line-engraver, William Rollinson, practised aquatint; the E. B. Holden sale included a view of the New York Custom House, with the original drawing, both by Rollinson. His *View of New York from Long Island* (1801) was from a drawing by J. Wood. Rollinson used stipple and aquatint in a portrait of Washington after Savage, and in the portraits by Samuel Folwell aquatint and stipple also appeared in a combination "rather pleasing in effect, though showing an unpractised hand." Abner Reed, a stipple-engraver, aquatinted a portrait of Rev. Jonathan Edwards, after Molthrop, as well as a series of *Six Views, in Aquatinta taken from Nature* (Hartford, 1810). To occasional aquatints by line-engravers there are to be added views by William Kneass and J. I. Pease (*Fort Niagara*, 1814), and one by F. Shallus, poor enough but with a certain freedom (in sky effect) in contrast with his fearful line portrait of Captain Cook. J. Bower of Philadelphia did a *Bombardment of Fort McHenry*. And so on.

Particularly identified with the art in those early days was William Strickland, the architect. He did small views, such as *View on the Susquehannah* from a drawing by J. L. Morton ("Port Folio," Feb., 1816), scenes in the War of 1812 ("Analectic Magazine"), and portraits of heroes of the war, Hull, Decatur, Jackson, Lawrence, McDonough, and a full-length of Meriwether Lewis, *St. Memim* [sic!] *Pinxt*, done in coarse grain. The use of aquatint for portraits was not common at any time. A thin volume published in Baltimore in 1815, "The Art of Colouring and Painting Landscapes in Water Colours . . . By an Amateur," has ten plates by Strickland, colored by hand. Still another landscape aquatinter was

J. Drayton,—and a good print colorist to boot (*View near Bordentown, engraved and colored by J. Drayton*).

Caricature, too, is represented here: in some of the plates of William Charles (*John Bull and the Alexandrians, John Bull the Ship-Baker*) and in a later, unsigned picture of John Binns, *The Pedlar and his Pack*. Charles executed also plates after Rowlandson for the "Vicar of Wakefield" and the "Tour of Dr. Syntax," which he published.

The ground had been prepared when John Hill and W. J. Bennett, both Englishmen, came to this country in 1816. Their works mark the culmination of this short period of successful practice of the art. Hill, father of John William Hill and grandfather of John Henry Hill, executed a series of large plates after designs by Joshua Shaw (*Picturesque Views of American Scenery*, 1819) and W. G. Wall (the *Hudson River Portfolio*). This Hudson River series, an early tribute to the beauties of the "American Rhine," passed into the hands of Henry I. Megarey of New York, who issued an edition. There was some renumbering of the sheets, so that impressions exist with numbers different from those given in Stauffer's valuable work; e.g., 14, 2, 5, 20, instead of Stauffer's 5, 8, 10, 13, and so on. One of Hill's plates is the view of Broadway, New York City, at Canal Street, *Drawn and etched by T. Horner, aquatinted by J. Hill, printed by W. Neale*, 1836. (This giving credit to the printer is not uncommon on nineteenth century copper-plates, J. Neale, Rollinson, Andrew Maverick, and later Butler

New York from Governor's Island
Aquatint, after W. G. Wall, by John Hill

& Long, Kimmel & Co., J. E. Gavit and W. Pate being
among the names encountered.)

Hill, a good craftsman, appropriately used a coarser,
more open grain for these large plates, which were colored by hand. For his earliest works, the small magazine plates, in black-and-white, such as *Haddel's Point,
S. C., Richmond, Va., and York Springs, Va.,* all after
C. Fraser, he used a much closer grain, an exemplification
of the necessity of adjusting means to end.

Bennett, who became an N.A., signed plates well
known to collectors of views, particularly New York City
views, two of the most interesting plates being *South
Street, N. Y.,* and *Fulton Street,* both from his own
drawings. Among his plates for the "New Mirror" is
one of *Hay Sloops on the North River* (1843); "Fanny
Kemble thought the sloops of the North River the most
picturesque things she had seen in this country." His
larger pieces include *New York from Brooklyn Heights.
Painted by J. W. Hill* (1837), *New York taken from the
Bay near Bedlow's Island. Painted by J. G. Chapman,
Engraved by J. W.* [sic!] *Bennett,* printed in colors,
View of the Great Fire 1835 and *View of the Ruins after
the Great Fire,* both from paintings by N. Calyo, a scenic
artist, views of Baltimore, Boston and Troy, from his
own designs, and one of Buffalo after J. W. Hill. One
plate in which Bennett had a hand was a departure into
figure work: the portrait of Mrs. Maeder, late Miss
Clara Fisher, *engraved by Stephen H. Gimber and Wm.
J. Bennett from the original picture by Inman.* G. Lehman painted, engraved and hand-colored a series of Penn-

sylvania views (1829) and Annin & Smith, engravers and lithographers, tried their hand at aquatinting as well.

All the work spoken of is in flat tints, rather sharply circumscribed and consequently without gradations (excepting such as are effected through water-color washes), and with a resultant occasional stage-scenery effect. There was stray use of aquatint until well into the fifties, notably for large views. Robert Havell, the English engraver, who did plates for Audubon's book on birds, executed a view of Baltimore (1847), and two panoramic ones of New York City (1844), which latter he published at Sing Sing. Henry Papprill engraved two large views of New York City (1849), one *as seen from Governor's Island,* after F. Catherwood, the other (re-issued 1855 with necessary changes in names on signboards) *from St. Paul's Church,* after J. W. Hill. Hill designed also the large *New York City from Brooklyn,* engraved by *Himly,* printed by McQueen, London, 1855. Sigmund Himely, a Swiss who worked in Paris, did two other pictures of the metropolis, one (1851) painted by Heine, J. Kummer and Doepler (Heine and Doepler spent some time in this country), the other, *Vue de New York. Prise de Weahawk,* after Garneray, published in Paris, possibly much earlier. Another foreign-made view of the city is the well-known *Winter Scene in Broadway* (1857) by P. Girardet after H. Sebron, who was in New York City at the same time as Doepler. Line-engraving, and later on also lithography, took the place of aquatint as a means of reproducing pictures of landscape.

It was not until the movement for painter-etching took

OLD DAM
Aquatint by James D. Smillie

place in the seventies and eighties, that one man at least turned his attention again to the disused art. That was James D. Smillie; and he used aquatint as a painter art, as a medium for direct expression. In *An old Dam near Montrose* and *Old Houses near Boulogne,* he showed a mastery of technique which merged the flat, even tints into each other with more than a semblance merely of a gradual passing from light to shadow. With him, too, we find variation of method to suit the particular purpose: *Fairground, Montrose, with Sheep* shows a crayonlike effect, *Pansies* is done with a very coarse grain.

Charles F. W. Mielatz, a craftsman ever experimenting, similarly disclosed somewhat unexpected possibilities in painter-aquatint. In his *The Wave* the art through scraping and other manipulations acquired a pliancy, a fullness of delicate gradation that once seemed hardly possible. Moreover, this is an interesting piece of colorprinting in two tints, bluish green above and yellowish below, the two mingling in the center, the printing done from one plate at one time, the color having been applied *à la poupée.* Again, the etching, *Grand Central Depot at Night* (1889), has a light tint of aquatint, which took off the sharp edge of the etched lines and modulated their incisiveness into something like the suaver effect of softground etching. Finally, in *Winter Night,* he employed organdy, or something like it, to regulate the grain of the aquatint. The textile was laid onto a plate covered with etching ground and run through the press, exposing the copper wherever it was thus pressed through the ground. The plate was then subjected to the action of acid, and after that aquatinted. The process is therefore in a measure akin to what is known as "sandpaper mezzotint." Mielatz used aquatint in its more usual form, and as a reproductive art, in a series of New York City views done for the "Society of Iconophiles" after pictures on Staffordshire pottery, the proofs printed in blue ink.

Usually, however, aquatint is employed as an accessory to the etched line, either to add a tone or to serve as a basis to hold color. J. S. King, using it to get tones in reproductive etchings, applied the acid with feather or brush in order to avoid the characteristic sharp edges. John Henry Hill, in an etched view of Niagara, applied the grain on the falling water and foam with a delicacy similar to that of the sky of *Dunstanborough Castle* in Turner's *Liber Studiorum*. His *Moonlight on the Androscoggin*, entirely in aquatint, was published in the "American Art Review." C. A. Vanderhoof sometimes made a restricted use of the medium. Helen Hyde aquatinted a Japanese subject with the flat effect of Japanese wood-block tints. W. F. Hopson employed aquatint as an accessory. Likewise Addison T. Millar, to add tone to some of his etchings, for instance *The Sheepfold, Laren* (1904) and *Moonrise, the Shipyard* (1905). Millar sometimes washed a drawing on a plate with prepared ink, then covered the plate with etching ground, immersed it in water, thereby dissolving the ink and lifting off the ground above it, baring the plate wherever it had been drawn upon. Aquatint was then applied, taking effect on the bared portions. Joseph Pennell, easily master of processes, turned from line to tone in a number of subjects, with results which moved Campbell Dodgson to speak of his "fascinating methods."

Mary Cassatt did some aquatints in black, but used the process more notably in a fine grain, to hold color, in her dry-points intended to be printed with something of the effect of Japanese chromo-xylographs. Vaughan Trowbridge employed the aquatint ground in practical purity, to express light and shade and tone by "stopping out," and as a means for holding color, with a certain aquarelle-like vivacity. George Senseney combined the suave qualities of soft-ground etching with aquatint in prints of a noteworthy spontaneity in tonal effect. "The Senseney prints," wrote Huneker, "attract you by their air of sweetness, their soft magnetism, their harmonious ensemble in tonalities." The same two media have occasionally been blended by Lester G. Hornby, in color-work as well as in black-and-white. They were used also, with the addition of rouletting, in *Road to the Beach*, by Mielatz. That artist, always of a strongly experimental bent, ever and again followed the alluring by-paths of color-printing, his last important work having been an engrossing reproduction of *Woman and Macaws*, by George Luks. And there are the figure pieces, of an exotically decorative charm, by Vojtech Preissig, who came to us from Bohemia.

More recently, Arthur B. Davies, avid of expression in ever new media, has employed aquatint as he has lithography, to evolve figures that live in a world of their own, placed in attitudes studied but not posed, examples of beauty for beauty's sake. He weaves various influences subtly into the pattern of his own views. His work in painting, in etching, in lithography is all marked by the same striving,—"spiritual adventures in search of expression," Henry Tyrrell calls it.

John Taylor Arms, developing "a strong desire for tonal expression," turned to aquatint, using it at times in its purity, but also modeling with burnisher or scraper. F. K. Detwiller is still another who has adopted this medium, using it in his depictions of shipping activities during the war, a series made for the government.

The record of American achievement in this art of pleasing effects embraces practically all its possibilities, presented with noteworthy craftsmanship.

There are other methods of producing tints and tones on copper plates. Foul biting, sulphur, scotch-stone, and experiments such as etching zinc with rain-water (made by Mielatz), are noted in the chapter devoted to etching. Sandpaper mezzotint Pennell has used occasionally to produce grained tint.

The monotype may as well be considered with miscellaneous processes here. It is produced by painting on the plate with printer's ink, or oil colors (Bacher used "burnt sienna or ivory black with a medium"), worked up with rags, brushes, stumps, brush-handles, fingers,—any instruments to suit the artist's fancy and serve his purpose. With the ink or color still wet, the plate is run through the press, with a resultant impression on paper that must of course be, in each case, unique. The process has had a peculiar attraction for artists, from Castiglione's time to the present day. The monotypist within the proper limits of the art works with unrestrained freedom while at the same time considerable demands are made on his dexterity and experience in order that the best results may be foreseen and produced. S. R. Koehler says: "The first to show such impressions publicly in America was Wm. M. Chase in New York; soon afterward Charles H. Walker in Boston discovered the process independently, and has since applied it with particular preference, and Peter Moran and others followed them." Dr. Charles H. Miller, N.A., in Rotterdam in 1879 bought a monotype, a head of a girl of a Carrièrelike mistiness, inscribed *T. Cremona dip. I. Ciconi inc. 1874.* This he showed to fellow members of the Art Club of New York, and it was subsequently exhibited in that city. Thereupon, said Mr. Miller, "Mr. Chase and others experimented with the fascinating possibilities" of this process. Chase showed a monotype at a black-and-white show at the Academy (N. Y.) in 1881, and Peter Moran's exhibits at the first etching show in Philadelphia (1882–83) included some specimens of this alluring art. Christian Brinton records the enthusiasm of Joseph Jefferson for this medium, and the work in colors of Prof. Rufus Sheldon. Otto H. Bacher's method was employed, as Bacher records in his "With Whistler in Venice," by Duveneck and his class "as a means of amusement," under the name of "Bachertype."

In recent years the process has again attracted increased attention among artists. The late Louis Loeb, Augustus Koopman, and Charles Warren Eaton have practised it. Loeb, Albert Sterner and E. Peixotto were among the members of a monotype club formed in New York City under the presidency of Leslie Cauldwell, according to Brinton. Eaton showed some prints, rich in effect, at the exhibition of the American Water Color Society in 1910, where there were also several interesting ones in color—*Girl at the Bath Tub, Girl near Mirror*— by Everett Shinn, who called them "pastel monotypes." C. F. W. Mielatz used the process with touches of color, in reproducing certain picturesque spots in New York City, in a series of plates reproduced in photogravure for the Society of Iconophiles (1908). He also executed a number of other monotypes, getting interesting effects with a pigment not intended for art or even color purposes at all, drawing in broad strokes which contracted when the plate was heated. In 1911, Albert Sterner held in New York an exhibition of monotypes, among them *The Echo, The Model* and *The Gray Vase,* which lastnamed the "Evening Post" singled out for "the wonderful lights on the woman's flesh" and a "serenity of color"; *My boy* was characterized as a "remarkable piece of mellow color." Sterner, working with brush, cloth or fingers, modeling with rapid energy, has shown what results training, fine, sensitive, artistic temperament and flexibility of method can effect in this medium. E. Haskell, whom A. E. Gallatin well described as "always a student and experimenter," whose "point of view is invariably fresh and engaging," quite naturally extended his activities to the production of monotypes, "some of which have been worked in pastel." Eugene Higgins, too, tried his hand at this process, which offered rich possibilities for the rendering of his style, with its dark recesses of mysterious shadow, its subdued mellow lights. All proper use of such processes by artists is to be commended. It gives new viewpoints, arouses interest, protects from the rut.

CHAPTER VII

WOOD-ENGRAVING

THE wood-block is a vehicle of strong characteristics and great possibilities. For four centuries, before the advent of the ubiquitous half-tone, it served the people in the close relation offered by its universal use in book illustration. It was utilized in the coarsest work and the finest, in roughly cut posters and in delicately elaborate reproductions of works of art, in vigorous facsimile line and in richly tender tones. Woodcut illustrations appeared in the earliest books printed in Europe. For a while it sank into decay, so that in the eighteenth century the copper-plate, both in etched and engraved form, took possession also of the field of book-illustration, and wood-engraving was relegated to the chapbook and other like means of reaching the common people. Thomas Bewick opened the way for new and hitherto unthought-of possibilities.

America formed, quite naturally, no exception to the general rule. The parallel with European conditions may be drawn even to this extent that the first engraving known to have been executed in this country was on wood. This was a portrait of the Rev. Richard Mather, supposed to have been engraved by John Foster. This engraver did also the *seal and arms of ye colony* (in "General Laws and Liberties of the Massachusetts Colony,"

RICHARD MATHER
By John Foster. The first known wood-engraving
executed in the colonies.

1672) and a map of New England (1677). This map,
issued with Rev. W. Hubbard's narrative of Indian
troubles, was the first one engraved in this country.
Subsequent response to what needs our colonies had for
portraiture or views came practically all in copper-engraving. The rougher effects of the woodcut methods of the
day appeared in printer's stock ornaments, newspaper
titles and occasional cuts, even in paper currency, printed
from the wood-block or from type-metal. There was,
for instance, the title design of the "Boston Gazette"
(March 11, 1771) representing Britannia and various
attributes. Or such early attempts at newspaper cartooning as the snake divided into pieces representing the
individual colonies, with the device *Unite or die* or *Join
or die,* which appeared in various papers before the Revolution. This is attributed to Benjamin Franklin. In
"Father Abraham's Almanac" for 1759 there is a frontispiece representing a man at a telescope, signed *H. D.;*
the theory that the engraver is Henry Dawkins is invit-
ingly obvious. There were such ambitious attempts as
the series of profile portraits, each representing a man
wearing a cocked hat. All are either printed from the
same block or copied from the same original, but they are
labeled, respectively, *Bradley, Governor of Rhode Island,
Columbus, Henry Lee, Samuel Adams* and *Richard
Howel.* A few instances of known eighteenth century
engravers are noted in Stauffer and elsewhere; Thomas
Sparrow and Francis Dewing (who did also calico printing), both engravers on copper, produced also some
woodcuts. The fragmentary appearance of this infor-

mation is in accord with the sporadic nature of the work described. With us the renascence came, as in England, through the "white line." Late in the eighteenth century, Dr. Alexander Anderson, having first tried copper-engraving, and then cutting in relief on type-metal for newspapers, saw work by Bewick in 1793 and was led to try box-wood. He re-engraved Bewick cuts ("Quadrupeds," New York, 1804, and "Emblems of Mortality"), meanwhile studying medicine. He soon found much employment from various publishers; of one of them, Samuel Wood, Anderson himself says: "I did an infinity of cuts for his excellent set of small books." The amount of work he accomplished was enormous; the New York Public Library has about 8,000 proofs in old scrap-books, apparently including not many duplicates. Lossing says he did, on wood, "from sheet ballads, primers, business cards, tobacconist's devices, wrappers of playing cards, diplomas and newspaper cuts of every sort, to magazines, stately scientific treatises and large Bibles." An interesting example of his work, done at about his best period (1818), is the bust portrait of Washington (the one facing right!), printed from the original block as a frontispiece to "A Bibliography of American Books relating to Prints," by H. C. Levis (1910). It is dark in tone, the face vigorously modeled without cross-hatching, and the background *criblée* (white dots on a black ground). Two large engravings are recorded to his credit, *Returning from the Boar Hunt*, after Ridinger, a bold, vigorous piece of white-line engraving, and *Water-fowl* after

Teniers. These were copied, it is said, from copper-plates, but Anderson, though originally an engraver on copper, did not allow that fact to influence him in his work on wood. When copying Shakespeare cuts after Thurston by John Thompson, he has toned down the metallic luster of the original by adhering strictly to the white line and preserving the essential character of wood-engraving, instead of twisting it into an imitation of copper-plate. Wm. Clark, an old Philadelphia engraver, aptly quoted the "Port Folio," 1812, page 14, with reference to *Sherlic and Venvula,* from Ossian, by Anderson, shown at the exhibition of the Academy of Fine Arts: "We have at all times been delighted on viewing the works of this excellent, useful and unassuming artist. Engravings on wood, when finely executed, are of great importance, as they are printed with the letter press, take off large numbers of impressions, and are afforded at a low price, but the talent and skill necessary in this truly useful branch of the arts is not perhaps at present sufficiently appreciated." The recognition of Anderson and the inclusion of a wood-engraver's work in so early an art exhibition are as noteworthy as is the understanding of both the commercial and the artistic possibilities of wood-engraving shown in this notice. It further indicates Anderson's standing, that he was an honorary member of the National Academy of Design. Anderson had four pupils, Garret Lansing, William Morgan (who "abandoned the graver for the pencil"), John H. Hall, and his own daughter Anna. John H. Hall, who began in 1826, and in 1830 found employment with Carter, Andrews &

Co., did some of his best work, ornithological illustrations, in a spirit and manner showing that Bewick's influence had descended through Anderson to his pupil. He could be both delicate, as in some of his landscapes, and vigorous, as when he combined the white line and inky blacks.   In an announcement dated Albany, Oct. 20, 1826, he states that "it is a fact well attested, though not generally known, that engravings on boxwood, with proper usage, are more durable than either type-metal cuts or copper-plate engravings."

Abel Bowen, who began as early as 1805, brought the art to Boston about 1812, his apprentice, Nathaniel Dearborn, starting in business there for himself some two years later.   Much of Bowen's production consisted of copies for American editions of English books, for example the "Young Ladies' Book" (1830).   "Very remarkable for their fidelity to the original," says Linton of the cuts in the latter; "the distinguishing manner of each engraver is so exactly preserved that I was with difficulty convinced the cuts were not done from transfers."   William Croome, pupil of Bowen, worked somewhat similarly to his master; he subsequently turned to illustrating and to designing for bank-notes.   Other pupils of Bowen were G. Thomas Devereux, Mallory, Kilburn, B. F. Childs, George Loring Brown the painter and Hammatt Billings the architect; this in the thirties.

Bowen, a publisher of illustrated books, brought out "The Naval Monument" (1816), "A topographical and historical Description of Boston" (1817), and "Picture of Boston" (1829).   That form of activity is found in a number of other cases. John N. Barber of New Haven, "draughtsman, engraver, author, editor and publisher," issued a number of historical works, and, it is said, devoted his energies not so much to accomplishment in engraving as to preaching "the Gospel by means of pictures." For his book on Connecticut, he traveled about, collecting material and making sketches for the illustrations, just as Benson J. Lossing did, in later years, when preparing his "field books" of the Revolution and the War of 1812, the volume on the Hudson River, and similar books. Many of the cuts in these, signed *Lossing & Barritt,* were done, I am told, by R. B. Pierson. Several other engravers became known as publishers of illustrated books or periodicals. T. W. Strong issued "Yankee Notions," "Young America" and other serials. Joseph A. Adams was directly interested in the Harper Bible. Later in the century John Karst was projecting and publishing school books and A. V. S. Anthony was superintending for Osgood in Boston the preparation of finely illustrated books of poetry and other literature, planning text, pictures and all.

Returning to our earlier engravers, we find William Mason introducing the art to Philadelphia in 1810, followed by his pupil Gilbert. The latter, as I was informed by Wm. Clark (who himself began his apprenticeship in 1851), was connected with the "American Sunday School Union." Later there were Fairchild in Hartford and Horton in Baltimore. In 1829, Abraham J. Mason, an Englishman, came to America, was made an Associate of the National Academy in 1830, and became professor of wood-engraving at that institution, delivering also a course of lectures on his art. But although he also had a bookstore on Canal Street, New York City, he could not command a satisfactory income. These and other names are recorded, with interesting comment, in W. J. Linton's "History of Wood-engraving in America" (Boston, 1882).

Linton notes that in the forties illustrated books began to increase. The "Family Bible" was brought out by the Harpers in 1846, "embellished with 1,600 historical engravings by J. A. Adams, more than 1,400 of which are from original designs by J. G. Chapman," the exceptions being transfers of English cuts. Many of the smaller blocks were engraved by pupils of Adams. There was no use of the white line here; it was all straight facsimile work, faithful rendering of Chapman's lines, which latter were executed with a fineness and formal precision and cross-hatching reminiscent of copper-plate work. All of this had to be rendered literally, with a resultant mechanical hardness in the engraving. This feeling appears also in Chapman's "American Drawing Book," issued in several editions from 1847 on, with cuts by Kinnersley, Herrick, Howland, Wright, Bobbett, Bookhout; "the very perfection of mechanism," says Linton, but also "I know no other book like this, so good, so perfect in all it undertakes."

It was one evidence of the considerable English influence on American wood-engraving, this quality which led Linton to speak of Adams as a possible American Thompson, this tendency to apply the methods of copper-plate

THE LAST ARROW
Wood-engraving after J. G. Chapman
By J. A. Adams

engraving to the wood. Yet the "Harper Bible" in drawing, engraving and printing was a very remarkable production for its time. Linton calls attention particularly to Adams's inventiveness and skill in overcoming difficulties in preparing his engraved blocks for the press, and states that his "printing of his own engraving is equal to the best of any time." And of his engraving he says that the best work, such as the *Massacre of the Innocents* and *Jacob's Dream,* is "yet unequaled in this country [this in 1882!] and worthy to rank beside the best of the great old time in England." The reference to English influence recalls the stimulating infusion of British blood through the addition of such men as Albert Bobbett, John Andrew, George H. Thomas and Robert Carter ("Frank Leslie") to the ranks of our native engravers.

The increasing skill of our illustrators counteracted on the engravers. Not only was facsimile reproduction of pencil drawings called for, but washes placed on the block by the artist had to be rendered in lines. That developed interpretation. By 1852, in which year the Putnams issued Irving's "Sketch Book" and the "Knickerbocker History of New York," we had such able craftsmen as H. W. Herrick and E. J. Whitney (both designers also) and B. F. Childs to cut on wood the illustrations in a worthy manner. The "Sketch Book," at its time "the most beautifully got-up book that had appeared," had illustrations by Darley, Hoppin, William Hart and others, engraved by Richardson; the "Knickerbocker History" was illustrated by Darley alone. To these and other issues from the presses of the Harpers and the Putnams there came a third strong influence toward the advance of American wood-engraving and book-illustration,—the American Tract Society. Engraving became more delicate and clear in line, tints became smoother and greater attention was paid to tone. Kinnersley, Annin, Hayes, J. H. Richardson, Benjamin F. Childs, Bogert, Jocelyn, Bobbett, Edmonds and Whitney are names found in the juvenile literature published by the Society. Whitney's work rather stands out, his engraving of Sir John Gilbert's drawings being particulalry noteworthy, and some birds by Childs and Kinnersley after Herrick are of special interest. To the names already mentioned are to be added those of D. C. Hitchock, S. P. Avery, W. Roberts, W. Howland, Bobbett & Edmonds, Bobbett & Hooper, J. W. and N. Orr, Jocelyn & Annin, Morse, Redding, Orr & Andrews, Richardson & Co., Richardson & Cox, Kingdon & Boyd. The frequent occurrence of firm names indicates commercialization of production.

About the fifties or sixties there came also the use of tint-blocks, in the manner of the old chiaroscuro prints. Much less elaborate, however; it was simply a matter of using an extra block to print one tint,—say red, or blue, or light yellowish brown,—in which some high lights, a few clouds for instance, had been cut out so as to appear white in the print.

Wood-engraving was now the principal reproductive medium through which art was brought before the greater public. It served for the illustration of books (including the schoolbook with its obvious influence on

the impressionable young mind), magazines, weekly illustrated journals, comic papers, and for such an occasional
cut as might appear in the daily press, the "Herald" of
New York, for instance. The illustrated daily did not
exist in those days, but there were sporadic outbursts in
the one-issue "blanket sheets."

All this magazine and periodical work necessitated a
haste that neutralized much of the good effect which the
possibility of larger, broader treatment may have had in
counteracting the tendency to mere technical finesse.
During the War, especially, illustrators and engravers
no doubt had to work against time.

While wood-engraving served temporary needs, it also
answered more and more the demand for pictorial instruction through the reproduction of works of art as well
as of beauty of natural scenery.

In the late sixties and the seventies there came an
increasing improvement in technique, which found employment in growing plans for elaborately illustrated
books. Gift books, *éditions de luxe* of the poets, volumes
of travel and description were issued with a wealth of
illustrations. Very likely there were not a few cases in
which such undertakings were not well advised, had no
raison d'être beyond the production of a seller, an elegant adornment for the drawing-room table. No doubt,
too, much of the engraving in these elaborate publications
showed "an average of creditable mediocrity." Yet on
the whole the tendency toward refinement must have
tended also to refine public taste, and the encouragement

afforded both designers and engravers no doubt resulted in mutual influence for good between the two.

Linton declaimed vigorously against fineness, meaningless niggling delicacy, weak dexterity. But he is careful to except from this condemnation the fineness that is necessary and fitting, such as is found in Henry Marsh's exquisitely delicate rendering of the downy, evanescent bloom on the wings of moths, the flabby softness of caterpillars, the horny hardness of beetles, in Harris's "Insects injurious to Vegetation" (1862) or in Closson's *Winifred Dysart* after George Fuller.

A. V. S. Anthony's "tasteful supervision," during 1866–89, of the books published by Osgood of Boston, notably the quarto edition of Longfellow's works, had a good effect on the development of the art. Anthony was himself an engraver of distinguished ability, and elegance in style. Other engravers at this time were J. P. Davis, Berlett, Kilburn & Mallory, Annin, Hayes, and John Andrew, under whose "careful superintendence" the engravings for the book "Pioneers in the Settlement of America" were executed. A noteworthy stimulus to good engraving was afforded by the publication of "Picturesque America" (1872–74). In those two profusely illustrated volumes, opportunity came to engravers such as John Tinkey, Morse, Harley, Filmer, Halliwell, J. A. Bogert, Langridge, Karst, N. Orr, J. H. Richardson, Anthony, Annin (whose *Walls of the Grand Cañon,* after Thomas Moran, is a particularly careful and fine example), F. O. Quartley, Slader, Henry Linton, Measom, Cranston, Robert Hoskin, Palmer, Alfred Harral, and

W. J. Linton, the last eight Englishmen, some of whom became acclimated here. The "calm elegance and delicacy" of Hoskin, who was not carried away by the "new school," was emphasized by S. R. Koehler.

Among the artists of English birth W. J. Linton was prominent. His work has distinction, is "firm and honest" (which he himself called ' the first qualification of an engraver"), exemplifies his theory that the engraver should draw with the graver, and illustrates his devotion to the expressiveness of the line and its possibilities in rendering form, texture, substance and distances. Said he: "The art of engraving is discoverable, even by the uninitiated, in the intention of the lines." In spite of a certain direct vigor and boldness ("coarseness" he designates it), his method could produce such an interesting effect of light and tone as *The Mayflower at Sea* after Granville Perkins. In engraving and writing he exerted a strong plea for the engraver as an interpreting artist, yet his own vigorous individuality found adapting changes of expression to suit the personality of the various artists upon whose work he was engaged.

The cuts in "Picturesque America" form an interesting collection of well-engraved landscapes. The student of the art has rich opportunity here for suggestive comparison of differences in treatment. Koehler calls the book an epoch-making work, and quotes Linton as saying that it contains the best landscapes cut in America. The "Art Journal" begun by the Appletons in 1875 is to be noted, as is the "Aldine, or Art Journal of America" (begun in

1871), which latter included cuts by Davis & Spier, and early work by Juengling and Cole.

The number of talented and adaptative craftsmen, not a few of them of English or German birth, was increasing. At the same time the development of technique brought about a tendency to greater elaboration, to more careful rendering of various textures and of color values. And this was strongly influenced by the alliance between the wood-block and the camera. Before there was devised the process of photographing on to the block the drawing, painting or object to be reproduced, the drawing had to be executed directly on the wood with pencil or pen, in lines that had to be cut in facsimile by the engraver. At most, there were added washes which the engraver had to render in lines. But now the original might be executed in any medium and size; pencil, charcoal, oils or water color might be used. It was photographed on to the wood-block, and the engraver translated it into his own language. Furthermore, he did not destroy the original by cutting it away as he engraved the block, but the photograph on the block was to him simply a guide, while the original stood before him. The possibilities thus opened up were seized upon, and there was formed a distinctly American school of wood-engraving, which enjoyed a lucrative period of brilliant achievement. The wish to render tones and color values led these new engravers to be deeply absorbed in the imitation of textures, to the extent that even the brush-marks of paintings were faithfully reproduced. Henry Marsh, in some blocks after drawings by John La Farge (e.g., for

"Songs of the old Dramatists," Boston, 1873, or those illustrating scenes in the Arabian Nights), done with a solid richness of effect, proved the adaptability of his art. Such cuts, and others by other engravers, in a measure led the way to the daring effects of the new school. In Bogert's *Caught by the Snow* (which appeared in "St. Nicholas") after T. Moran, "a cut full of refinement and delicacy, without sacrifice of effect," there may be seen, for example, how long, sweeping lines, effectively crossed in white, could be made to indicate whirling snow.

CHAPTER VIII

THE "NEW SCHOOL" OF WOOD-ENGRAVING

WITH the wakening of new aims, of new ideals, there came changes in technique to meet changing demands. Broken, short lines, scattered in whatever direction seemed best fitted to reproduce a given detail, took the place of the more regularly cut and longer sweeps of the graver.

It has been contended that J. G. Smithwick's engraving of C. S. Reinhart's *Drumming out a Tory*, in "Harper's Weekly" for February 3, 1877, cut, as Koehler says, "spot for spot," was the first published application of the new method. Again, Timothy Cole in 1906 wrote James E. Kelly that *The Gillie Boy*, from a drawing by Kelly, was the first thing of this kind which he engraved and the first ever done, and that he "will always regret . . . that his modesty prevented him from signing it." This appeared in "Scribner's" for August, 1877. But the illustrations engraved by Frederick Juengling (the "boldest and most inconsiderate experimenter among the pioneers of the new school," says Koehler) for articles dealing with the New York police force, the New York aquarium, "A Railroad in the Clouds," etc., appearing in "Scribner's Monthly" for 1877, made the first obvious, continued assertion of the new point of view. The drawings for these illustrations were executed by James E. Kelly, slapped down in broad brush-marks, blocked in with a disdain of finish.

Care was taken to reproduce this style faithfully. The first Kelly illustration that has come to my notice appears on page 581 of "Scribner's" for March, 1877; it bears no engraver's name, and is comparatively timid. The second, on page 585, is signed with J. G. Smithwick's initials. But, as already said, it is with the Kelly-Juengling cuts that the new method sets in with full swing. In these, designer and engraver coincided; here was the opportunity to state the newly discovered possibilities of the boxwood and graver in straightforward, unmistakable terms. They came as a shrill trumpet blast to gather adherents to the banner of the new dispensation. Artists, engravers, art editors and the public were fairly caught in the intoxication of this delight in astonishing achievement. One strong voice was raised in warning, that of W. J. Linton. He laid down his principles in an article on "Art in Engraving on Wood," which appeared in the "Atlantic Monthly," and for which he was denounced with some acrimony. Opposition drew from his pen a little volume entitled "Some practical Hints on Wood-Engraving for the Instruction of Reviewers and the Public" (Boston, 1879). Finally he issued his "History of Wood-Engraving in America" (1882). The critical and historical account of the development of the art, particularly during 1840–70, will always make this an indispensable book of reference. The portion relating to the work of the "new school" is of interest and value on account of the comments on the numerous examples given. Linton, while evidently striving to be fair (he finds much to praise), protested vehemently against an undue and slavish devotion to textures and tones, to ultra-refinement. He found, too often, the essential sacrificed to the unessential, while at the same time the very distinction of substance aimed at was missed. As an instance, among many, he pointed out Juengling's remarkably clever *Professor,* after Duveneck, with lip, cheek, eye, hair, coat and background "all of the same wooden texture." As a result, says he, lines of demarcation indicated by differences in color are lost, and the *Professor's* cranium—the hair having faded into the background—appears misshapen and deeply gashed. He deplored so much real talent in all this new work misapplied, "spent on endeavors to rival steel line-engraving or etching, in following brush-marks, in pretending to imitate crayon work, charcoal or lithography." It was the tendency to render substance rather than spirit to which he objected. He insisted on the importance of the line, and of "drawing with the graver." That implied, with Linton, despite a certain flexibility of technique, an adherence to some conventions, a translation into the language of the engraver.

On the other hand, Timothy Cole more recently, speaking of the changes brought about in modern wood-engraving, says: "At last it became apparent that the old conventions were inadequate and that they had to go by the board. The line *had* to be tampered with in order faithfully to render the qualities characteristic of the artist's painting. In other words, the painting came to be deemed more important than the exploitation of the engraver's skill in the production of lines. All the old conception of reproducing textures—a certain sort of line for this and another sort of line for that—had to go." All very true, yet it was "exploitation of the engraver's skill" which called forth Linton's severest strictures. It is a question whether Cole, in the maturity of his power, has not to a certain extent approached Linton's point of view.

As to photographing on the block, Linton points out that it was done in the London "Cornhill" days, long before the advent of our "new school." And when met by the statement that "the freest handling is not attainable [by the designer] on the limited surface of a block," he asks: "Was Holbein cramped when he drew the Day of Judgment on a block three inches by two?" Linton made a strong plea for the status of the engraver as a thinking artist, who must interpret the original in his own language and way, and not slavishly imitate it *ad absurdum*. There was a basis of common sense and of esthetic reason in Linton's strictures.

The late Sylvester Rosa Koehler summed up the matter in sane language. American wood-engraving, he wrote, began to go its own way; the evolution was "justified, indeed necessary." He continues: "Linton bases on the erroneous assumption that wood-engraving through its material and its tools is irrevocably confined within the limits of what has already been accomplished," while, in fact, "wood-engraving must adjust itself to the character of contemporary art." And that contemporary art, that new movement of the seventies, he points out, was under the influence of France, of the "reign of technique and color," and in its turn naturally influenced wood-engraving and illustration, so that the purely technical side, "the how rather than the what," became predominant. The delicate pencil drawing had already given way to a great extent to wash drawings on the block, and now came large paintings, photographed in reduced form on the block. "Here, then, the wood-engraver was confronted by a new problem:—he was no longer to draw, he was to paint!" Some silly and ugly work resulted. "The boldness of the manner degenerated into coarseness; emancipation from abandoned academic rules seemed best proven by impudently violating all laws of nature and art, and particularly all demands of beauty." Gradations of tone and color, textures, the quality of pulsating air, all the things which the painter rendered through differences in handling of the brush, the superposition of layers of color, had to be translated by the engraver with his one instrument, the burin. The imitative spirit went so far as the indication of the grain of the paper in white spots in water colors. "In the one-sided striving for tonality . . . the textures of the materials represented are but too often entirely overlooked." Koehler's conclusion is that all these efforts eventually bore good fruit. The final impression that he gives is that in the belief in certain underlying eternal laws of fitness and beauty, and of the necessary integrity of the line, he and Linton are, after all, on common ground. Linton ends his "History" by saying of the men of the "new school": "Notwithstanding all my censures, the revival of wood-engraving is in their hands. They will outgrow their mistakes."

The fact remains that the "new school" did its work and did it well. After we have eliminated what was ill-advised so very much remains that we can continue to feel great and justified pride in the results of the movement. It left the mark of its achievement indelibly inscribed in the annals of wood-engraving. Not a few of the engravers identified with this "new school" were of foreign birth and early foreign training, but their talents were enlisted by an impetus carried to its highest development here. J. F. Jungling's block after Whistler's drypoint of Riault, the engraver, and of Daubigny's etched portrait of himself, showed what the imitative care of the "new school" could accomplish in straight line facsimile work. John G. Smithwick was for some time in partnership with Frank French, among whose works was a volume of "Home Fairies and Heart Flowers" (1886), heads of children from his own drawings, with text by Miss Sangster. Richard Alexander Müller's ability was well exemplified in *On the old Sod,* from the painting by William Magrath. There were, furthermore, S. S. Kilburn, William H. Morse, E. Schladitz, H. W. Peckwell, Richard George Tietze, William Miller, W. M. Aikman, S. G. Putnam, J. W. Evans, F. H. Wellington, F. W. Putnam, Victor Bernström, E. H. Del'Orme, Van Ness, J. H. E. Whitney, M. Haider and Miss Caroline Powell. All craftsmen with whom technical ability and artistic feeling produced the best results. Miss Powell, like

Mrs. Anna Botsford Comstock (devoted particularly to natural history subjects), studied at the engraving school for women at Cooper Institute, New York City. This school was established in 1859 and continued until 1890 or '91, being managed successively by Robert O'Brien (1859–67), Linton (1868–70), Miss Charlotte B. Cogswell (1871–80) and J. P. Davis (1880–90).

Thomas D. Sugden, an old engraver who learned his art with T. W. Strong, and who for years was in charge of the block and plate department of The Century Co., has compiled a manuscript volume, "Remarks on Wood Engraving, by One-o-them" (1904), unconventional comments accompanying a number of proofs.

Not a few of the engravers became identified with some specialty in style or subject, or became best known through some particular engraving. Thomas Johnson, who excelled in portraits, won praise for "calm and appropriate treatment." Gustav Kruell long devoted himself to portraiture, producing work such as the vigorous head of Fletcher Harper, and the smaller heads in the series of musicians by himself and Johnson (1878). He developed a style of strength and distinction, in which a proper appreciation of tried convention and tradition is modified by a sane adaptation of new methods. His large portraits of Wendell Phillips, W. T. Sherman, Robert E. Lee, Beethoven, Darwin (with small "side whiskers"), Webster, Hawthorne and Lincoln (clean-shaven), gave him much opportunity for personal expression, rendering in the richness of his burin-stroke the matter-of-fact truthfulness of the camera's point of view. The personalities he pictures rise out of the impersonal reflection of the photograph into a fresh and most lively characterization.

Frank S. King, who later turned to engraving on copper, numbered among his blocks such quite different undertakings as a series after Burne-Jones, a portrait of Modjeska after Carolus Duran, *The Fog* after F. S. Church and finished productions akin to Marsh's insects, for instance a peacock's feather ("Harper's Monthly," 1878) from a drawing by W. H. Gibson. His *Lobster Pot* ("Scribner's Monthly") won strong approval from Linton because "the rock and the water are really distinct substances, and the lobsters have the form and texture of lobsters."

W. B. Closson delighted and excelled in the reproduction of hazy, vaguely defined effects such as appear in the lightness and delicacy of his engraving from a drawing by William Rimmer (*Magdalen*), with its effect of soft, broken, crayon or charcoal lines, or even more in his excellent *Winifred Dysart* after George Fuller. Later he engraved blocks from his own designs, the preference for not too sharply circumscribed forms still evident. Elbridge Kingsley was particularly happy in presenting the rich, succulent foliage of Rousseau or Diaz, or the joyous hymn to nature that Corot sang, or D. W. Tryon's dreams of misty evening. His engravings executed from nature were transcripts of mood rather than of cold form, visions rather than views. He did fifteen illustrations "engraved directly from nature" for Whittier's "Poems of Nature."

Ernst Heinemann successfully reflected the airy, translucent manner of F. S. Church in that picture of a mer-
maid riding on a horse dimly outlined in a swirling wave,
or in *Nymphe des Eaux* ("L'Art," November, 1889).
But he showed also command of entirely different manners in the *Guitar Player* of Frans Hals, *The Studio* after
T. Ribot (medal, Buffalo Exposition of 1901), or his
best, the Plantin proof-readers. Influenced by the spirit
of the new school, he was not carried away by its vagaries.

John P. Davis, one of the older men, changed his style
and produced such blocks as the *Dartmouth Moors* after
R. Swain Gifford, in which Linton, while criticising on
technical grounds, finds the tone "of admirable quality."
He, a link between the old and the new, was the last secretary of the Society of American Wood Engravers.

Cole and Wolf developed each an absolutely distinct
style, a manner of expression born of a long experience
which engendered a remarkable development of technique, placed always fully at the service of the particular
artist whose spirit was being drawn from the canvas at
a given time. That is the essential feature in the work
of these two men, the regard for the personality behind
the canvas. They are concerned not so much with that
delight in the power over tools that may lead to a camera-
like imitation of every brush-mark or sweep of the
palette-knife, but rather in the transposition, into the
language of the burin, of what the painter has said with
brush and color. In the case of Cole, who was called to
"Scribner's Monthly" by its art editor, A. W. Drake,
as early as 1875, this is done with a simplicity of method,

THE HAYWAIN

After John Constable.   Wood-engraving by Timothy Cole

a broad, bold directness of expression, a contemplative attitude, that give his translations a personal distinction. It is that which constitutes the importance of his series after the Italian, Dutch, English, Spanish and French masters. Such a sympathetically critical temperament was naturally attracted by the art of other days, which he has illumined also in written comment. "He handles his tool," says Miss E. L. Cary, "as a painter handles his brush, with the same freedom and dexterous control, and the same variation of stroke to meet various problems." Cole has shown manifold resources, "from the wildest unbridledness to the faultlessly classical line," as Koehler once said. His art has long since become clarified into the expression of calm and serene sureness.

In Wolf we find suavity and *raffinement* dominant. Wolf, devoted particularly to the moderns, brought to his task sensitive adaptativeness, discriminating understanding and distinguished skill. These have served to disclose or recall the beauties of art of various periods. He copied, in a spirit in harmony with the intentions of the artists, Corot; Jongers's portrait of W. T. Evans; the portrait of a girl and Balthasar Carlos, both by Velasquez; Ver Meer's *Young Woman at a Window;* Whistler's *Miss Alexander* and Manet's *Boy with a Sword.* As an interpreter of contemporary American figure painting, he reflected the best spirit of that art in terms of his own and with sympathetic appreciation, in blocks after J. Alden Weir, Horatio Walker, J. W. Alexander, W. M. Chase, E. Tarbell. James G. Huneker said of him: "He has attacked all schools, all styles, from Frans Hals to Homer Martin, from interiors by Vermeer to the subtle tonal graduations of Whistler's mother. . . . The line . . . is clean and significant. He has the sense of tactile values. Vitality there is . . ., above all virility in company with poetic distinction."

Honors in plenty came to our engravers at exhibitions here and abroad. Most of the engravers of the "new school" were identified with the "Society of American Wood Engravers," which issued in 1882, through the Harpers, a "Portfolio," a noteworthy monument to that period of brilliant achievement. There was also other collective presentation. The Scribners brought out "A Portfolio of Proof Impressions selected from Scribner's Monthly and Saint Nicholas" (1879); a second series with the same title (1881); and a selection from both: "Selected Proofs from the First and Second Portfolios of Illustrations from Scribner's Monthly and Saint Nicholas" (1881). The first series included Cole's *Gillie Boy,* as well as his engraving of Whistler's *Study in White,* and Linton's *Grand Cañon of the Colorado* after T. Moran. Still another collection of proofs was the "Longfellow Portfolio" (1881) of seventy-five plates, issued by Houghton, Mifflin & Co.

An interesting undertaking was the edition of Poe's "Raven" (1884) with illustrations by Doré cut on wood by Americans: Juengling, Claudius, Tietze, W. Zimmermann, Kruell, French, Bernstrom, Hoskin, R. A. Müller, King, G. J. Buechner, R. Staudenbaur and R. Schelling. Huneker asserts that Doré's French engravers made everything of his work, while the Americans engraved

GIRL AND PEONIES

After Irving R. Wiles.   Wood-engraving by Henry Wolf

him too literally, the inference being that they showed up his weaknesses instead of glossing them over.

There are various public collections of the productions of this American school. Particularly large ones in the Boston Museum of Fine Arts, the Congressional Library at Washington and the New York Public Library; others on the walls of the Young Men's Christian Association in Orange, N. J., in the Newark Public Library and in the public library of Springfield, Mass. ("Aston collection"). The work of certain individual artists may be studied in collections of noteworthy fullness in certain places: Wolf in the National Gallery at Washington, and the Lotos Club, New York City; Elbridge Kingsley at Mount Holyoke College and the New York Public Library. This New York institution's noteworthy collection of nearly five hundred pieces by Juengling includes a number of interesting proofs of small sections of various blocks, pulled on little scraps of paper; thus, the heads of John Brown and one of the soldiers and various hands, feet and other portions in *John Brown going to Execution,* after Thomas Hovenden, are each repeated a number of times on bits of paper an inch and a half square, or less, showing how the engraver progressively proved various portions of his block. Henry Wolf once told me that, as far as he knew, Juengling and he were the only ones to practise this method. Adequate records of the achievements of this interesting and brilliant phase of American art are thus preserved.

CHAPTER IX

PAINTER-WOOD-ENGRAVING

FROM A BOOK-PLATE BY G. W. PLANK

THE development of reproductive wood-engraving in the United States was carried to the limit of possibilities in the suggestion of tones and textures. The glorious period of success was short in duration. The photo-mechanical processes, particularly the now ubiquitous half-tone, swept all before them, and soon only two noteworthy members of the group of men who made American wood-engraving famous were still regularly practising the art as a reproductive process,—Cole and Wolf, to whom was added W. G. Watt, following with distinguished understanding in this path. Some entered the service of the photo-mechanical processes which supplanted wood-engraving, and added to the plate of the half-tone that engraving by hand which emphasizes light and shade and corrects the dull uniformity of the screen. F. S. King (whose "printer's devil" plate is noted among collectors) and Walter Aikman turned to copper-engraving.

Experiments have been pointed to as showing that the shallow half-tone plate will not generally give as good an electrotype as will the wood-block with its possibilities of deeper lines. The block, as William Aspenwall Brad-

NOTE.—The illustration above is from a book-plate by G. W. Plank and is used by the courtesy of Charles Scribner's Sons.

ley points out, gives clean-cut, sharply defined printing surfaces, instead of the monotonous, uniform mesh of the half-tone screen which, besides its deadly mechanical effect, is apt to smudge in printing. Bradley, when art editor of the "Delineator," put his idea to the test, in engravings by F. H. Wellington and others. But a general resumption of wood-engraving as a means of reproducing paintings has not taken place.

The decay of wood-engraving has been deplored in print and speech not a few times, and not infrequently in apparent forgetfulness of the fact that not only will necessity insure the survival of that which fits its case, but in this case the revival is already with us. But the art has arisen in a new form, or rather there is a renascence of an old form.

To-day our production in wood-block printing, and its near relative, linoleum printing, lies in the direction of "original" or "painter" engraving. That implies artist and engraver in one person, the block being used, as is the etching plate or the lithographic stone, as a direct medium of expression for the artist, an autographic art. Thus the artist's design is transmitted directly to his public, without the intervention of a professional engraver. Painter-wood-engraving has come to its own.

The desire for original work firs. took the form of engraving direct from nature by some of the men who had helped to bring reproductive wood-engraving to its high state of development. The original work of Kingsley, who printed some of his blocks in colors, and of Closson has already been spoken of. Others—the late

Victor Bernström, Henry Wolf, Frank French,—felt the impulse of original creation and brought to its service their long training. Wolf saw "Lower New York in a Mist" and showed it with a delicacy, a "silvery tone," that recalls Whistler's rhapsody concerning the fairyland which London at night opened up to him. Wm. G. Watt, too, has engraved his own designs on the wood. The result, with all these, is generally completeness of effect, the natural outcome of the engravers' previous activity. The spaces of their composition are filled with lines to indicate tone or local color.

In the hands of the artists who are not professional wood-engravers, but who turn to wood and graver as one of the means through which to find an outlet for what they see and feel, the medium is usually employed in a somewhat different way. Here, there is apt to be indication rather than fulfilment, decorative effect of line or space rather than insistence on detail.

In this use of the wood-block the tendency is toward simplicity in execution, few lines, flat tones of black or color, the use of the plank cut with the grain instead of the block cut across the grain. And there is felt the influence of the early facsimile cuts and of the Japanese color print. But these influences, in work which is worthy of serious consideration, appear in assimilation, not in imitation. Pure, unadulterated archaizing is rarely more than a sport, a stunt, the artist projecting himself backward into a time which is not his own living, pulsating present. The key-note in these prints is modernity; they

LOWER NEW YORK
Wood engraving by Henry Wolf

are of to-day, and none the less original because based on experience of the past.

A number of artists have exemplified the widely vary-ing possibilities of individual expression in this art of simple, straightforward and yet subtle effects, responsive to the evoking touch of personal intent. This display of variety in conception, treatment and result is based pri-marily on an understanding of the peculiar nature of the tools used, on a recognition of both the range and the limits of their inherent potentiality. To know how to produce effects without torturing the instrument beyond its proper functions is as necessary in art as it is in literature to produce word-pictures without straining the language.

In the increasing use of the wood-block by American artists there appears not only the individual note but also the reflection of modern points of view, ideas, ideals, which integrate the spots of individuality into groups of approximately common aims. It's a loose classification, however, for the spirit of individualism shines forth in differences subtly expressed here, vigorously there. The clean-cut blacks of Mildred McMillen contrast with the rolling, rough-hewn, scumbled lines of Birger Sandzen, the precision and reticent delicacy of Rudolph Ruzicka with the bold cutting of Tod Lindenmuth, the sculptur-esque realism of J. J. A. Murphy with the decorativeness of Horace Brodsky, the light tints of A. W. Dow with the complete color effects of Gustave Baumann.

Certain artists, while differing in style and aims, may conveniently be considered together because of a general

tendency toward realism. Most of them have some connection with deep-rooted traditions in wood-engraving,
traditions of the old days of facsimile cutting on the
plank. One, indeed, Howard McCormick, with a rugged
insistence on pictorial completeness, recalls our American
school of the eighteen-eighties, but only at a distance; no
trained line here, but a free, flickering touch which gives
an impression of pulsating life. Drawing with the graver,

Lankes   Courtesy of Charles Scribner's Sons
SLEIGH RIDE

brushing almost. A method well adapted in its vigor to
his reproduction of Gutzon Borglum's bust of Lincoln.
Usually, however, he engraves after his own designs, as
in his series of Mexican subjects. Tod Lindenmuth also
works for distance, and gets effects of detail by suggestion
of detail which is not there. With Sandzen the rugged
line turns into a sweeping gesture which at times rolls
gnarled trees and clouds into convolutions like those of a
finger print. Robustness, likewise, is the outstanding

quality of J. J. Lankes, with a muffled undertone of sympathetic human interest in his bits of rural life. More suave is the vigor, changing in manner with the purpose, of W. A. Dwiggins, always direct, happy and sufficient. Vigor is still the word for J. J. A. Murphy. Quite personal and natural, with thoughtful entry into his subjects, and with a fine sense of omission and of balanced composition, he guides his technic in terms of the mind to produce results of a sculpturesque effect. His wife, Cecil Buller Murphy, has a similar bigness in execution. In her nudes there is no attempt to go beyond the simplest outline to indicate the soft firmness of flesh, yet it is indicated. Childe Hassam, again, uses a tint block with white cross-hatching to arrive at results similar to those in his paintings and etchings of the human body.

Sanity, directness, restraint, and honest craftsmanship mark the work of Rudolph Ruzicka. He has observed and reproduced the beauties and interests of urban aspect with a delicate taste, a contemplative attitude, and quiet humor. In A. Allen Lewis a frank archaism in manner is joined to a distinctly individual expression, and a direct and simple vigor, his work bearing a vague and attractive flavor of the art of the old masters. Decorative quality, grace of line, and a "quaint and underlying concept" are qualities aptly attributed to the prints of George Wolfe Plank, which show "an appreciation of the traditions . . . , with a modernism that is beautifully informed and discriminating." The list is growing almost as one writes. Harold Haven Brown has expressed the simplicity and vigor inherent in the very nature of the block, as have Carl Oscar Borg (*Hopi Patriarch*), C. Bertram Hartman (of a decorative intent), W. G. Reindel and Walter H. Vanderburgh. E. L. Tinker has illustrated on linoleum his impressions of New Orleans.

Ruzicka   Courtesy of Charles Scribner's Sons

NEW YORK FROM THE MANHATTAN BRIDGE

And A. B. Davies brings to the wood-block the same inquiring spirit that has led him to other picture-printing processes. Quite recently the "Century," which, with "Scribner's," was once so closely identified with our brilliant period of reproductive wood-engraving, has been publishing cuts by artists of the youngest generation: C. O. Woodbury, Bernhardt Kleboe (who has a loose, easy stroke in simple winter scenes and the like), A. Majer, H. Pullinger, and L. F. Wilford (the structural textures of whose buildings are convincingly interesting).

The reality of every-day life is thrown out of focus in figures such as those by John Storrs, of a monumental quality that stamps a group of soldiers, for example, as a type of the warrior rather than a picture of present-day

Lewis   Courtesy of Charles Scribner's Sons
HEAD-PIECE FROM "JOURNEYS TO BAGDAD" BY CHARLES S. BROOKS

"doughboys." This feeling of an alignment of the world into linear arrangement to express mental attitudes is also Rockwell Kent's. His nudes stride this world of problems and tragedies and ecstasies with a gesture that recalls Blake, without calling for further comparison; Kent needs no such crutch.

Thence the step is natural to the decorative effect which is the key-note of cuts by Hunt Diederich, George Biddle, Horace Brodsky, William and Marguerite Zorach. A matter of conventionalities and swirling lines, going from a certain central impulse to divergent individualities. Where Brodsky offers strong juxtaposition of absolute black and white, which at times becomes silhouette, Diederich remodels men and animals into proper shape for the measured cavortings that fit into his decorative scheme. And with the Zorachs form is schematized even more into a matter of design, of balance, of intertwining patterns almost geometrical.

The spirit of revolt, of the desire to get away from the usual, of avoiding any charge of looking at the past, now rampant in painting and sculpture, is felt also in the graphic arts. Particularly is the wood-block, by its very technique and its adaptability to archaizing or primitive effects, a ready vehicle for such tendencies. "Expression-ism," however, is not as evident here as in Europe, but instead a strongly expressed if odd decorative quality and a withdrawal from material facts which takes you back to the vicinity of Blake, and sometimes an uncouth direct-ness rivalling the *images d'Epinal.*

A frank, humorous leaning towards earlier methods is indulged in by John Held, Jr., borrowing from early nineteenth-century chapbooks or similar popular print-ings, as in his *Bygone Days,* a bar-room scene, or his jolly old sailing ships. In his *Mate of the Lille-Elena* he moves toward the methods of the old-time theater-poster carver, whose materials,—wood-carver's tools ground down to the length of a boxwood graver, the blade being grooved to prevent splitting in the soft basswood, free from knots—were well utilized by James Britton in some posters done for the Connecticut League of Art Students, etc., years ago, with bold, broad effect. Harry Townsend has announced the Painter Gravers' exhibition with the

directness which the mural advertisement demands, and
Adolph Treidler, his poster-making abilities evident, digs
out form with an almost tactile effect.

The mention of posters recalls other uses to which the
wood-block has been put. Book-plates form an interesting specialty, cultivated by Ruzicka, George W. Plank,
A. Allen Lewis, and W. F. Hopson, the art of the last-
named long since clarified into a sure and calm taste and
craftsmanship. Holiday cards for individuals embody
happy conceits by Ruzicka, Lewis, and F. T. Chapman,
and the art has been felicitously applied to commercial
purposes by Murphy, Chapman, Percy A. Grassby,
Ruzicka, and C. B. Falls.

This last matter is one of some importance, because
the block print has qualities of simplicity, boldness, directness and vigor that make it peculiarly applicable to advertising art, and because it emphasizes the everlasting
law of the necessity of harmony between the picture and
the printed text. J. J. A. Murphy has illustrated here
the possibilities of the woodcut in designs that are symbolical by the force of related suggestion, decorative, yet
rugged and virile, different indeed from the quality of
feminine lissomeness that descends to anemic inanity in
much of our production.

The matter of harmonious agreement with type is particularly applicable, of course, in book illustration, and
the recent entry of the wood-block into this sphere will
be noted in its place.

In the course of the tendency to get beyond black and
white, Lewis, Ruzicka, Grassby, and Childe Hassam have

used, with modifications, the old chiaroscuro method, employed centuries ago to reproduce wash-drawings with white high lights. The process consists in adding to the black design a tint printed from a separate block, with the lights cut out in white. The texture of the wood, in Lewis's work for instance, produces a mottling of delicate variations. Ruzicka sometimes employs several tints to suggest color effect. From this, one steps on naturally to color printing, in which the influence of the Japanese has been very strong.

When Arthur W. Dow brought out his *Ipswich Prints,* "simple color themes," in which the principles of color-printing from wood-blocks are well illustrated, Ernest F. Fenollosa, writing of those experiments in a few flat tints, emphasized the characteristics of the process. "The artist," said he, "is as free with his blocks as the painter with his palette. . . . Pigment washed upon the wood, and allowed to press the sheet with a touch as delicate as a hand's caress, clings shyly only to the outer fibers, . . . leaving the deep wells of light in the valleys, the whiteness of the paper's inner heart, to glow up through it and dilute its solid color with a medium of pure luminosity." And further: "This method . . . strengthens the artist's constructive sense in that it forces him to deal with simple factors. It stimulates the faculty of design. . . . Mr. Dow's application of it to Western expression and use remains an epoch-making event."

Since then, that method has been applied in ways that reflected changing tendencies, general and individual, in a variety of manners, ranging from merest color suggestion to a chromatic vehemence that ends in practically ignoring the character of the medium. The Japanese manner is insisted upon in the case of Miss Helen Hyde, who, furthermore, lived in Japan and chose Japanese subjects. She presented delicate and subdued color harmonies, such as we see them in old Japanese prints. Yet there is an element of Occidental observation. The gesture is Japanese, the language is English—with an accent. B. J. Olssen-Nordfeldt, evidently influenced by the landscapes of Hokusai and Hiroshige, rests somewhat more obviously on the line. And in the latter he seems to see picturesque rather than decorative possibilities,—foamy wave tops circumscribed into rigidity by curly lines which yet in themselves have the restlessness of irregular rhythms. He gets away farther than Miss Hyde from the land of Fuji Yama, despite the still evident influence of its art. Yet more Occidental are the grace and charm of rhythmic line of Mrs. Bertha Lum.

Hugh M. Eaton, Elizabeth Gardiner, Harry De Maine, Mildred Fritz, Juliette S. Nichols exemplify as many different ways of color printing, which in some cases turns into a reduction into juxtaposed tints of the artist's seeking rather than nature's. An avowedly decorative use of color and form in combination appears in the studies of birds by H. M. Baer and in the Russian dancers by Mrs. W. M. Ivins, Jr., graceful weldings of tint and form, some with a touch of Bakst, others with a faint suggestion of children's books of the Greenaway period. Gustave Baumann strives for a completeness of realistic color effect, without losing sight of the wood-block, while the color prints, often bold in line, of Margaret Patterson, Edna Boies Hopkins, Elizabeth Colwell (straightforward yet subtle), and others almost suggest actual work in oil or body color rather than printing. These artists of the Provincetown group are much concerned with technique, yet frankly reject any expression of the medium, suppressing the character of the wood, in fact, so that their color prints partake of the nature of monotypes. The fact that most of the women in this field work in color may be noted in passing, as well as the fact that an unusual collection of the work of Ethel Mars is to be found in the Library of Art founded in Paris by Doucet. Also, as an oddly humorous contribution to color-printing, there may be listed the little book "Poker Rubaiyat" (1902) by Kirke La Shelle, with illustrations done by F. Holme with a jack-knife on poplar.

In all this contemporary work there is, quite apart from the question of quality, a variety of an extensiveness and richness not dreamed of in other days. And it reflects its time, our time, a period of many minds, ideas and ideals, and some aberrations. The wood-block, like the copper-plate and the lithographic process, offers bypaths for incursions, for occasional changes of activity on the part of artists working in other media. It has the possibilities of a safety-valve, it presents a chance of escape from the danger of routine, a road of return to the artist's own self.

Clearly, here is an art which, with all its characteristic of vigorous simplicity, can be moulded, without loss of its nature, to the manner of each individual artist. A medium as much worth our attention, in its way, and within its limitations,—limitations are always to be understood in any medium—as is etching. Clearly, too, the amateur or collector, in this garden of latent delights, must attend to some weeding. We cannot escape here, any more than we do in etching or any other art, the entrance of the glib one. It's so tempting to be able to perpetuate one's drawing by putting it down on a plate or block or stone from which impressions can be taken,— and perhaps sold! It's comparatively easy to make prints, but much more difficult to make good ones. After all, part of the pleasure of the game lies in the hunt, the comparison, the choice. And the exercise of those prerogatives, the activities of sorting, will help also to keep up the good name of wood-engraving. And to keep the block print, that buxom maid now being introduced to so many would-be practitioners, from the indignities which, in Whistler's metaphorical pleasantry, the more elegant etching had to endure when, with easy familiarity, the passing gallant chucked her under the chin.

CHAPTER X

LITHOGRAPHY: A BUSINESS, AN ART

LITHOGRAPHY found its greatest development here through its commercial possibilities. Nevertheless, the first attempts in the art, which had been taken up enthusiastically by artists in Germany and France, were made here, too, by a painter, Bass Otis, in two little landscapes (1819–20). Joseph Jackson ("Pennsylvania Magazine of History," 1913) thought that they were antedated by Otis's portrait of Abner Kneeland (1818), but that was executed on copper in a mixture of line, stipple and aquatint. The two drawings mentioned have little to recommend them but the interest of priority. They gave no hint of the possibilities exploited even at that time abroad. Our distinguished countryman in England, Benjamin West, and his son Raphael, had tried both crayon and pen on the stone as early as 1801 and 1802. But over here we had, apparently, not been in a hurry to test the newly discovered medium. Yet Dr. S. L. Mitchill, according to the "National Intelligencer" of Jan. 8, 1808, had a lithographic stone and ink in his possession at that time.

However, hardly seven years after Otis's essays appeared, Rembrandt Peale was awarded the silver medal of the Franklin Institute for his copy, on stone, of his own portrait of Washington. Peale, in this work, showed

The two earliest known lithographs produced in the United States
Both by Bass Otis

an understanding of the process which is not so apparent in other lithographs from his hand,—the larger head of Washington, and the smaller portraits of John Warren, M.D., Rev. John E. Abbott, etc.

Painter-lithography, as an autographic art practised by the artist similarly to etching, could not find much expression in a land in which the conditions of social and political development left little time for the cultivation of art. Still, artistic interest was not entirely wanting, even in commercial work, when men such as Henry Inman (who formed a partnership with C. G. Childs), Thomas Sully, Rembrandt Peale, and Thomas Doughty were taking part in the development of the new process. Much work of these early days was signed instead of bearing only the trade-mark of a firm name. But one finds also the signatures of geniuses deservedly unknown.

The commercial importance of the new reproductive process was evident from the beginning. As early as 1825 John Pendleton was engaged in the business of lithographic printing in Boston, and Anthony Imbert in New York at about the same time, and firms soon sprang up in Philadelphia and other cities. Much of the work produced was poor. Maverick, the New York engraver, busied himself also with lithography, one of his works being *Daughter of Charles B. Calmody* (1829) after Lawrence. Among the prints he issued is a view of Wall Street, New York City, the rarity and interest of which is in inverse proportion to its artistic value. It is signed *H. R.*, which presumably stands for Hugh Reinagle, who signed in full a view of St. Paul's, in the same city, printed by Pendleton. In Philadelphia, Cephas G. Childs similarly practised lithography as well as engraving. He became associated in 1831 with Henry Inman, a versatile painter, with facility in his crayon drawings on stone. These include portraits, a view of Mount Vernon in which the branches of trees outline a spectral Washington, and the particularly well done *Scraps* (1831), including the figure of a little nude boy on a stone, a graceful and delicate bit of crayon work.

The services of other artists were enlisted in the cause of the "grease crayon." Such were four who occasionally drew for Imbert: Archibald Robertson (*Grand Canal Celebration, 1825*), A. J. Davis the architect (whose New York City views are well known to collectors), George Catlin the Indian painter, and David Claypoole Johnston (whose work is characterized by the colorless uniform gray of his portrait of Webster, after Chester Harding, 1831). G. Marsiglia, N.A., drew at least one view (*Niagara Falls*) for Imbert. Still other painters gave some attention to lithography, but not much of their work calls for special commendation. Lambdin's portrait of Robert Owen has an amateurish aspect, and the *Tomb of Washington, at Mount Vernon,* by the landscape painter Thomas Doughty, done *from a drawing made on the spot by J. R. Smith,* and printed in 1832 by Childs and Inman, is not prominently good. Doughty did *from nature and on stone* some fairly acceptable animal studies (*Summer Duck, Newfoundland Dog,* etc., published in the "Cabinet of Natural History," 1830) for Childs and Inman, as did J. G. Clonney, the *genre*

PATRIÆ PATER

WASHINGTON
Lithograph by Rembrandt Peale

painter, somewhat later, for Mesier. Thomas Cole made attempts on the stone, notably *The Good Shepherd,* with a delicate background of trees and clouds, published in 1849, printed in tints by Sarony & Major. John William Hill, one of the American circle of Pre-Raphaelites, signed *Hackett's Town* (1845) and *Rockland Lake,* both for Endicott & Co.

Meanwhile there was an increase in professional lithographic artists. They, too, often signed their work, thus accenting the dignity of the artist in contrast with the lithographic firm name, although often there was little to dignify by the name of art. Thomas Edwards, of Boston, was one of the first to draw in the crayon manner, and in portraits such as the one of *James Tilton, M.D.,* the want of familiarity with the new medium is quite apparent. His *Jacob Perkins* (1826, printed by Pendleton) is more free in execution. F. Alexander, William Hoogland and J. R. Penniman (who did a portrait of Clay for Michelin & Creifeld, New York, 1844) were other Boston artists, and the garrulous William Dunlap commends the work of John Bisbee and John Crawley Junior, employed by Endicott and Swett. A picture of Washington Hotel, Broadway, New York (1833) was *drawn from nature and on stone by Moses Sweett,* while the name is spelled Swett on other prints, such as those in the "American Turf Register" (volume 1, 1830), or the *Irving . . . addressing his Countrymen after an Absence of 17 years.* Other names met with are R. Cooke, J. M. Roberts and Charles Toppan under some Imbert prints, W. Ball, W. Kelly, P. Hoas, E. Jones.

The interest in all this is antiquarian; the work is poor.
There were furthermore J. H. Colon (Inauguration of
Washington, about 1830), A. Hoffy (Tompkins Blues of
New York, City Troop of Philadelphia, colored plates
by P. S. Duval, 1839, published in "Military Magazine
and Record of the Volunteers of the U. S.") and R. J.
Rayner (portrait of Washington after Stuart). G. Lehman, like Hubard (portrait of Andrew Jackson, 1833),
lithographed for Childs & Inman; I have seen a flamingo
drawn by him from nature, of a noteworthy delicacy, as
well as a lithotint in colors, *The Pirates' Well.* In the
thirties some of Pendleton's prints were signed by J. H.
Bufford, who later was in business for himself. His
drawing of Inman's portrait of Wirt (Pendleton) is the
best by him that I have seen.

Signatures increase as we go on in chronological
sequence: Bouvier, Penniman (1844), C. W. Burton
(panoramic view of New York, 1849). F. J. Fritsch's
pretentious pictures of the *38th Regiment, Jefferson
Guards* (1843) and the *First Division* (1844) both por-
tray New York State Artillery organizations with the
impartial inclusiveness that Banning Cock's company felt
should have been accorded them in Rembrandt's famous
"Night Watch." The interest in these two colored prints
lies in the fact that the first shows the City Hall and the
second Castle Garden, in New York. Charles Gildemeister signed a View of the Narrows and a View of the
Hudson River from Fort Lee, both published by Seitz in
1851; G. W. Fasel drew *Heroic Deeds of former Times,*
six scenes in Indian warfare (Seitz: 1851), and Bach-

mann and Th. Benecke views in New York City. Gustavus Pfau and Hardtmuth, who both did portraits for
Nagel & Weingärtner, J. H. Sherwin (1858) and C.
Koppel (Jefferson Davis, bust portrait, nearly life-size,
1865), may also serve to indicate not necessarily importance, but the prevalence of signed work.
The enlarging proportion of German names in this
later work will be noted. But much of the earliest work
showed French influence. Among Imbert's artists we find
the names of F. Duponchel (1825), J. Bauncou and
Canova (a poor portrait of Richard Riker),—presumably brought over from France as P. S. Duval was by
Childs & Inman to take charge of the lithographic department added to their general engraving business. Pendleton, too, had studied the art in Paris and brought the
materials with him. The painter and engraver Hugh
Bridport's portrait of John Vaughan, after T. Sully, also
shows French influence and is somewhat in the style of
his pupil, Albert Newsam (1809-64), a deaf-mute. Newsam was an assiduous student of French models. That
is apparent in his larger portrait of W. Rawle, which
stands out prominently from his many smaller colorless
portraits, and notably in the portrait of John G. Wat-
mough after Inman, in the style of Grevedon, his finest
effort. Newsam produced many of his earlier and best
works for Childs & Inman, and was active for years in
the service of their successor Duval. He was most successful when copying portraits, for when he drew directly
from the life he faithfully reproduced the tired look of
the sitters whom he could not animate on account of his

bodily misfortune. Two collectors—D. M. Stauffer and Charles Roberts—directed their energies in his direction, and the Pennsylvania Historical Society has a number of proofs which once belonged to Newsam. Childs himself produced creditable portraits, such as those of Miss Clara Fisher, John Adams (partly done with the scraper) and Gen. A. Macomb. The first shows deep, rich shadows in the hair; the last, printed by Pendleton, Kearny & Childs, is of a soft, miniature-like effect.

The technique in this early work was that of the crayon drawing, with occasional use of the scraper, the stroke of the crayon being usually lost in a uniform, often grayish, tint. An especially effective example of this style is found in M. E. D. Brown's portrait of William P. Dewees, after Neagle, printed by Lehman and Duval, 1833. Its deep, inky shadows and indefinite contours make it one of our most interesting early examples of lithographic portraiture. In other work Brown fell much below the standard which he himself had set in this stunning portrait.

From the late thirties to the early fifties a little group of portrait artists turned out very respectable work, with an occasional infusion of decidedly artistic feeling. Charles Fenderich's political notabilities, issued 1837–1841 in Washington under the firm name of Charles Fenderich & Co., are rather uniformly dark, but fairly well modeled. His *Garret D. Wall* is the freest drawing by him that I have seen. F. D'Avignon likewise served his portraits in a lineless sauce of crayon tint; he ran to rich, shimmering grays instead of the heavy blacks that others affected. The portraits after daguerreotypes by Brady, "Gallery of illustrious Americans" (1850), are his most familiar work; *Baron Stow* (Bufford, Boston: 1859) one of his best in execution. A contrast is offered in his delicate miniature likeness of Ralph Izard (Boston, 1844). The firm of D'Avignon & Brainerd existed in Boston in 1859. Fabronius, a Belgian, who came to Philadelphia in 1855 and worked for Rosenthal, Duval and Prang, did good portraits. Martin Thurwanger, an Alsatian, who was in this country during 1850–55, employed the less-used medium, pen and ink, for carefully executed portraits, such as that of E. Biddle. J. Lion, a Frenchman working in Louisiana for many years, made a series of portraits of the legislature of 1836, never published in collected form. His portrait of J. J. Morgan (1846) shows a little similarity in manner to the lithographs of Léon Noël. William Beer, of the Howard Memorial Library, wrote me that "the most celebrated head by Lion is one of Audubon," and that Gaspar Cusachs has about 100 lithographs by this artist. Much later, early in the eighties, Max Rosenthal did two hundred or so of small heads of Revolutionary and other notabilities with a light, smooth touch.

If the crayon tint is in evidence in the drawings of most of the men who have been mentioned, the line is evident in those of L. Grozelier (portraits of Charles Sumner, Lyman Beecher, 1854, and N. P. Banks, 1856) and C. G. Crehen (portraits of W. S. Mount, 1850, and J. C. Fremont, 1856). The former drew for Duval and for J. H. Bufford (in the fifties); the latter for Nagel & Weingärtner. Both of them had something of the manner of the Frenchman Julien, whose "drawing models" were so familiar in our boyhood days. Vincent Collyer, similarly, in his large *Crayon studies from life,* gave a suggestion of the style of Josephine Ducollet's *modèles de dessin.* And Jules Emile Saintin, a French painter who spent some years in this country, did a good portrait of Stephen A. Douglas (1860).

Lithography drew not a few engravers to its service, either as draughtsmen, or as managers or owners of establishments executing engravings and lithographs. Childs and Maverick have been referred to. V. Balch drew upon stone a portrait of Dr. Samuel L. Mitchill, published by Imbert. Annin & Smith, says Stauffer, "were for some time engaged in the lithographic business under the name of the Annin & Smith Senefelder Lithographic Co., of Boston. In 1831 they sold out the lithographic business to W. S. Pendleton, who continued the business as the Senefelder Co. of the same city." John Cheney drew on stone for Boston lithographers two tender, silvery-gray landscapes and a figure-piece, *The Broken Heart.* S. H. Gimber did poor lithographs. James Akin, a "jack of all trades," stippled and lithographed. J. B. Martin, of Richmond, executed a portrait of John Randolph of Roanoke, printed by Childs. John Rubens Smith, who practised in various media, brought out *A Compendium of Picturesque Anatomy . . . on four Folio Lithographic Plates* (Boston, 1827); James Smillie, the line-engraver, drew for lithographic reproduction a *View of Union Park, lith. by Sarony &*

Major, 1849; Kimmel & Forster (*The Preservers of our Union,* 1864) and H. B. Hall are credited with some work on the stone. J. E. Gavit had an engraving and lithographic establishment.

A large proportion of the production of the first half of the nineteenth century consisted of portraiture, but other fields were not neglected. There is a little gallery of landscape art, pictures mainly of topographical and local interest. The somewhat dry "Views of Philadelphia and its vicinity," from paintings by J. C. Wild, "published by J. T. Bowen at his lithographic and print colouring establishment" (1848), and "Scenery of the White Mountains, with 16 plates from drawings of Isaac Sprague. By William Oakes" (Boston, 1848: B. W. Thayer & Co.). Or the numerous views signed by Mrs. Frances F. Palmer in the forties and fifties, and published, some by F. & S. Palmer and many by Currier & Ives. Not only views of large cities (e.g., *View of New York from Weehawken,* 1849, or *Suburban Gothic Villa, Murray Hill,* New York), but vistas of small towns and villages, responding to local pride. E. Whitefield signed a number of views, among them one of *Brooklyn from the United States Hotel, New York* (1846).

Two particularly fine examples of semi-commercial landscape work are *Taghanic Fall,* put on stone by D. Glasgow (died Jan. 29, 1858, aged 24) after a drawing from nature by E. Whitefield, and *Catterskill Falls,* by Charles Parsons. Both are good, workmanlike productions, somewhat in the manner of J. D. Harding, or Calame. Charles Parsons executed a number of drawings, particularly pictures of noted vessels, and a view of New York City (1858).

Lithography, for a while, was used in book-illustration. An early effort is the title-page design of "The Daughter's Own Book" (Boston, 1833), a female figure in the manner of the French romantic period, done by *Pendleton's Lithography*. Pendleton printed many illustrations, among them those for A. Bigelow's "Travels in Malta and Sicily" (1831). Hawthorne's "Visit to the Celestial City" was published in 1844 by the American Sunday School Union with droll lithographic plates. In the fifties, sixties and seventies firms such as Sarony, Major & Knapp and Julius Bien were active in this field. Characteristic examples of the work of the first-named are "Graphic Scenes of the Japan Expedition, by W. Heine, executed in colors and tints" (1856), and *Compositions* for Judd's "Margaret" (1856) drawn in outline by F. O. C. Darley and put on stone by Konrad Huber, and other similar work by Darley and J. W. Ehninger. Long before, in 1843, Sinclair of Philadelphia had printed outline *Scenes in Indian Life, drawn and etched on Stone by Darley*. Bien's product included the illustrations for "The House that Jack Built," "Five Little Pigs," etc., by H. L. Stephens, issued 1864–65 in editions of 100 copies, and the "Fables of Æsop" (1867) by the same artist.

Lithography was allied also to the comic art, in humorous weeklies such as "Puck," "Judge" or "The Wasp," as well as in separate sheets such as Thomas Worth's gaudily colored caricatures of negro life (*Darktown Fire Brigade* and the like). These last were printed and published by the New York firm of Currier & Ives (N. Currier, 1836–57, Currier & Ives, 1857–1901), who for many years before and after the Civil War issued a pictorial record of happenings,—battles, shipwrecks,—as well as portraits, views, and sporting prints, and war-time cartoons. Also prints with no reference to specific events, such as the series of six dealing with *The Life of a Fireman* by L. Maurer and Charles Parsons, or the *Summer Scenes in New York Harbor* (1869) by Parsons and Atwater, or scenes in country life. Such prints were issued also by John L. Magee, of Philadelphia, in the fifties. Similar in purpose but better in execution were *Lincoln on his Death-bed* and *Grant's Council of War*, by Peter Krämer.

A field in which the stone crowded out the wood-block was that of the theatrical poster. The artists Matt Morgan and H. A. Ogden and the firms Strobridge Lithographic Co., A. S. Seer and W. J. Morgan have been particularly identified with this form of lithographic activity, into which there have been occasional incursions from without, so by Ernest Haskell and B. J. Rosenmeyer.

As in other countries, the music cover was the province of lithography, from the days of Pendleton to those of H. A. Thomas. A title-vignette for a song, printed by Pendleton, 1831, is signed *Lopez;* another piece of sheet music bears a portrait of Clay (Thayer & Co.'s Lithograph, 1844); and J. D. Smillie designed a vignette or two. Many marches and quicksteps were dedicated to military bodies; their title designs form a record, amazing and amusing, of militia uniforms of 1830–60.

Many of the names mentioned represent material for the history of commercial lithography. Such considerations take us naturally into the record of firms. Beside those named elsewhere in this chapter there were Childs & Lehman, Lehman & Duval (who lithographed the plates in J. O. Lewis's "Aboriginal Port-Folio," 1835), Kennedy & Lucas, P. S. Duval & Co., Pendleton, Kearny & Childs, George Harris, T. S. Wagner, and T. S. Sinclair in Philadelphia; Endicott & Sweet, later Endicott (1832–90), G. Hayward, Heppenheimer & Maurer, Schumacher & Ettlinger, Sackett & Wilhelms, J. Ottmann, Ferdinand Mayer, in New York; T. Moore, successor of Pendleton, and himself succeeded by Thayer, W. Sharp & Co., in Boston; Wegner, Brueckner & Mueller in Pittsburg (A. D. Wegner drew portraits); R. H. Pease in Albany; D. W. Kellogg in Hartford; and similar establishments in Washington, Philadelphia, Baltimore and other cities in the third to sixth decades of the century. In more recent times the list becomes too long for full citation. These firms were kept busy supplying demands for comic papers, posters, chromos, advertisements, cigar-box labels, cigarette cards, Christmas and other cards, supplements to periodicals, and the numerous other forms of pictorial production which came from the lithographic press. Not a few of the firms became united in the American Lithographic Co.

A large proportion of the later work has been in color. Printed in color, that is, not hand-coloring such as it is

found in *Grandpapa's Pet, Drawn and lithotinted by John
H. Richards expressly for Miss Leslie's Magazine, the
first Specimen of this Art ever produced in the United
States, Lith. of P. S. Duval, Phila.* Early efforts in color-
printing are encountered occasionally. For example, the
cover, *printed in colors by E. W. Bouvé, Boston,* of "The
Waif," edited by Longfellow (Cambridge, 1845). Or
the bust portrait of Washington *lithographed and printed
in oil Colors by P. S. Duval & Son, Philadelphia.* Or
the *Interior View of Independence Hall, Philadelphia*
(1856), *on Stone by Max Rosenthal; Lithographed and
printed in Colors by L. N. Rosenthal.* The color-plates
in J. F. Reigart's "Life of Robert Fulton" (1856) were
produced by the same combination of designer and
printer. And I've come across some sheets of Indian
studies, with title, by Ferdinand Pettrick, in black crayon
with brown washes (printed) with white high lights,
printed by E. Weber, Baltimore, 1842. Max Rosenthal,
who came to Philadelphia in 1849, we are told, "made
the chromo-lithographic plates for what is believed to be
the first fully illustrated book by this process in the
United States, 'Wild Scenes and Wild Hunters.' In 1854
he did an interior view of the old Masonic Temple in
Philadelphia, 22 by 25 inches, the largest chromo-litho-
graph that had been made in the country up to that time."
Christian Schussele, an Alsatian, who came to Philadelphia in 1848, worked for Duval and subsequently turned
to painting, is said to have learned chromo-lithography
from Engelmann and introduced it here. He designed a
card and the title for "Godey's" for 1850 for *P. S.*

Duval's Lithographic & Color Printing Establishment.
The preface of the "Iris," 1851–52, speaks of the color
prints which Schussele-Duval did for that "Souvenir."
Then came Julius Bien's large undertaking, the plates for
the 1860 re-issue of Audubon's "Birds."

A name of particular significance in the annals of
lithographic color-printing is that of Louis Prang, who
issued many prints, including reproductions of paintings.
The culmination of his achievement is found in the rendition of ceramic ware in the W. T. Walters collection,
in a sumptuous folio (Baltimore, 1884). Finally, there
are the color-plates by the Forbes Co. in "The Bishop
Collection. Investigations and Studies in Jade. Catalogue" (1906).

With great improvement in commercial lithography
there came comparatively few instances of artistic force
or individuality as we find it in the work, say, of Sarony,
Morgan or Keppler to some extent. The incentive to
original work, "painter-lithography," weakened.

Lithography passed into a long serfdom of commercial
activity. The word "commercial," be it understood, in
such a case practically always means, not that the art has
been commercialized, but that it has been cheapened or
debased by commercial interests. Any attempt to link
good art with commerce, in a combination that makes
art a co-operator and not a slave, can only be greeted
with satisfaction, and has worked well where it has taken
place.

The line bounding original work is not always easy to
draw absolutely. Napoleon Sarony, identified with litho-

One of the "Campagne Sketches"
A series of lithographs by Winslow Homer

graphic printing houses from his thirteenth year, signed some pieces, executed with a graceful and facile touch and in a smooth manner. Shall David D. Neal's *Captain John Paty* and A. Nahl's *Thomas O. Larkin* (1863), both the work of California painters, be considered as original or as commercial lithographs? Or Seymour J. Guy's large certificate issued to subscribers to the Brooklyn and Long Island Fair in aid of the U. S. Sanitary Commission? Or the *Campagne* [sic!] *Sketches,* drawn with crayon and some scraping by Winslow Homer, during the Civil War, and published by Prang & Co. of Boston? Or even S. S. Frizzell's suave rendering, with crayon and some touches of the scraper, of W. M. Hunt's *Elaine* (1866)? Decision is not quite so difficult if it be borne in mind that the fact that a painter happens to make a drawing for a lithographic house does not *per se* constitute the result a "painter-lithograph." It is a matter of expression of individuality.

W. M. Hunt, in the sixties, showed true painter qualities in some studies of a flower girl, a Savoyard (hurdy-gurdy player) and other simple subjects treated with feeling for tone and color. In 1870 G. W. Nichols of New York published a series of lithographs by painters, *Twilight* by A. Delessard, *Twilight* by F. Rondel after a painting by George Inness, *Plato* by F. B. Mayer, *Hagar and Ishmael,* a strong bit of work by Edwin White, who showed here the same quiet richness that marks some of his paintings. George Inness, Eastman Johnson (1860) and J. F. Cropsey also dallied with the crayon.

To these names must be added those of Thomas

Moran and J. Foxcroft Cole. Moran expressed on the stone his love of bold, scenic effects, towering mountains, forest giants, vistas of wild, stern nature. Two of his best-known lithographs are *Solitude* (a wood-interior: No. 1 of his *Studies and Pictures,* 1868) and *South Shore of Lake Superior* (1869), a strong and picturesque performance. A contrast to his vigor and sweep is offered in the eight *pastorals* of Cole (six of them issued by L. Prang & Co. in 1870 as part 1 of an "Album of American Artists"), simple in subject and treatment, with a quiet charm. Cole, like Winslow Homer and Eastman Johnson, was originally a lithographer; Homer's *œuvre* includes a number of humorous little cards of soldier life during the Civil War, issued by Prang.

There was promising material but the period of active interest was short. About 1896 Montague Marks, editor of the "Art Amateur," enlisted the attention of J. Carroll Beckwith, J. Alden Weir, H. W. Ranger, F. Hopkinson Smith, Joseph Lauber, J. G. Brown, Ruger Donoho and Cleveland Coxe, who at his instigation made attempts in lithography. A particular understanding of the medium was shown by Weir (who used the scraper in some characteristic studies of home life) and Ranger, whose *On the Seine* is an admirable rendition of a rainy day, with sky of tremulous gray and reflecting glint of wet stones. That is as far as it went. Marks's idea of an "American Society of Painter Lithographers" was not realized. With so little to record, one feels grateful for any further sign of intelligent and discriminating interest in the art. C. A. Vanderhoof, the etcher, once used the stone for a

FLOWER GIRL
Lithograph by William M. Hunt

VIEW ON THE SEINE

series of magazine covers. And C. F. W. Mielatz showed
the same devotion to the nooks and corners of New York
City, which we know in his etchings, in a series of 12 lithographs issued by the New York "Society of Iconophiles."
This same society a few years ago brought out a set of
skyscraper studies by Joseph Pennell.

The last name recalls the painter-lithographs by American artists produced abroad.

Whistler was introduced to lithography by T. R. Way,
who says that he found in it "a medium which is more
sympathetic and personal even than the copper-plate."
He made the medium peculiarly a means of expression
for his nervously sensitive artistic personality. Some of
the greatest masters of lithography had accustomed us to
velvety blacks, to dark notes of a rich resonance, to tones.
Whistler did away with tones (except in his few lithotints), gave us crayon drawings in which the insistence
was on the line, limited in quantity to the least possible,
tremulous in its sensitive response to passing mood. With
joyous spontaneity he set down impressions of shifting
grace in form and movement, with a touch as light as air,
of an evanescent suggestiveness, sometimes heightened by
spots of color. He added a highly interesting variant to
the illustrations of technical possibilities in lithography.

Whistler singled out the crispness of Pennell's "Spanish" series for special mention. Pennell has made interesting trials of various resources of the stone, as in
Poitiers: Church of St. Hilaire, or in those prints showing a castle on a hill, to the right of a broad road, with
rich unctuous blacks, produced by crayon, brush and rags,

with lights brought out by the scraper. But the pure line of the crayon is found in his numerous drawings for Irving's "Alhambra" and the "Highways and By-ways" series of books on English counties, and in the *Spanish* and *Holland* series of lithographs. In the last-named, more satiety of effect is gained; this, finally, in his views of the *Rouen Cathedral,* sounds in deep, booming notes of black that throw the delicate treatment of decorated form into effective relief. Most recently he has sung a resounding hymn in praise of the *Wonder of Work* at the Panama Canal and in industrial centers.

John S. Sargent's studies of draped models drawn on transfer paper, show broad crayon-strokes and rich, dark shadows, forming an interesting contrast to the pencil-drawing-like manner of Whistler and illustrating the pliability of the medium. E. A. Abbey is said to have made some attempts, of which I have seen only a carica-ture of Sir John Hare, the actor. And Mary Cassatt, of Paris, is represented solely by a *Lady in a theatre box* (1891), an "early and only attempt," as she says. Among Robert J. Wickenden's prints are *La Mère Panneçaye* (a character study of an old Frenchwoman, rendered with loving appreciation) and *La Rentrée du Troupeau,* shown at the Salon of 1894 and published in "Les Peintres Lithographes."

To-day artistic lithography, or, better said, lithography for the artist, has begun to have a living present in this country. Ten years ago one was almost limited to the consideration of past performances. Then, the use of the process by American artists was sporadic and rare.

LIMEHOUSE
Lithotint by J. A. M. Whistler

Lithography played the rôle of a stepchild beside etching. It emitted but a feeble peep in the chorus of our art. To-day, to continue the use of the metaphor, it is heard in a voice rich, varied, sometimes subtle, not always discriminating, and fairly voluminous.

We are getting away from the idea that because for many years lithography has been preponderatingly used for commercial ends, it is something beneath the artist's notice. The very manysidedness and suppleness of this process, which made it so useful an aid to commerce, makes it equally and pre-eminently a means by which the artist can express his individuality and mood. The process is autographic, reproducing the drawing as the artist makes it. You might well say, it is the drawing itself.

There is in lithography, as in etching, the facile practitioner. It is easy enough to make a drawing on stone or transfer-paper, have it printed from, and delight in the dignity of an edition and the possibility of sales. More than one of us have been hoping, praying, working, writing, agitating for a revival of lithography. Now that it is under way, one need not be discouraged if not all of the results are what one would have liked. The best will inevitably float to the top eventually, the rest will subside to the sediment of the deservedly forgotten.

"Lithography," says Joseph Pennell, "is the simplest and most abused of all the graphic arts, and is the most wonderful." It offers a sensitive response to the artist's touch. Its resources are marvellously rich. The artist may use crayon, pen, or brush, he may scrape out lights from washes or rub in tones with stump or rags, he may apply spatter-work or stipple. Lines may be drawn in the incisiveness of pen and ink, or the broad, quivering strokes of the crayon, or the sweep of the brush. Delicacy and vigor, tenderness or brilliancy are at command. The keyboard of tones on the stone ranges from grays of the delicacy of silver-point to blacks of the richness and depth of mezzotint or dry-point. Furthermore, the stone offers possibilities of color-printing to those who prefer that to black and white. And if desired the drawing may be made on paper and transferred to the stone.

Yet with all this remarkable range of possibilities, lithography has a character of its own which must be understood and respected. Differences in handling the process run from the live to the dead. Where one shows a loving, sympathetic, searching study of the nature of the medium, another will produce dry statements, drawings that might as well be in pencil, that give you the feeling that they were not done in lithography because the artist liked that form of art and found that it responded to his temperament or temporary mood, but because it offered a quick and easy method of reproducing his design for the market.

When working in this medium, as in any medium, the artist must understand it, respect it, love it. The activity in poster design engendered by the various "drives" during the late war brought it home forcibly to more than one of our artists that you have to understand a process in order to employ it. So they learned to go into the lithographic printing shop, take off their coats, work with the printer and learn of his needs and difficulties. Simply to paint a poster or other design which has to be done over by a lithographic artist will not prove satisfactory, least of all to the original designer.

The war, it seems, gave a certain impetus to the use of lithography by our artists. At all events the process served a number of them to depict figures, scenes, and activities in the great conflict. Pershing and others were portrayed by Leo Mielziner, the forward struggle of the Allied armies was observed and recorded in its more intimate aspect, more from the standpoint of the individual soldier, by Kerr Eby and Captain Harry Townsend. The ravages of war at Rheims, Verdun, and elsewhere, were shown by Howard Leigh. Incitement to effort was furnished in dramatic compositions—cartoons they may be called, for purpose of classification—by George Bellows. The gigantic work at home, in munition-plants and ship-yards, was set down picturesquely by Joseph Pennell, Vernon Howe Bailey, Herbert Pullinger, and Thornton Oakley.

Many contemporary American lithographs have already been seen, both in one-man shows and in collective exhibitions such as the one held at the New York Public Library in 1920 and in the gallery of the National Arts Club, New York. The work already produced runs an interesting scale of possibilities in handling, in technique, and discloses a pleasing and promising variety of temperaments and minds, to which these technical privileges have afforded richly adequate means of expression. Here is the utmost delicacy of pearly grays, as in the picture of haze-enveloped nymphs by the water-side, in which Bolton Brown, with subtlety in printing, repeats the evanescence of the shimmering, eye-confusing colors of his paintings. And not far off—if you happen to run down the alphabetical list of artists—is the massive force of Bellows's broad, heavy crayon strokes and resounding array of darks and lights. Here is straight realism, as that of Adolph Treidler, and an imaginative quality that is quite of to-day. And that though it may be in touch with the past, as in the case of Rockwell Kent, with a certain kinship to Blake. Again there is plain, straightforward study of nature, as in the tree forms which Sears Gallegher gives with the effect of a crayon or pencil sketch, and the large drawings by Birger Sandzén, in which rugose and swirling lines bind trees and clouds into a big decorative pattern that recalls the convolutions of a finger-print, and that somehow, again, breathes the free, clear spirit of the West.

Still pursuing the always alluring sport of contrasting temperaments and methods, one may place side by side city scenes and buildings by certain artists who have found strong interest in these. Hassam, with sureness of eye and light definiteness of touch, has here, as in his etchings, explained his outlook on things through air and sunlight. George Elmer Browne, in such a piece as *The Old Mill*, produces a colorful painter-quality in statement vigorous and sane. Ernest Haskell, avid pursuer of processes, has a Whistler-like lightness in his *Ruined Pier, Staten Island*. He has worked delicately with crayon and scraper, sometimes with a suggestion of the

MORNING
Lithograph by Bolton Brown

LITTLE ARKANSAS RIVER
Lithograph by Birger Sandzen

silvery grays of the early days of the art. Howard Leigh
in his drawings of cathedrals and other monumental
structures gives not so much architectural renderings or
decorative detail as massive impressions of massive con-
structions imbued with a dramatic element born of their
picturesque qualities. Vernon Howe Bailey brings to his
task the important equipment, not too common, of sure
draftsmanship. Before the skyscraper of New York, at
the docks among great vessels, in huge and busy plants
and at sight of towering smoke-stacks, everywhere the
same clear view and presentation, the suave swing of line,
the matter-of-course yet subtle sweep of composition. A
natural manner that makes the selection of the right
view-point so apparently inevitable that you take it for
granted. And somehow, sometimes, your thoughts go
to Pennell at sight of this.

Joseph Pennell was in the game with Whistler. He is
still at work to-day, telling of the beauty and activity
of the life around us, and agitating for a better understanding of this medium. He bridges earlier days and
the present, that live, hustling, eager, inquisitive, impressionable and somewhat unrestrainedly and unthink-
ingly individualistic present, in which the latest achievement to record is that of Arthur B. Davies. A dozen
or more years ago this insatiable trier of processes made
a number of experiments in lithography, delightful in
their spirit of adventurous discovery, no two alike in
method of production. It was like a sensitive preluding
performance, a running over the keys, a testing of the
various stops of this instrument of rare possibilities.

Then, quite recently, he exhibited in New York a lot of lithographs in color which were, in their way, a revelation, not only of Davies, but of lithography. Whistler, Toulouse-Lautrec, Ibels, Lunois are some of the names that rise to memory at the thought of color-lithography for artists. They represent so many different methods of combinations of the stone, colored inks, and the artist. Davies has added another. This tireless experimenter, ever alert to try out the new idea or process, ever making characteristic and sensitive response to the veering tendencies of the day, who will pull different proofs of the same lithograph in different color combinations, is, of course, attracted by the medium for what it will yield in expression of himself. His figures live in a world of their own, an exemplification of beauty for beauty's sake.

From these imaginings one turns naturally to other figure pieces. Rockwell Kent's symbolical presentation of man in terms of typical experience. Albert Sterner's studies, of a reserved richness, always within the medium and always individual, running from his early distinguished portraits and the reality of *The Cards* to the daintily imagined *Amour Mort*. His portraits include the characteristic one of Martin Birnbaum, which leads to a field in which W. Oberhardt has shown facile observation of salient traits, as in the heads of Pennell, John Gelert, and Edward Borein. S. J. Woolf's study of Mark Twain, W. J. Duncan's full length of Robert C. Holliday of the "Walking-Stick Papers," the late F. Walter Taylor's head of Joseph Pennell are illustrations of the sporadic or more or less habitual practice of por-

AUTUMN
Lithograph by R. B. Davies

THE CARDS
Lithograph by Albert Sterner

traiture. And, stepping backward a bit, one can add to this record the rather unusual poster portraits of Mrs. Fiske, by Ernest Haskell, flung on the stone with a nervous pertness which strikes a note of that actress's characteristic utterance. And there is—or isn't—that portrait of Ernest Lawson, by W. J. Glackens, so unfindable that it is becoming semimythical.

C. Washburn has turned at times from etching to lithography, W. B. van Ingen showed drawings of Chicago parks in 1922, and Mahonri Young has digressed to this medium, well suited to his vigorous crayon strokes. Violet Oakley, E. Watson, and others have thrown more than a glance in this direction.

The prize-fight scenes and other pieces by George Bellows at times go beyond the author's engrossment with problems of chiaroscuro, and his attitude of sympathetically and smilingly observant aloofness, into a spirit of satire reservedly expressed. A humorously tolerant comment on his fellow man appears in the street scenes by John Sloan, whose brotherly interest in humanity does not show the bitterness of the overzealous reformer. Sloan, moreover, modern in spirit and outlook, yet builds solidly on the firm foundation of tradition in the matter of technique. Jerome Myers has put down on stone his types of New York's East Side, where W. J. Duncan has found *McSorley's Ale House* an appealing subject. Among newcomers Adolph Dehn was praised by the "N. Y. Herald" for his "scenes of the city, the kaleidoscope of cabarets and night life, of war profiteers and beggars, presented with an unusual mastery of form and space and the utmost economy of line. There is humor in his trenchant observation of life."

From such thoughtfully amused observers of their fellow men the transition is easy to notice of the fact that crayon has in recent years crowded out the pen in the hands of political cartoonists such as Boardman Robinson, Cesare, John Cassel, Rollin Kirby. Over much of this the spirit of Daumier hovers as a strong source of inspiration. While these drawings were reproduced by "process," they have a lithographic "feel," and Robinson and Cesare, in fact, have worked directly in lithography.

At the end one is reduced, by very breathlessness through accumulation of citations in evidence, to the simple repetition of the fact that this most pliable and adaptable instrument may be played upon in as many ways as there are personalities worth while to take it up. Delicacy or vigor, realism or imagination, whatever the demand of subject or temperament, lithography stands ready to serve with a chameleon-like change of manner in adaptation to the need of the moment.

And here in our country, too, the use of this flexible medium has shown a wide diversity of styles and temperaments and moods.

TENEMENT ROOFS
Lithograph by John Sloan

CHAPTER XI

THE ILLUSTRATORS

THE history of the reproductive processes is to a great extent the history of book-illustration. Line-engraving, etching, mezzotint, aquatint, lithography and wood-engraving have each had its period of application to the elucidation or adornment of the printed page. Particularly wood-engraving. Its office as an agent of pleasure and of pictorial instruction in connection with the printing press was of long duration, until it was supplanted by the half-tone process.

In the eighteenth century, what little we had of book-illustration—an occasional portrait or map—was done in copper-engraving. With the Revolution there came some native illustration of current events, and activity increased when political independence was assured. We were beginning to take breath while building up the nation, and to note natural beauties around us; also, pride in national achievements and local development called for tangible pictorial records.

Periodical literature played an important part in the fostering of engraving on copper and steel in the nineteenth century. The "New York Mirror" (begun 1823) published good work, particularly views. Then came "Family Magazine" (in the thirties), "Picture Gallery" (1843) and "Godey's Lady's Book." The last-named informed its readers that no plates so fine were to be found in any magazine and that they were from designs expressly for "Godey's." That is the best that can be said of them: poor as they were, they were generally after paintings or drawings by Americans. George G. White, C. Schussele, Mrs. Lily Martin Spencer, P. F. Rothermel, H. L. Stephens, E. Brown, John R. Chapin, James Hamiltqn, Dallas, William Croome and H. Bispham were those whose works were thus reproduced between 1840–65.

Literary annuals, "tokens" and "keepsakes," were likewise illustrated with steel plates (in line or mezzotint), as were the various "elegant publications, suited for the drawing-room table," as one advertisement put it,—collections of sentimental "beauties" of the poets, volumes of local description, immortalizations of cemeteries. The steel-engraving as a means of illustration survived until after the Civil War. For example, in F. O. C. Darley's characteristic vignettes for Houghton and Mifflin's edition of Dickens. Or in the rather mechanical plates after paintings by Alonzo Chappel in the "National Portrait Gallery of Eminent Americans" (1862) and other publications of Johnson, Fry & Co. Chappel based his work on fairly careful study of historical data. He collaborated with Darley in the illustration of the Stratford edition of Shakespeare, edited by W. C. Bryant (1886), the last important work by either of them.

The Cruikshank-Phiz-Leech period of etched book-illustration in England had a slight reflex in our country.

There was some use of lithography for book-illustration,—beginning in the thirties and applied in black-and-white, in tints, and even in the full colors of chromo-lithography. Darley's "Scenes in Indian Life" (1843), his illustrations for Irving's "Rip Van Winkle" (1848: American Art Union), "Legend of Sleepy Hollow" (American Art Union, 1849), Judd's "Margaret" (1856), all in outline, were etched on stone. John W. Ehninger employed the same process for his outline plates for Irving's "Dolph Heyliger" (1851); his drawings for "Ye Legend of St. Gwendoline" (1867) were reproduced by photography, an unusual method, "because," said H. C. Bunner ("Harper's," October, 1892), "they were considered too delicate to entrust to the engraver's burin."

During this time, wood-engraving, with its peculiar possibilities of direct and harmonious combination with the type-printed page, was coming to its own. From the rehabilitation of wood-engraving in the days of Anderson, to its consummate development about two or three decades ago, its application as a means of adornment and as a source of, and impetus to, pictorial instruction in connection with the printed page was far-reaching in extent. Growing demand for illustration of historical works, schoolbooks and fiction called into being the professional illustrator, a class which rapidly increased in numbers and ability.

With the forties there set in an impetus toward freer and more artistic drawing on the block. A particularly noteworthy undertaking was the Harper Bible, with about 1,400 drawings by John Gadsby Chapman, executed in the spirit of the steel-engraving. Somewhat freer, yet with something of the feeling of the English artist John Thurston, were the Shakespeare illustrations (1853) of T. H. Matteson, perhaps his best work. William Croome illustrated John Frost's "Book of the Navy" (1843), "Songs for the People" (1849), and other works with some spirit. And Hammatt Billings, wood-engraver and architect, illustrated Whittier's poems (1849), Waverley Novels (1857–59) and writings of H. B. Stowe, Dickens, Pellico, S. S. Goodrich and others, in the fifties.

With the opening of this new period there appeared one who still stands as perhaps our most noteworthy example of an "all around" illustrator—Felix O. C. Darley. Darley's industry was as great as his facility and versatility, and for years the phrase "illustrated by Darley" appeared with never-failing regularity in announcements of new books. The swing of his style, his grasp of individual action and the movement of groups, give his work distinction. His illustrations are really illustrations and not drawings without any appreciable reference to the text, or pictures of "swagger" young men with stern brows, massive chins and padded shoulders, and the ever-beautiful young woman whom we are tickled to-day to accept as the type of an American girl. Before the mind's eye there rise his early Philadelphia street scenes, occasional "comics," title designs (as for "The Lantern"), the illustrations for Irving's "Knickerbocker History of New York," Poe, Wm. Gilmore Simms, stories of Western and Southern life, juveniles, Frank Forester's sporting books, Tristram Shandy, Joseph C. Neal's humor,

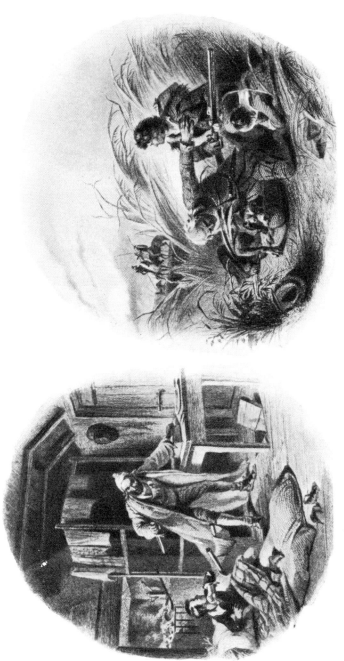

A Scene from "Oliver Twist"   A Scene from Cooper's "Leather Stocking Tales"

Illustrations, engraved on steel, from designs by Felix O. C. Darley

"Nick of the Woods," T. B. Thorpe ("the bee hunter"), Cooper (over 500 designs), Dickens, Lossing's "Our Country" (500 drawings), the outline compositions mentioned and the later works, Evangeline and the Shakespeare plates, numerous bank-note vignettes, and large Civil War framing prints, *March to the Sea,* etc. The mere quantity is astonishing, but respect for this artist is much increased when one realizes the high average merit of it all. Such unceasing demand inevitably developed a manner, but at its best it approached so closely to a style as to challenge a definition of difference. Rough preparatory sketches for a number of designs to be drawn on the block, rich little conceptions of vignettes, interesting pencil notes, the line massed to block out movement and composition, detailed studies from nature, show how facts carefully observed, noted and stored up formed the foundation for Darley's easy presentation. The vigor of his style finds a certain reflection in the drawings of Jacob A. Dallas, Frederick M. Coffin, and Elias J. Whitney.

In the fifties, efforts to establish illustrated magazines had influence on illustration. In the earliest ones, the "International Monthly" (New York, volumes 1–5: 1850–52), "National Magazine" (New York, volume 1, 1852) and "United States Magazine" (N. Y., 1854–57), the cuts were mainly copied from other sources. But the last-named had some drawings by John R. Chapin, as well as those for Major Jack Downing's "Letters" (1857) by J. H. Howard (who illustrated also Downing's "My thirty Years out of the Senate," 1859), and all three had portraits by Samuel Wallin. Wallin, much in demand, drew all the heads in the "Illustrated American Biography" (1853–55), re-issued as A. D. Jones's "American Portrait Gallery." He was better than J. A. Oertel, had more aplomb, but it is interesting to compare his portraits, always done with the same recognizable curves, manner more evident than characterization, with such a careful production as August Will's portrait of Alexander Anderson ("Child's Paper," 1867).

In California, book and magazine illustration, with other evidences of civilization, came close in the wake of American settlement in 1849. Pioneers in Pacific coast illustrating were Charles Nahl, who drew with a Teutonic character, and H. Eastman, publisher of "Hutchins' California Magazine."

In the meantime, "Harper's Magazine" had come in 1851 to stay. The publishers made haste slowly in the art department, but gradually the illustrations increased and improved. Among the artists in the first decade were Frank Bellew, Chapin, Coffin, W. H. Davenport, Darley, Dallas, C. E. Doepler, Hinsdale, D. C. Hitchcock (the "Hitchie" of Vedder's "Digressions of V.," 1910), Augustus Hoppin (illustrator of "Nothing to Wear," 1857, and of books by W. D. Howells, G. W. Curtis, and B. P. Shillaber), E. F. Mullen, Thwaites, H. L. Stephens, B. J. Lossing, T. Addison Richards and David H. Strother ("Porte Crayon"). The last three were artist authors, frequently illustrating their own writings. Lossing drew the illustrations for nearly all of his popular books, such as the "Field Books" of the Revolution and the War of 1812, and "The Hudson from the Wilderness to the Sea." It appears that his landscape sketches were re-drawn on the wood by Runge. T. Addison Richards was the first artist in this country to make a specialty of drawing acceptable landscape illustrations on the wood. He furnished drawings and text for "Romance of American Landscape" and other volumes. "Porte Crayon" illustrated Southern life with pen and pencil in "Virginia illustrated." Other artist-authors were T. B. Thorpe, Capt. George H. Derby (John Phoenix), H. W. Herbert ("Frank Forester" of sporting books fame), Thomas Butler Gunn ("Physiology of the New York Boarding House"), Augustus Hoppin, Charles C. Perkins, G. G. White, C. A. Barry and H. W. Herrick, the last three responsible for hand-books on drawing and painting. A. F. Mathews, W. Keith and Alexander F. Harmer appeared in the "Californian" in a similar dual capacity. In later years the tribe increased greatly: Livingston Hopkins, J. Carter Beard, Dan C. Beard ("The American Boy's Handy Book," 1883), Palmer Cox ("Brownie" books), A. F. Jaccaci, Wm. Hamilton Gibson, Frank D. Millet, Mary Hallock Foote, W. H. McDougall, C. S. Reinhart, Frank French, A. C. Redwood (stories of the war from the Southern standpoint), W. H. Shelton, Frederic Remington, George Wharton Edwards, George Gibbs, E. Seton Thompson and many more illustrated text of their own making. Some were rather better known as writers, who added the force of graphic representation to their written word, as did also Frank B. Mayer, Edward Strahan ("Earl Shinn"), W. Mackay Laffan, Wm. H. Bishop, Roger Riordan.

But this was a divagation, and we return to the Harper artists, of whom Carl Emil Doepler, a German with a facile style, was in this country during 1849–55. Among his many designs were those for J. S. C. Abbott's "Life of Napoleon" and the Jacob Abbott "Rollo" books.

A factor of note was the spread of illustrated weekly journalism. In 1851 T. W. Strong brought out the first illustrated weekly worthy of note, the "Illustrated American News." Dallas drew the title, and the illustrations were signed by Bellew, C. J. Brown, G. T. Devereux, Elliot, Egbert, Chapin, D. C. Hitchcock, John H. Goater, Hoppin, McDonough, Magee, Masson, W. R. Miller, E. Purcell, Howell and Wallin. This publication ended the same year and was followed January 4, 1853, by the "Illustrated News" (issued by P. T. Barnum and Beach, of the "Sun"), which lived a year and passed into "Gleason's Pictorial," of Boston, in which city Ballou also issued illustrated publications. These unsuccessful efforts were followed by "Frank Leslie's Illustrated Newspaper" in 1855 and "Harper's Weekly" in 1857. Among Leslie's artists were Joseph Becker, Albert Berghaus and Georgiana A. Davis (who later drew for the Salvation Army's "War Cry"). There must be noted also the "New York Illustrated News" (1859–62), with A. R. Waud, Lumley, Eytinge and Nast. The "Southern Illustrated News" (beginning in 1862), like the Palmetto series of schoolbooks or the novels by Clara Mühlbach issued in wall-paper covers, or the illustrated edition of the "Adventures of Philip," marked the brave attempt of the South to cultivate the gentler arts of peace under adverse circumstances.

In the seventies and eighties New York even had a daily illustrated paper, the "Daily Graphic." Philip G. Cusachs was at one time its art-manager; photo-lithography was the reproductive process used. Later, S. H. Horgan, I am told, brought out in this publication the first half-tone published in a daily. As for the daily newspaper, there were occasional cuts in the "Atlas" (1842), "Mercury" and "Herald," and Valerian Gribayédoff notes that the "Pittsburgh Telegraph" in 1875 commenced using woodcuts. But illustration as a regular feature came with "Truth" (New York) in 1877. Not illustration of current events as we understand it to-day, for as it took two or three days to turn out a cut by the "soft metal process," stock illustrations were used again and again. In 1883 illustration was tried by "The World" (New York), with which Gribayédoff came into contact the following year. Other papers followed suit, as well as the American Press Association, with S. H. Horgan as art manager. Among the newspaper artists of the following years were H. Coultaus and J. Knickerbocker of the "New York Herald," and John Durkin and O. H. von Gottschalk of the "Sun." The "Ben Day" process of quick mechanical production of tints by "rapid shading mediums" was a time-saver. To-day the newspaper illustrator has largely given place to the photograph reproduced in the half-tone, with results questionable in effect, but speedy of attainment.

If, in the earlier days of the nineteenth century, illustrations in newspapers were practically non-existent, we had the occasional "blanket sheet" of one issue, such as that brought out during the Mexican War, "Brother Jonathan: Great Pictorial Battle Sheet" (New York, 1847). This was an amusing mixture of bona-fide portraits of American generals, and French and other foreign cuts doing duty as delineations of Mexican life, a pretty example of the bare-faced "fake."

In the literature relating to the Civil War the names of Alfred R. and William Waud, Christian Schussele, T. R. Davis, Arthur Lumley, F. B. Schell often appeared, the last two being artist correspondents in the field, as was also Winslow Homer. No doubt engravers and artists often had to work against time in those troublous days. A collection of pencil drawings (preserved in the New York Public Library), made in the field by Frank Leslie's artists, to be re-drawn on the block in the home office, shows under what conditions the work was done. The artists made short-cuts for the "re-drawers," adding written memoranda to guide them.

In the improvement in the reproduction of illustrations by wood-engraving the influence of "Picturesque America" (1872–74) was noteworthy. In that book landscape artists had their opportunity, particularly Thomas Moran, Harry Fenn and J. D. Woodward. Fenn, suggester and principal illustrator of the publication, was prominently identified also with "Picturesque Europe" and "Picturesque Palestine," beside executing designs for Whittier's "Ballads of New England," 1870, and "Snow-Bound," 1881. Woodward's skilful pencil was so much in demand that in 1881 he wrote to T. D. Sugden that he was "driven within an inch of my life." Other artists identified with landscape art were Henry Bisbing and John A. Hows ("Forest Scenes," 1864, and "Forest Pictures in the Adirondacks," 1865). The latter drew for "Appleton's Journal" (begun 1869), as did also R. S. Gifford, Granville Perkins (marine subjects his specialty), J. Hill, E. Forbes, A. C. Warren, Thomas Hogan (long associated with Frank H. Schell), W. M. Cary (Western scenes), W. L. Sheppard (illustrator of John Esten Cooke's novels and of Carlton McCarthy's "Life in the C. S. A."), Frank Beard, Alfred Kappes, Will H. Low, Charles G. Bush, Winslow Homer, Paul Frenzeny, Darley and W. J. Hennessy. The last-named one's twelve drawings of Edwin Booth in as many characters, engraved by W. J. Linton, 1872, are well known. At about the same time there were running "Every Saturday," "Our Young Folks" (Boston, 1865–73), the "Riverside Magazine" (1867-70) and "Scribner's Monthly" (begun 1871). Further illustrators were E. B. Bensell, J. McNevin, W. Momberger, Thomas Nast (illustrations for "Robinson Crusoe"), I. Pranischnikoff. Sol Eytinge, Jr., drew illustrations for Dickens, which won the praise of that author, and for Lowell's "Vision of Sir Launfal."

Women artists entered this field. Among the earliest were Jessie Curtis (subsequently Mrs. Shepherd), dainty but undistinguished Addie Ledyard and Mary A. Hallock (later Mrs. Foote), who illustrated books by Longfellow, Hawthorne and herself. In the eighties and nineties, came M. L. D. Watson, Irene E. Jerome ("Nature's Hallelujah," 1886, "The Message of the Bluebird," 1886), Ida Waugh, Mrs. Jessie McDermott Walcott (child subjects), Allegra Eggleston (daughter of Edward), Helen Rosa Lossing ("H. Rosa," daughter of Benson J.), L. B. Humphrey, L. J. Bridgman, Mrs. Allingham, Maud Humphreys, not a few of them at most pleasingly pretty in their work. Mrs. Alice Barber Stephens and Mrs. Foote, through the breadth and vigor of drawings, stand out from the rest. They connect directly with the present day, when Blanche Ostertag, Sarah S. Stilwell Weber, May Wilson Preston, Rose O'Neill (whose style has varied from a pleasing though vigorous charm to a bold modeling with massed and curved pen-strokes), and those products of the influence of Pyle, —Elizabeth Shippen Green, Violet Oakley, Charlotte Harding and Jessie Willcox Smith (children a specialty) exemplify various possibilities resulting from the application of the female temperament to illustration.

This diversion, brought about by the convenient classification by sex, was anachronistic. We are supposed to be still in the seventies, and there are yet to be noted some designs by John La Farge, illustrations for "Enoch Arden," scenes from the Arabian Nights, and the drawing "The Wolf Charmer," that strange composition, entering the "region of mystery," yet with a compelling sense of reality. Occupied with the fundamental spirit of a literary production, he, as Cortissoz said, "steeping himself in reflection, brought all manner of constructive thought to the development of his work."

The domain of the schoolbook was developed to a noteworthy extent. George G. White, Henry F. Farny, Alfred Fredericks and others signed the woodcut illustrations in the "readers." The preface of E. J. Lewis's "American Sportsman," 1857, in which White made his début, emphasized his ability as a delineator of animals. He had a leaning toward the style of Sir John Gilbert, and eventually became connnected with "sporting" and religious publications, employing a staff of helpers.

The influence of the illustrated press continued. Henry James wrote of the "art of illustration in black and white, to which American periodical literature has lately given such an impetus, and which has returned the good office by conferring a great distinction on our magazines." Joseph Pennell says: "The principal credit for this development must be ascribed to the intelligent support which Mr. A. W. Drake, art editor of the 'Century,' then 'Scribner's Monthly,' was the first to give."

Late in the seventies came that new movement in wood-engraving, emphasized with éclat in Juengling's cuts after James E. Kelly's remarkably free drawings for "Scribner's." In these designs, the line was absent; it was painted illustration, which we see in preponderance to-day. And yet the eighties brought also a widespread employment of the medium which is essentially and incisively expressed in line,—pen-and-ink.

This artistic exploitation of the possibilities of the pen was exemplified notably by Abbey, C. S. Reinhart, Alfred Brennan, W. T. Smedley and Joseph Pennell, whose book on "Pen Drawing" is dedicated "to A. W. Drake, W.

Lewis Fraser, Charles Parsons, Richmond Seeley, four men who should be honored for their encouragement of pen drawing," this list including three Americans.

Edwin A. Abbey, "endowed," as Miss E. L. Cary says, "with the instinct for the exquisite and the old," reconstructed the seventeenth and eighteenth centuries for us in his drawings for "Old Songs" and Goldsmith's "She Stoops to Conquer" with a vividness and grace that quite obliterate the preparatory labor of historical and antiquarian studies. The light, caressing strokes of his pen graphically illustrated the easy craftsmanship which attains result with no trace of effort. "For grace and refinement," wrote Pennell, "he ranks second to none." In his famous Shakespeare illustrations W. H. Downes found refinement, tenderness, grace, rather than dramatic force or grandeur. Large human sympathies he did not express.

Charles Stanley Reinhart's forceful directness was joined to what some one has described as a "quick grasp and holding of characteristics of various national and social types." For C. D. Warner's "Their Pilgrimage" (1886) he furnished what Henry James termed a "rich and curious pictorial accompaniment"; his designs for G. P. Lathrop's "Spanish Vistas" are set down by the same authority as "delightful notes of an artist's quest of the sketchable." In contrast to the incisive rich blacks of Reinhart's technique is W. T. Smedley's more suave, repressed method, in harmony with the manners of the well-bred, comfortable middle class which he depicted with happy seizure of essential nature. He had a keen eye for the individualities which the monotonous same-

" THERE NEVER WAS ANYTHING THE LEAST SERIOUS BETWEEN US"
Illustration for Henry James's "Julia Bride," by W. T. Smedley

ness of fashionable attire often veils, as well as for the character that the very fit of the clothes themselves discloses to the observant eye.

A. B. Frost pictured with particular success our rural citizens. Joel Chandler Harris said of him: "The one characteristic that marks all the work of Mr. Frost, is its persistent and ever-present humor." Robert Bridges quotes F. Hopkinson Smith as saying that "no man laughs effectively with pen or brush who does not laugh with his own soul first." He gives us real people, who meet our sympathy and interest, and not the foolish "rube" of the comic sheets. In his "Sports and Games in the Open" (1899), with their joy in out-door life, we feel this same whole-souled, kindly absorption in the point-of-view of his characters. He illustrated A. W. Tourgee's "Hot Plowshares" (1883), but better known, more spontaneous, are his drawings for F. R. Stockton's "Rudder Range." His delightful treatment of two such different books as H. C. Bunner's "Story of a New York House" and "Uncle Remus" is to be noted. In delineating various types of American life he came across the negro, his *Music for the Dance* and a negro version of "the ant and the cricket" being characteristic efforts.

The black man was particularly cultivated by Edward W. Kemble ("Uncle Tom's Cabin"). Furthermore, in the apportionment of specialties, J. O. Davidson,—of whom Hopkinson Smith, I think, said he "knows our ships, especially the older ones, as no other artist knows them,"—M. J. Burns and F. S. Cozzens became identified with the sea and its ships; J. Carter Beard with animal life; and William Hamilton Gibson with animal and plant life. Gibson used pen and pencil in a number of volumes ("Sharp Eyes," "Happy Hunting Grounds," "Pastoral Days") to familiarize a larger public in a charming and graceful manner with characteristic features of that life and with "the idyllic qualities of nature." Gilbert Gaul, H. A. Ogden (with Revolutionary times as a sub-specialty), W. H. Shelton, Rufus F. Zogbaum and Thure de Thulstrup illustrated military matter. Thulstrup, though most at home in military art, had to treat the most varied subjects, and acquitted himself well, thanks to good draughtsmanship.

The West was pre-eminently the domain of Frederic Remington, who delineated its military types, frontiersmen, cowboys and Indians (once the subject of J. E. Taylor) with vehement realism and uncompromising fidelity, an unbiased and breezy freshness of perception. "What makes Remington's Indian sketches so real and so fine," wrote one critic, "is that he knows it all himself." Mrs. Schuyler Van Rensselaer, reviewing his illustrations for the "Song of Hiawatha" (1890), said: "Remington is always sincere, spirited, individual and interesting."

A great contrast to Remington's rough-and-ready use of pen-and-ink was Alfred Brennan's loving and insinuating courtship of the same medium. Pennell wrote that he "most certainly was and is the master of this school of American draughtsmen," the school referred to being a group showing "intelligent adaptation of the methods of Fortuny, Rico and Vierge, of the artists of 'Fliegende Blätter,' and of the draughtsmen of Japan" Harry

Watrous told me that Blum, Brennan and others spent
much time in the studio of Humphrey Moore, who, in
turn, was the friend and companion of Fortuny. Hence
these cross-influences. Those were the days when Fernand Harvey Lungren showed "great power of expression conveyed with very few and simple lines." Robert
F. Blum drew stunning Fortuny-like things such as his
portrait of Joseph Jefferson as "Bob Acres," and Reginald B. Birch, in his illustrations for "Little Lord Faunt-
leroy," combined charm and sweetness and the artistic
sense in a noteworthy manner. Brennan, who had a vein
of extravagant fancy, was "unconventional and often
startling," and "an assiduous cultivator of whimsicality
as a fine art." He injected, into whatever he did, a
peculiar flavor which pervaded even when he was re-draw-
ing a photograph. In those days, photographs were re-
drawn in pen-and-ink, by men such as Kenyon Cox, Otto
H. Bacher, Wiles, Thulstrup, Henry F. Farny, and W.
H. Drake.

Plenty more illustrators were actively engaged in this
period of the eighties: E. H. Garrett, Frank T. Merrill,
Henry Sandham (Canadian subjects), Frank M. Greg-
ory, Frederick Dielman (Susan Warner's "Wide, Wide
World," 1888, and "Queechy," 1893), Charles Graham,
W. A. Rogers, C. A. Vanderhoof, Alfred Fredericks.
John W. Alexander drew some noteworthy portraits,—
that of Walt Whitman, for instance. In the nineties, B.
West Clinedinst, H. Denman, Eric Pape, Charles Cope-
land, Charles Broughton, H. C. Edwards, W. Granville

Smith and André Castaigne in various ways answered to the demand for illustration.

Many of the artists named were professional illustrators, entirely devoted to their specialty. Some were painters who placed themselves at the service of the sister art for a limited period or occasionally. Among these was Walter Shirlaw, who in his drawings for Edward Eggleston's "Roxy," or in magazine illustrations picturing rolling mills, etc., retained his predilection for rich, succulent tones and broad decorative effects. Pennell finds that he "gave some of the most artistic renderings of commonplace things ever produced in America." In what one writer calls the "shifting membership" of the craft, there were temporarily enlisted also the painters Childe Hassam, Irving R. Wiles, W. L. Metcalf, E. W. Deming, Francis Day and E. H. Blashfield, who emphasized pictorially the results of antiquarian and historical research, in "Italian Cities," by Mrs. Blashfield and himself.

Three noteworthy instances of an incursion by a painter into the domain of illustration are found in Kenyon Cox's pictures for Rossetti's "Blessed Damozel," Will H. Low's "illustrative designs" for the "Lamia" of Keats (1885), and Elihu Vedder's accompaniment of drawings for the Rubaiyat of Omar Khayyam (1884). The last-named gain much from the circumstance that each page of the book is drawn, text as well as the surrounding design, by the same hand. That emphasizes the advantage and importance of having the book, as a mechanical product, "cast in one piece," although in this case the text was drawn, not printed. This matter of unity in the design of a book was exemplified in a measure also by the 1887 edition of "Odes and Sonnets" by Keats, for which W. H. Low designed not only illustrations, and decorative floral panels, but the cover and lining papers as well. Copious illustrations with a decorative element were also those by Wm. Martin Johnson for "Ben Hur" (1891) and Reade's "The Cloister and the Hearth" (1893), Albert Herter's for Cable's "Creole Days" and "Grandissimes," and Ludvig Sandoe Ipsen's for Mrs. Browning's "Love Sonnets" (1886), described as a magnificent piece of decorative book-making; "Nothing like this has ever been done in this country before," wrote R. H. Stoddard. It was a time of holiday books and sumptuously illustrated editions, graced by the work of George Wharton Edwards (Spenser's "Epithalamion," 1895), Wm. St. John Harper (Keats's "Endymion," 1888), W. L. Taylor (Owen Meredith's "The Earl's Return," 1886, Tennyson's "Holy Grail," 1887), and with archaizing effect, the brothers Rhead—George W., Frederick and Louis ("Pilgrim's Progress," 1898).

In the early nineties a gaily serious mood found expression in short-lived periodicals such as the "Knight Errant" (Boston), "Lark" (sponsored in San Francisco by Gelett Burgess, of "Goops" fame), and the "Chap Book" (Chicago). Artist-contributors to the last included Will Bradley, John Sloan, Fred Richardson, Gardner C. Teall, Claude F. Bragdon, Robert Wagner, and Frank Hazenplug, the latter emphasizing the decorative spirit that marked not a few of the drawings.

The facile entrance of painters into this field indicates influences at work which characterize our book-illustration in these later days. The freedom in the choice of materials and in the size of the original drawing which the artist gained through the method of photographing the drawing on to the wood-block and through the subsequent use of the half-tone, would naturally draw the painter occasionally into the service of the sister art.

A noteworthy connecting link between the last generation and the present was Howard Pyle, by reason of thirty years of prominent attainment, and through alertness of point of view and his serious attitude toward his art. His realism, while stern, was never crass. With a style that seemed at first sight inflexible he combined a keenness of observation that served him in the treatment of scenes in widely different lands, times and strata of society. "Versatile," one would say, were there not the fear of a by-taste, in that term, of glib facility. The periods and subjects which he covered were varied: seventeenth century England and France, the American Revolution and our Civil War, buccaneers, Robin Hood, the divers and fishermen of our coasts, Holmes's "One Hoss Shay" and "Autocrat of the Breakfast Table." For a time he was his own author, writing of Robin Hood, or "The Buccaneers and Marooners of America" (1890). "Nowhere," wrote Hopkinson Smith, "have I seen text better idealized or illustrations better described than in that series of articles by Pyle on the 'Buccaneers.'" His picture of a seaman *marooned* sticks in the memory with all the pounding emphasis of its simple dramatic force.

VIEWING THE BATTLE OF BUNKER HILL
By Howard Pyle

Pyle became particularly identified with the authoritative illustration of eighteenth century America. To quote Samuel Isham: "Pyle is the only man who seems to know thoroughly the colonial and revolutionary epoch. . . . He has represented the founders of the Republic as they were,—sturdy, hard-headed folk, with strong characters and few graces, who wore the rather rigid costumes of the time with dignity and not like singers in comic opera or dancing masters." His historical correctness was free from pedantry through the success with which he projected himself into time, place and spirit of each scene. Pyle preserved to the end a steadfast, virile thoroughness in his presentation of essential characteristics. His use of the pen, with an archaic flavor that caused Pennell to characterize him as "a careful student of Duerer," was pretty well abandoned, later on, for that of the brush. He painted his illustrations; that fact, in itself, brings him in touch with the younger men of this day, who are to a great extent availing themselves of this method of working for reproduction.

Yet one of the first men to come to mind among our illustrators of the present time, Charles Dana Gibson, has used pen-and-ink almost exclusively, and has in its use achieved his finest successes. From his earlier manner, in which he delineated *Bishop Gullem, Jonathan Trump, Penelope Peachblow* and *Dolly Flicker* in various combinations to fit evanescent jokes in the comic press, with close-set lines to form tones and local color, he developed into a free insistence on the line *per se*. His command of the pen is noteworthy; he has used it rarely in illustration proper, usually in what for lack of a better term has been called "cartooning." The Gibson Girl, rare creature of his fancy, wove her spell.   But Gibson broadened out, widened his outlook on humanity, which, with a smile, he presented in its failings and virtues, in continued performances such as the "Education of Mr. Pipp" (1899) and in single leaves from the book of life, scenes in drawing-room and street, on ferry boat and in the world of the stage.   The point is made by insisting enough on. the obvious not to trouble the beholder with too much subtlety of thought or observation.   The manner of presentation, the technique, obviously adequate, satisfies both the average citizen and the artist or connoisseur.

The "American girl" and her entourage engaged the attention of Howard Chandler Christy, A. B. Wenzell, Henry Hutt, Harrison Fisher, prominent figures in a group which strongly represents certain tendencies and characteristics of recent illustration.   Extraordinary technical facility is put to the task of evoking types of girl and man, ideals of stately elegance and statuesquely athletic vigor that appeal to many.   It puts the beholder in a wonderful land where all is "swell," where beauty and luxury reign, a sort of enchanted isle without the sensuous languor of Cythère, the fine perfume of the automobile pervading it all.   This long array of girls and men of impeccable appearance is interrupted in the case of James Montgomery Flagg.   To dash and facility he joins an evident strong sense of humor, a saving grace which restores balance, bringing us more into accord with things as they are.   Flagg, like Gibson, is active not so much as an illustrator, but as a producer of individual drawings emphasizing each some particular idea, a form that enters the realm of pictorial satire. The art of book-illustrating, which has its finest success in the intelligent wedding of picture and text, unfolding originality within limits set, is practised, in these times, by a number of able and discriminating artists. Consideration of present-day illustration must be based on the principles of the art. Illustration must elucidate the text or adorn it; it may do both, but at all events it must be in harmony with the text. I have not in mind the occasional lapse, the oversight that produces an unwarranted change in appearance of a character, or an anachronism in costume, or the construction of a scene distinctly different from the author's description. Our illustration has suffered from a tendency to parade cleverness in place of thoroughness, to dazzle the eye by a display of glittering superficiality. The burden of duty toward art is borne rather too lightly when the same heroic "full dress" type is employed to represent both the society man and the Italian excursion-boat fiddler. Oliver Herford, in "The Astonishing Tale of a Pen-and-Ink Puppet, or The Gentle Art of Illustrating," from one drawing of a man and one of a girl constructed manikins which he readjusted into caricatures of the "he and she" drawings familiar to readers of books and magazines. Luckily we are not wholly dominated by this school, although it has often held the center of the stage, brilliant in the lime-light's glare. If there have been "stars" not free from glittering rant, we have also had a very good stock company.

Arthur I. Keller, prominently identified with *de luxe* editions of American classics (Longfellow's "Hanging of the Crane," etc.), known also as the illustrator of Wister's "Virginian," F. H. Smith's "Caleb West" and other books, shows conscientious study of the authors' intentions and characters, embodied in a style that is free and spontaneous. The author speaks to us in the pictures through a discriminating personality that has added life to the characters visualized for us. He seems particularly happy in the representation of groups of people in their temporary mental and physical relations.

Work such as that constitutes the real backbone of modern illustration; cleverness, the use of dashing types, a brilliant, "swagger" style are not in themselves the sole elements of the best art. Serious accomplishment appeared also in the illustrations of the late Walter Appleton Clark, F. C. Yohn, the late Louis Loeb and Albert Sterner. Sterner's drawings for "Prue and I," by G. W. Curtis, "preserved the very essence and sweetness of the aroma of [this] charming story." Other names familiar to the public in the recent years of the ubiquitous illustration are W. J. Aylward, George Varian, Stanley M. Arthurs, Jay Hambidge, the Kinneys, Clifford Carleton, Orson Lowell, Franklin Booth, W. D. Stevens, Frederic D. Steele, Jules Guerin (a painter of delicate visions of city scenes), J. R. Shaver, Thomas Fogarty, W. L. Jacobs, C. Allan Gilbert, C. K. Linson, G. Wright, Reuterdahl, F. Luis Mora, F. Gruger, E. L. Blumenschein,

Illustration by Arthur I. Keller.   From "Tomorrow's Tangle,"
by Geraldine Bonner

Lucius W. Hitchcock, Ernest C. Peixotto, Vernon Howe Bailey, W. J. Glackens, John Cecil Clay, Gordon Grant, N. C. Wyeth, Victor S. Perard, and a group of Californians: L. Maynard Dixon, A. F. Mathews, Albertine Randall Wheeler, Alexander F. Harmer, H. J. Breuer, Charles Witkowski, drawing for the "Californian." If they do not all exemplify fully the illustrator's function to illustrate, they do accentuate the great advance in the general level of technique.

We have had and have illustrators who link arms with the author and interest us in what they have to say about him. And there are others who also, with knowledge of printing, serve the cause of the book beautiful. The photo-mechanical processes have done incalculable good in facilitating and cheapening publication, and have brought good art where it was not brought before. But they have not been an entirely unmixed good. The ease of reproducing drawings done in wash or oils has dimmed to sight the essential significance of the line. The close relation between printing-type and the line-drawn illustration, ornament or initial, is apt to be overlooked. Recognition of the importance of this harmony between component parts has caused the production of books with type, pictures, end papers and covers designed by one artist. W. H. Bradley, B. G. Goodhue, T. M. Cleland, W. A. Dwiggins and E. B. Edwards have been identified with this spirit in book-making. If there is shown more frequently a regard for the book as a product, in itself, in its entirety, of craftsmanship governed by good taste, we may be content with such a counterbalance to the deteriorating effects of over-production.

The fact that drawing in line, as contrasted with drawing in tones (wash drawing, painting) is seen increasingly in illustration to-day, is decidedly significant. The line in the illustration echoes, and finds its echo in, the line of the type. W. A. Dwiggins has ingeniously pointed out that one reason why the line in this combination appeals to us is that in both cases use is made of the white of the paper as an integral part of the composition. Photo-engraving (the line plate, zinc etching) here offers a cheap and true medium of facsimile reproduction not only of pen drawings, but also work in pencil, crayon and char-coal. We are already seeing the forming of a group of draughtsmen in line: the late J. C. Coll, F. Luis Mora, W. J. Duncan, Kerr Eby, John Wolcott Adams, Wallace Morgan, Charles Sarka.

The service rendered to the people by wood-engraving through five centuries came to a very large extent in the form of book illustration. And to-day, now and then, some of our "painter-engravers" get an opportunity to exercise their craft in the adornment of a book. In such cases—for instance Mrs. Charles MacVeagh's "Foun-tains of Papal Rome" and "Journeys to Bagdad," by Charles S. Brooks, Ruzicka the illustrator of the former. Lewis of the latter—even though the artists have not had full opportunity to direct in the wedding of type and decoration, there is yet impetus toward harmony between the two. Wood-engraving, a relief process as is type-cutting, is a peculiarly effective and proper element in the realization of this fundamental factor in the making of decorated books.

The sense of appropriateness that fits the proper medium to the end in view, obtains here as in any art. It cannot, of course, be exercised toward the production of a book harmonious in all its parts unless those concerned —illustrator, printer, binder—also are in harmonious accord. In the end, it is after all more important that we produce well—not necessarily sumptuously—illustrated books, than that we produce many of them.

CHAPTER XII

CARICATURE

THE corrective force of pictorial satire did not enter as a factor into the political development of this country until the first low rumblings of the revolutionary thunderstorm made themselves heard. In the clash between French and British interests, in the uncertain times when the Revolution cast its shadows before, and during the war itself, caricature had its part, but its execution was mainly foreign. Not only in the countries unfriendly to England, in France, Holland and Spain, but in England itself did these sharp attacks on the policy of the mother country appear. Mr. R. T. Haines Halsey's collection of cartoons of this period offers a remarkable review of the nature and extent of this pictorial comment. In our present day of facile reproduction, when every daily paper appears to have its cartoonist, when every little political local happening is humorously pictured next day, these two and a half hundred cartoons may not appear a great number. But when we consider that every one had to be engraved on copper, the output seems decidedly large. These old cartoons comment on more general and far-reaching events and principles than the little happenings, or acts of individuals, of minor importance, which so frequently form the subject of the pictorial joke of our daily press, thrown away on the day it is published.

These old cartoons, often quite crude, are of interest and value as historical documents; in them, contemporary opinion is mirrored. In them the struggle between France and England for supremacy in the New World is reflected, and the rise of Scotch influence at the English court. Then comes the Stamp Act period (to 1773), with prints nearly all friendly to America; in one of them, referring to budget troubles, an Indian appears *taxed without representation*. The Boston Port Bill (1774) called forth a series of mezzotints in London; one deals with the resolution of the women of Edenton, N. C., to drink no more tea and wear no more British clothes. The largest group was that dealing with the Revolution, and it consisted of English, Dutch and French engravings. The British caricatures, on the whole, were not unfriendly to the colonies. They show a tendency to treat America as a wayward child, a dupe of her confederates *Monsieur Louis Baboon* (France), *Don Diego* (Spain) and *Mynheer Frog* (Holland), which three are frequently and vigorously attacked, as is the home government. The American rattlesnake holding two British armies (Burgoyne's and Cornwallis's) in its coils, and ready for a third, is a striking production. The chapter is closed by a picture published in 1783, with the inscription:

"Britannia: 'Come, come, shake hands, and let's be friends.'

"America: 'With all my heart, I've gained my ends.' "

This period called forth a few caricatures by colonial talent, notably some by Paul Revere, allegorical compositions, *A View of the Years 1765* and *Stamp Act repealed* (the obelisk print, 1766), both dealing with the Stamp Act, and caricatures: *The Rescinders, The Able Doctor, or America swallowing the Bitter Draught* (tea forced down her throat), June, 1774, *The Mitred Minuet* around the Quebec Bill, October, 1774, and *America in Distress,* February, 1775, the last three published in the "Royal American Magazine." Sometimes an event of local interest would occasion a satirical design of home manufacture, the work of engraving which might fall to one with a sense of humor or not. Nathaniel Hurd in 1762 caricatured Dr. Seth Hudson and a certain Mr. Howe, convicted of counterfeiting. Henry Dawkins is credited with several large plates "caricaturing events in the political history of Philadelphia in 1764." One of these was probably the one showing *the advance of the Paxton boys upon Philadelphia* (1764), suggested by C. R. Hildeburn to be by James Claypoole, Jr., but believed by Stauffer to be probably the work of Dawkins. Two of these plates, relating to the election of 1764 and the "Paxton Boys," are reproduced in P. L. Ford's "Many-sided Franklin" (New York, 1899). Franklin is associated with the invention of two of the most noted satirical designs of the day. One was the device of a serpent, cut into pieces, one for each colony, with the motto *Join or die* or *Unite or die.* This appeared in the "Pennsylvania Gazette," the "Boston Gazette" and the "Boston News Letter" in 1754, the "Boston Evening Post" in 1765 (Stamp Act period), and again before the Revolution, in the "Pennsylvania Journal," 1774. The

POLITICAL CARICATURE: AMERICA SWALLOWING THE BITTER DRAUGHT
Engraving by Paul Revere

loyal papers roundly condemned this cut, a writer in "Rivington's Royal Gazette" calling it a "scandalous and saucy reflection." The other Franklin cut represented Britain dismembered, a limbless trunk, turning tearful eyes to heaven, while beside her lie her legs, arms, hands and feet, representing the colonies, cut off and leaving her helpless (1774). James Parton calls attention to another newspaper heading, the row of Boston Massacre coffins, mutely voicing the colonists' protest. And there was a bit of pictorial humor *post festum,* the nine copperplates by E. Tisdale illustrating the 1795 edition of Trumbull's "McFingal."

The period about the end of the Revolution was not notably productive of caricature. Perhaps the cause is to be found in the fact that despite the politico-military cabaling of some generals during the war and the growing difference between Federal and Republican principles afterward, the country was united in the struggle for national existence. Dissenting opinion grew, however. William Maclay commented in his "Diary" on the excessive adulation of Washington and the monarchical tendencies of his followers. Opposition to the "Father of his Country" took pictorial form as well. Lossing, in "Our Country" (Vol. 2, p. 1123), records that on the day after Washington's arrival in New York, as president-elect, a caricature appeared, "full of disloyal and profane allusions." In it the president was shown mounted on an ass, in the arms of his body servant Billy. Colonel David Humphreys, leading the animal, is "chanting hosannahs and birthday odes," while the devil remarks that "the glorious time has come to pass when David shall conduct an ass." Yet in the catalogue of the E. B. Holden sale, No. 1088 is described as the "only known caricature of Washington." This represents "Mrs. General Washington, bestowing thirteen stripes on Britannia" with the lash.

Most of the caricatures of the day were anti-Federalist, but the idol of the Republican Party came in for at least one vigorous pictorial knock. In a pamphlet by Robert G. Harper, probably issued in 1797, entitled "Observations on the Dispute between the U. S. and France," the frontispiece presents a caricature of Jefferson in allusion to his alleged atheistic tendencies and his attachment to the cause of the French Revolution. The doctrines of Thomas Paine were dealt with in a large and poor plate entitled *Church and State,* signed *B. Picart,* and issued, we are told, by H. D. Robinson, New York, "about 1800."

A very crude print depicted an exchange of amenities in Congress (1798), of a kind that has occurred much more recently in Washington, Matthew Lyon and Roger Griswold being the members implicated. Under this caricature were these lines:

> "He in a trice struck Lyon thrice
> Upon the head, enrag'd, sir,
> Who seiz'd the tongs to ease his wrongs
> And Griswold thus engag'd, sir."

The plate is reproduced in the "Historical Magazine" for January, 1864, where reference is made also to a caricature of an earlier fracas between these two gentlemen, in which Lyon is represented as the king of beasts on his hind legs. That was a record of a personal intermezzo. Of more significance was the comment on the proceeding which to this day is termed "gerrymandering." In 1811 the Massachusetts legislature rearranged the senatorial districts of the state so as to secure power to the Democrats, Governor Gerry signing the measure. In Essex County the arrangement as to towns was "particularly absurd." Gilbert Stuart, seeing a map on which the towns thus selected were indicated by particular colors, noted the similarity to some monstrous animal. Indicating the same with a few touches, he said to Russell, of the "Boston Sentinel," "that will do for a salamander." "Salamander," was the reply; "call it Gerrymander." With the War of 1812 home product in comic art became a little more prominent. Quincy's opposition to the "War act" of the Administration (1812) roused bitter attacks in squibs, epigrams and caricatures. One of the last, by William Charles, entitled *Josiah the First,* pictured Quincy as a king (in reference to his political domination), with crown and scepter, with an inscription in which he proclaimed himself *King of New England, Nova Scotia and Passamaquoddy* and *Grand Master of the Noble Order of the Two Codfishes.* The Embargo Act of April 14, 1812, was strongly denounced by anti-administration speakers and newspapers, and the land trade with Canada, which had become suddenly arrested by it, was represented by a bewildered serpent, stopped by two trees labeled respectively Embargo and Non-

Intervention. The Gallic cock stands by, joyously crowing. The passage of the Embargo Act in December, 1813, designed to prevent the furnishing of supplies to the enemy and the importation of British manufactures in professedly neutral vessels, evoked a caricature designed and engraved by Alexander Anderson. A former embargo, during Jefferson's administration, was called by the opposition Federalists "a terrapin policy." In recollection of that, Anderson has the act of 1813 personified by a monstrous terrapin who has seized a violator of the law by the seat of his breeches, he crying out, *Oh! this cursed o-grab-me* [embargo spelled backward]! The fling was aimed at the New England people, supposed to be saving their coasts from devastation, and filling their pockets at the same time, by supplying the British cruisers with provisions. On the repeal of the measure, the "Death of the Embargo" was celebrated in verses in the "Federal Republican," subsequently republished in the "Evening Post" (New York) with a design by John Wesley Jarvis, also engraved by Anderson, whose burin thus served both sides. The cut illustrates a poem entitled the *Terrapin's Address*, and beginning:

"Reflect, my friend, as you pass by,
As *you* are *now*, so once was I."

These war prints were reproduced in Lossing's "Field Book of the War of 1812."

The Hartford Convention naturally called forth Democratic attacks. The administration party issued a handbill (reproduced in "Harper's Popular Cyclopedia of

U. S. History") in which the Federal Party is represented by the devil and the Democratic by a comely young
woman with a palm leaf. The most noteworthy caricatures of the war were the prints by William Charles, who
practised his art successively in New York and Philadelphia, where he had a book and print shop. His caricatures are typical of the Rowlandson-Gillray period; one
of them, *John Bull making a new Batch of Ships to send
to the Lakes,* inspired by Gillray. While not remarkable,
they have a rough humor which no doubt made them
popular. A noteworthy one was *A Wasp on a Frolic, or
a Sting for John Bull,* giving expression to the exultation
at the victory of the "Wasp" over the "Frolic," with
the obvious conceit of a huge wasp stinging John Bull.
Another one (September, 1813) celebrated Perry's victory in a pun on the word "perry," the name for the
fresh juice of the pear, apt to produce uncomfortable
digestive phenomena. King George, seated, his hand on
his stomach, writhing in pain, rejects offers of more
"Perry" from Queen Charlotte, who holds an open bottle,
from which is spouting foam bearing the names of the
American vessels in the battle. The humor of the print
is emphasized in a ballad of the day:

> "On Erie's wave, while Barclay brave
> With *Charlotte* making merry,
> He chanced to take the belly-ache
> We drenched him so with Perry."

"Charlotte" was one of the British vessels, and a pun on
the queen's name is intended. Charles issued also prints

relating to embargo (*The Cat let out of the Bag*, a later impression of which has the title *The Tory Editor and his Apes giving their pitiful Advice to the American Sailors*), the *Hartford Convention, or Leap, no Leap*, and the ones entitled *John Bull and the Baltimoreans, Johnny Bull and the Alexandrians* (he demands their flour, tobacco, provisions, ships, "everything except your porter and perry. . . . I've had enough of them already") and *Bruin become Mediator or Negotiations for Peace.* Another naval victory, that of the "Hornet" over the "Peacock," February, 1813, brought Amos Doolittle into caricature. His engraving (reproduced in Lossing's "War of 1812," showed an immense hornet, alighting, with the cry *Free trades and sailor's rights, you old rascal,* on the head of a bull with the wings and tail of a peacock.

The years immediately succeeding the war do not appear to have borne much fruit in comic art. Occasionally you will come across a print such as the etching *Democracy against the Unnatural Union. Trial Oct. 14, 1817. Designed and executed by one who has neither place nor pension,* or the colored aquatint showing John Binns carrying a pile of coffins, from which emerge Henry Clay and J. Q. Adams. It is entitled *The Pedlar and his Pack, or the Desperate Effort, an Over Balance.*

As Charles had been a rough reflex of Gillray, so David Claypoole Johnston (1797–1865) was a weak dilution of Cruikshank. Johnston evidently had no easy time to make ends meet; he did many things and used various methods: portraits in lithography and stipple, book illustrations and caricatures in etching. The last

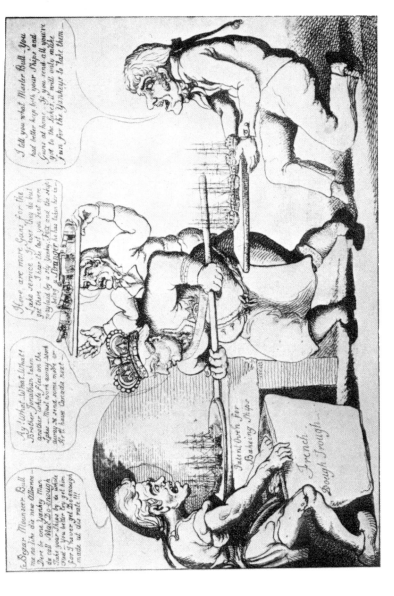

A Caricature of the War of 1812
By William Charles

he issued in oblong quarto booklets, under the title *Scraps*, during the thirties and forties, in the manner of Cruikshank's *Sketch Book*. On the last sheet of one of the parts he depicted himself figuring the price charged for each sheet—two cents "and no charge for letter press matter." A fair example of his work may be found in "Outlines illustrative of the Journal of F—— A—— K—— Drawn & etched by Mr——" (Boston, 1835), rather heavy and a bit coarse. A political squib by him was issued as late as 1863, a sheet on Jefferson Davis, *The house that Jeff built*. Scharf and Westcott, in their "History of Philadelphia," tell us that his hits at dandies and local militia officers were resented and libel suits threatened, so that he temporarily abandoned art for the stage. Another Philadelphia caricaturist was Edward W. Clay (1792–1857). His *The Nation's Bulwark. A well-disciplined Militia* (*Sketches of Character, No. 1*, 1829) is good-natured raillery; the nation's defenders shown include portraits of actual individuals, among them C. G. Childs. Like Johnston he did many things, drew views of Philadelphia for Childs, engraved in stipple, drew on stone, designed for line-engravers. James Akin drew and published *A down[w]right Gabbler*, directed at the eccentric and outspoken reformer Fanny Wright, who was lecturing in 1833–36.

The period between the War of 1812 and the Civil War had its good share of events to stir the public mind and exercise slowly growing facility in caricature. Caricature is the common and convenient name for pictorial satire, but the humor in the cartoons issued in separate sheets, down through the Civil War, lies not in any distortion in the drawing but in the underlying idea. The remarks of the various persons in the pictures are inclosed in loops issuing from their mouths, a manner always marking a distinctly lower grade of the art, as in so many of the dreary continuous series drawn out through successive issues of our present-day newspapers. The designer generally employed a number of figures to emphasize his point. He often offered a résumé, so to speak, of the collective activity of a group of politicians and statesmen during a given period. To-day, pictorial comments, frequently issued, deal each with some detail of the political situation, some individual affair or personality, and therefore often show a minimum of effort to emphasize a general principle. In those ante-bellum days, lithography appeared as a vehicle for caricature at an early date. *A new Map of the United States, with the additional Territories on an improved Plan. Exhibiting a View of the Rocky Mountains surveyed by a Company of Winnebago Indians in 1828,* from Imbert's establishment, is perhaps one of the earliest examples of the entrance into caricature of the lithographic art. The latter was employed a little later by H. R. Robinson, and then by Currier & Ives, whose long series of sheets remain a store-house of interest to the student of the American phase of what the French call *imagerie populaire.*

With the first administration of Jackson, caricature in this country became a more frequently employed factor in political contests. Jackson's robust personality formed good material for caricatures, both those assailing and those defending him in the fight against the United States Bank, the affair of the "Kitchen Cabinet," and so forth. A favorite device of the caricaturist, the race between rival candidates for nomination or election, appears in *A Foot-Race*, an etching showing Jackson and others. *Jackson clearing his Kitchen* and *Rats leaving a fallen House*, etchings published in 1831 and referring to the dissolution of the Kitchen Cabinet, were designed by Edward W. Clay, who drew also *A Boston Notion for the World's Fair* (1844), aimed at the Abolition movement. Parton's reference to burlesque processions during the presidential campaign of 1832 is *à propos*. The hickory pole, Nicholas Biddle as "Old Nick," and other features which figured therein, are akin to the catchwords employed by the cartoonists of that time. The war on the U. S. Bank (1837) called forth the shinplaster caricature, *Great Locofoco Juggernaut*, in which Van Buren appears, and the two lithographs, *The Modern Balaam and his Ass* and *New Edition of Macbeth, Bankoh's Ghost*, the last signed *C* and *printed and published by H. R. Robinson*. *Sub-treasurers taking long Steps*, also published by Robinson (1838), is signed *Grennell*. Still another publication by Robinson is a little volume by "Junius Junior," entitled "The Vision of Judgment" (1838), with Jackson caricatures signed *N. Sarony*. The candidate's race idea appears again in *The Great American Steeplechase for 1844* (issued 1843 by H. R. Robinson).

Then the Mexican War became the topic of interest,

but apparently not with the quantitative result in the field of caricature that one might perhaps have expected to find. The few pieces which I have discovered are marked by amused disdain for the opponent. *Uncle Sam's Taylorifics* (the Yankee snipping a Mexican in two with a huge pair of shears) and *The Mexican Commander enjoying the Prospect opposite Matamoras* (1846), a lithograph by Sarony & Major, copyrighted by T. W. Strong, and drawn with unusual freedom, illustrate this spirit of complacent superiority.

Of these caricatures drawn on stone and issued in separate sheets, those published by Nathaniel Currier, who entered the field about 1848, are best known and most numerous. It is an interesting series, this lot of cartoons of ante-bellum and war-time days, recalling much detail of our political history. They appeared irregularly, at the time of stirring public events, mostly as concomitants of presidential campaigns. In 1848, Marcy, Cass, Douglas, Buchanan and Houston, towed "up Salt River" by fox-bodied Van Buren, are labeled *Loco Foco Candidates traveling*. Fillmore protects the "government crib" in *Fancied Security, or the Rats on a Bender*. Webster, Scott and Pierce take part in the *Great Foot Race for the Presidential Purse ($100,000 and Pickings) over the Union Course, 1852*. When the slavery and state's rights controversies came to a head in the movement which resulted in the formation of the Republican Party, public feeling ran high and the campaign of 1856 brought out much anti-Fremont material. In *The Great Republican Reform Party calling on their*

Candidate, Fremont is promising the prohibitionist, woman's rights lady, socialist, free love advocate, the Roman Catholic Church and the negro all they want. In *The Great Presidential Sweepstakes of 1856* Beecher and Greeley help along a sorry outfit containing Fremont, which appears again in *The Mustang Team*, particularly free in drawing. One feels, despite expressed contempt for the new party, the feeling of uncertainty engendered by the approach of that irrepressible conflict, to which so many tried to close their eyes. Some phases of the slavery controversy had been touched upon by the satirist's pencil. For instance in *E. C.'s* depiction of Buchanan and the slave question, or *Practical illustration of the fugitive slave law* (the slaveholder astride of Webster on all-fours) or *What's Sauce for the Goose is sauce for the Gander*, a lithograph by *E. W. C.,*—E. W. Clay, —dealing with Northern protection of fugitive slaves. In most cases the pictures showed pro-slavery leanings. Abolitionism was repeatedly attacked, with especial emphasis on the dire effects of miscegenation. So in *Prof. Pompey magnetizing an Abolition Lady* (a lithograph issued by T. W. Strong), and *An Amalgamation Polka*, a lithograph by E. W. Clay. Buchanan's attitude gave rise to such cartoons as L. Maurer's *Ostend Doctrine: Practical Democrats carrying out the Principle* with the president inactive, or *South Carolina's Ultimatum*, in which Gov. Pickens is shown as wanting Sumter, while Buchanan entreats: *Don't fire till I get out of office.* In another, Buchanan is riding the dragon of slavery, and exclaims, *Pull down that fence, and make way for the*

"Peculiar Institution," the fence being Mason and Dixon's line; Fremont strongly objects.

Lithography did not monopolize this specialty altogether. The woodcut served for a number of these comic sheets, T. W. Strong sometimes appearing as publisher, the designer usually anonymous, in one case signed: *J. H. Goater.* In one of Strong's cuts, *Little Bo Peep and her foolish Sheep,* the shepherdess, Columbia, seeing her sheep (the seceding states) departing, exclaims, *Sick 'em, Buck—I wish old Hickory were alive, he'd bring 'em back in no time.*

In the presidential campaign of 1860, political feeling was at a high tension. One cannot recall any cartoon issued in New York which really gave expression to the Union sentiments which the election of Lincoln and subsequent events were to fan into a roaring flame. A few designs of well-tempered Republicanism; as for the rest, evasive presentations of not fully relevant facts or of distorted views. In *The Rail Candidate,* the railsplitter, carried by Greeley and a negro astride a rail marked *Republican Platform,* complains: "I began to feel as if *this* rail would split me, it's the hardest stick I ever straddled." Other sheets in this series of lithographs are *The Nigger in the Woodpile, An Heir to the Throne* (Greeley and Lincoln complacently regarding the "heir," Barnum's "What-is-it?") and *The Impending Crisis,* both by Maurer, and *The irrepressible Conflict,* the last two dealing with Seward's failure to obtain the Republican nomination, and Greeley's agency in the matter. Joseph B. Bishop, who had his information from James M. Ives, stated that all of these caricatures of 1856 and 1860 were drawn by Louis Maurer. The latter, however, told me that they were not all by him, and identified a number of them as his work. These include, beside those which I have named as his, *The Great American Buck Hunt of 1856*, *The Political Gymnasium*, *Letting the Cat out of the Bag*, *Honest Abe taking them on the Half Shell*, *Storming the Castle* and *The Great Republican Party*. The Currier & Ives lithographs have been reproduced in a volume with the title: "Caricatures pertaining to the Civil War . . . 1856–72" (New York, 1892).

With the election of Lincoln the storm broke loose, and some of the caricatures produced in the white heat of excitement were among the most telling of the war. They were often not lithographed sheets, but sporadic woodcut issues. The conceit which showed the seceding states as mice scampering away from "Uncle Abe" in the guise of a cat, whose paw holds down a rodent labeled *Virginia*, and which is appropriately entitled *Virginia pausing*, opens up the long series of war-time pictures. In many cases they appeared on envelopes, a method of publication very much used for the dissemination of both Northern and Southern views; the designs and mottoes thus issued were numbered by hundreds. There was much patriotic fervor, occasional bitterness and more often good humor. *I'm glad I'm not in Dixie! Hooray! Hooray!; Come back here, you black Rascal!—Can't come back nohow, Massa, dis Chile's contraban'; Music by the Contra-Band* and *Good Noose for Traitors* (a picture of a hangman's rope left no doubt as to the pun intended), are sufficiently clear in title and are average examples of the kind of humor thus disseminated through the mails. I have seen seven different reproductions in reduced size, on envelopes, of a remarkably popular early war-time caricature by Frank Beard, *Why don't you take it?*, representing Davis as a greyhound slinking off before the ferocious air of a bulldog (Gen. Scott) guarding a rib of *prize beef* (Washington). D. M. Stauffer did several of these envelope designs in 1862. Others beside Beard made an early appearance in those days. Thomas Worth, for instance, in *The Voluntary Manner in which some of the Southern Volunteers enlist*, or Benjamin Day, who depicts Lincoln and Davis as prizefighters, in a lithograph entitled *Caving in, or a Rebel deeply humiliated.* A casual incursion into a vein of mild humor, on the part of E. B. & E. C. Kellogg, the Hartford lithographic firm, is entitled *Forward March—Uncle Sam's old Hens covering their Chickens on the way to Richmond,* the hens being the gunboats steaming up the river and spreading their wings over the chickens,—the soldiers marching on the banks. Another publisher's name out of the common is that of Hough, of Philadelphia, on a lithograph which proclaims *The Southern Confederacy a Fact,* because it has been acknowledged by the devil.

During the war Thomas Nast began in a series of emblematic drawings that life-work which made him famous. *Compromise with the South,* referring to the attitude of the Chicago Convention, made a notable hit in "Harper's Weekly," and was subsequently used as a campaign document. A. B. Paine quotes Lincoln:

"Thomas Nast has been our best recruiting sergeant."
Lincoln naturally held the center of the stage in many
of the pictorial lampoons of the war. The lukewarm or
straight anti-Lincoln productions apparently greatly out-
numbered those supporting him. Among the first may
be named such lithographs as *The political Rail Splitter*
driving the wedge "Irrepressible Conflict" into the log
"Union," splitting it into North and South, or the onc
by Joseph E. Baker of Boston, *Columbia demands her
Children,* she asking back her 500,000 sons, to which
Lincoln remarks, "That reminds me of a story." This
phrase was used against Lincoln in various ways, and his
love of humor was assailed most bitterly in a poorly
drawn sheet entitled *The Commander-in-Chief conciliat-
ing the Soldiers' Votes on the Battlefield,* representing
him amid dead and wounded soldiers, saying, to the
horror of the listeners: "Now, Marshal, sing us 'Picayune
Butler' or something else that's funny." On the other
hand, *Grand Sweepstakes for 1862 won by the celebrated
Horse Emancipation,* a lithograph signed *Potomac,*
signalizes approvingly an important act of Lincoln's
administration. Occasionally there was a cartoon strong
for Lincoln; such as *A little Game of Bagatelle, between
Old Abe the Railsplitter and Little Mac the Gunboat
General,* a lithograph published by J. L. Magee of Philadelphia, and signed *J. L. M. Your Plan and Mine* (Currier and Ives) put the case even more strongly in Lincoln's favor; he completely subdues the South and keeps
the negro free, while his opponent weakly attempts con-
ciliation and is ready to restore the black man to slavery.

Political caricature No. 2, 1864, pictures *Miscegenation as the Millennium of Abolitionism,* and No. 3 of the same series prophesies *The Abolition Catastrophe, or The November Smash-up.* But fate willed otherwise; Lincoln was re-elected, and the war was carried on to success for the North. Jefferson Davis's attempt to escape was chronicled in more or less humorous manner in more than one print, even in a pamphlet entitled "Jeff Petticoats," with "graphotype" illustrations "drawn by the celebrated artist Frank Bellew on the chemical blocks of the Intaglio and Graphotype Co. and engraved by them in the short time of two hours." These pictures usually did not go very much beyond the facts in the case, and there is really more point to the grim conception of *Jeff Davis on his own Platform or the last Act of Secession,* in which that prominent representative of the "lost cause" stands, with the hangman's noose about his neck.

Gen. McClellan came in for some share of pictorial applause and criticism, mirroring the hopes which he aroused and the general opinion of his generalship. He appears in masterly inactivity at his *Headquarters at Harrisburg Landing,* in a lithograph by *Potomac,* whose *The last Round* was pro-McClellan in spirit. *The old Bull Dog on the right Track* (Grant) is contrasted with the protesting "little Mac," to the latter's disadvantage. In *The true Issue, or that's what's the matter,* Lincoln and Davis are hauling at opposite sides of a map of the United States, the former proclaiming "No Peace without abolition" and the latter "No peace without separation," while McClellan stays their hands, with the sentiment "The Union must be preserved at all hazards." The presidential campaign of 1864 occasioned a number of cartoons friendly to this general in politics. One, by J. E. Baker, shows a wounded soldier forced by a negro guard to vote for Lincoln instead of the Democratic candidate, while the poll-clerks pretend not to see. The difficulties of his position were pictured three times at least in that familiar conception of a circus-rider with each foot on a horse, the equines striving in different directions. In the one, a reproduction of a pen-and-ink drawing somewhat in the style of Augustus Hoppin, the horses are labeled respectively *Letter of acceptance* and *Chicago Platform;* in the second, *Slow and Steady wins the Race,* Lincoln rides "Slow and Steady," while McClellan's two steeds are "Brag and Bluster" and "Fawn and Cringe"; in the third, *Little Mac in his great Two-Horse Act* is striving to control his mounts "Peace" and "War," with Lincoln as a clown standing by. This last sheet was one of T. W. Strong's woodcuts, the drawing by J. H. Howard, who designed also the engraving of McClellan as Hamlet holding the head of Lincoln: *I knew him, Horatio; a fellow of infinite jest. . . . Where be your gibes now?* And *The Grave of the Union, or Major Jack Downing's Dream, drawn by Zeke* (lithograph, Bromley & Co., 1864), represents Lincoln, Greeley *et al.* burying the Constitution and free speech.

There was some Confederate comic art. The Battle of Bull Run brought forth a derisive whoop in the shape of a very poor lithograph *from a pfothogr.,* and B. Duncan of Columbia, S. C., issued a series of better designed plates with the suggestive title *Dissolving Views of Richmond,* one signed with a monogram *J. W.* But the best designed Southern production was a series of etched *War Sketches* by V. Blada (pseudonym of Adalbert Volck), partly issued abroad (London, 1864). Drawn mainly in outline, these plates, free from caricature—except the slight exaggeration in such a case as *Valiant men "dat fite mit Sigel"*—are satirical and vigorous arraignments of Northern principles and practice. *Free Negroes in the North and in Hayti* are contrasted, and the *Substitute Office* is derided.

When we draw a line under the long Civil War column, and add up the total the sum is not very impressive qualitatively. The possibilities of the period were perhaps not fully grasped by our caricaturists. In fact, we had no commanding figure among them, and we must go to Tenniel's cartoons in London "Punch" to get comments more in accord with the importance of this four years' struggle. This is said without reference to the point of view expressed in Tenniel's drawings. As far as his treatment of Lincoln was concerned, he joined with Tom Taylor in an *amende honorable* when the president was struck down by the assassin's hand. Years have begun to envelop the events of those days in the haze of intervening time. We are able to regard even the bitterest examples of pictorial satire, both Northern and Southern, with more calmness of spirit, as documents mirroring the high-tension excitement of an exciting period.

The preponderance of the lithographed separate sheets in the field of caricature came to an end soon after the

Civil War. They continued to be issued, notably in the distorted, though in a rough way funny, "Darktown" negro comics of Thomas Worth, but as an effective weapon in the political arena they gave way before the work of the comic press and the cartoons in the weekly illustrated journals.

CHAPTER XIII

THE COMIC PAPER AND THE DAILY PRESS

THE comic paper entered more decidedly into the field of caricature not long after the Civil War. There had been previous attempts to found periodicals devoted to humor. "Yankee Doodle" appeared in 1856, with Charles Martin as the principal artist. "Yankee Notions, or, Whittlings of Jonathan's Jack-knife," issued monthly by T. W. Strong of New York, made its appearance in January, 1852, claimed a circulation of 150,000 by September, 1854, and lived about fifteen years. Augustus Hoppin had a full-page drawing in each number, and the contributing artists included John McLenan, Frank Bellew ("the triangle"), Thomas Butler Gunn, Magee, J. H. Howard, Dallas, Thomas Worth, M. A. Woolf, and "Carl," pseudonym of G. W. Carleton the publisher, who later put a little bird under his sketches.

McLenan was one of the most noteworthy of this group. His bohemian nature seemed reflected in carelessly sketchy drawing, and in rollicking humor in his "comics." A. V. S. Anthony told me that D. C. Hitchcock discovered McLenan working in a pork-packing establishment in Cincinnati, where he made sketches on the tops of barrels. Among books illustrated by him was "Nothing to Say" by Mortimer M. Thompson ("Doesticks"), issued at the time of the "Nothing to Wear" controversy. As an illustrator he turned his hand to various things, even Collins's "Woman in White," but it is as a comic artist that he made his mark.

There came and went other periodical vehicles for humor: "The Lantern," edited, like "The Bubble," by John Brougham; "John Donkey" (Philadelphia); "Young America"; "The Picayune" (outlet for the humor of Mortimer Thompson); "The Carpet Bag" in Boston, with B. P. Shillaber; "Mrs. Grundy" (three months in 1865, Nast and Stephens the artists, with a cover into which Nast crowded a hundred or so portraits of notables recognizable despite their minute size); "Phunny Phellow" (Nast again); "Jolly Joker"; "The Punster" (Mobile, early seventies), and others. C. G. Rosenberg even tried to establish a humorous daily, "Momus," in the fifties.

The best, from the literary standpoint, was "Vanity Fair" (New York), with Fitz-James O'Brien, "Artemus Ward," George Arnold and C. G. Leland among its writers, and Henry L. Stephens, E. F. Mullen (illustrator of "Artemus Ward: His Book"), J. H. Goater, W. Fiske, H. Helmick, Ben Day as its principal artists. Stephens did the cartoons. His drawings, despite mannerisms, had easy flow of line, but lacked the vigor of characterization necessary to a successful cartoonist. "Vanity Fair" held on from 1859 until 1863. Possibly the public had no stomach in those days for graceful fooling and literary humor. It was a time for vigorous blows in the field, on the rostrum, in the editorial column, from the caricaturist's pencil. There were references to incompetent officers advanced by political pull, or to dishonest contractors, as in the small cut by Elihu Vedder depicting some soldiers who find their blankets more suited to use as fishing nets than for their legitimate purpose. Or the pictorial comparison, *Heroes of the war* (penniless, maimed veterans) and *He rose by the war* (a fattened contractor). But there is not much that strikes you as a blow from the shoulder, a bull's-eye scored. When the cartoons do not show distinctly anti-administration feeling, they give a lukewarm impression. It is not so much the telling force of satire as the mildly humorous comment of an amused spectator. About the same characterization will describe the cartoons in "Punchinello" subsidized by Tweed (1870–71), also by Stephens. We meet other familiar names under the cuts in this journal: A. Hoppin, J. H. Howard, F. Bellew, W. Fiske, W. L. Sheppard; and some new ones: F. T. Merrill, George B. Bowlend, F. S. Cozzens. The South had its "Southern Punch," a file of which is in the Confederate Museum, Richmond.

With the advent of Thomas Nast the sledge-hammer force of pictorial satire was felt in all its potency. In 1862, amid the clamor for "peace at any price," Nast drew for "Harper's" a double-page emblematic picture entitled *Peace*. It showed Columbia weeping at a Union soldier's grave, while the dead one's companion, stripped of arms, is shaking hands with a Southern soldier armed to the teeth, with one foot on the grave. "That picture made his reputation," said "Petroleum V. Nasby," and added: "It was circulated by the million as a campaign document." Nast continued in this emblematic vein, often surrounding his central composition with a number of smaller ones. With the campaign of 1868 he entered definitely into political caricature. His strong defence of the Union cause, his arraignment of the Canal Ring in New York State and of the Tweed Ring in New York City were accomplished with fearless earnestness in cartoons that form imperishable pages in the annals of caricature. In the anti-Greeley compositions in the presidential campaign of 1872, Nast showed bitter, unrelenting ingenuity in probing and laying bare every little weakness. He had a remarkable power of emphasizing the salient characteristics of a face. In time his strength waned, and his manner dropped into a multitudinous display of labels all over the drawing. Nast of his best period is remembered with warm appreciation of his great service. Albert Bigelow Paine traces to him the introduction of various symbolical devices dear to the caricaturist,—the square paper cap of labor, the full dinner pail, the Tammany tiger, and the "inflation" rag baby of 1875.

Nast's best work was done for "Harper's Weekly." "Leslie's" early in the seventies brought over Matt Morgan as a rival to Nast. Morgan had been connected with "Fun," a number of his contributions to that journal being republished in a volume of "American War Cartoons," 1879, and the "Tomahawk," in London. He did not make his mark in this country as a political caricaturist. Keppler also cartooned for "Leslie's" before he started his New York "Puck." The "Daily Graphic" had Th. Wust, Charles S. Reinhart, Grant Hamilton, C. D.

Weldon, A. B. Frost, E. W. Kemble and Fernando Miranda as cartoonists. And Mirall drew very mild specimens of what the French call *portraits-charges* for "The Hour" in the eighties,—portraits of noted individuals, with a slight admixture of witty or satirical allusion. It was a sort of thing done in "Vanity Fair," of London, by Bellew in the "Fifth Avenue Journal," of New York, and notably in *Puckographs,* appearing in "Puck," drawn usually by Keppler and occasionally by J. A. Wales and F. Graetz.

Social caricature, as distinct from political, continued mainly in cuts on the last pages of weekly and monthly publications. There were the little "comics" in the "bric-à-brac" section of "Scribner's," in the late seventies, drawn by Livingston Hopkins (who subsequently cartooned for the Sydney, Australia, "Bulletin"), F. B. Opper, F. S. Church, E. A. Abbey, Mullen, Addie Ledyard, M. A. Woolf, Bellew and Howard Pyle. Elsewhere, too, appeared those little tail-end "comics," long a feature in our magazines. The "Book of cheerful Cats," by J. G. Francis (1892), was made up of contributions to "St. Nicholas" and other publications.

While Nast was cartooning "Harper's Weekly" into a political force, attempts to establish journals devoted to the comic art went on. Frederic Hudson, in his "Journalism in the United States" (1873), stated that the American public did not want its humor in weekly doses, but preferred it in the morning paper, with its breakfast coffee. Recounting different efforts to found a comic paper, he concluded: "and *Puck,* of St. Louis, how is he?"

Cartoon, "Puck," April 28, 1886, by   Courtesy of "Puck"
Joseph Keppler

"THAT'S WHAT'S THE MATTER"

Boss Tweed. "As long as I count the Votes, what are you going to do about it? say?"

One of the Anti-Tweed Cartoons in
"Harper's Weekly," by
Thomas Nast

This "Puck" was founded by Joseph Keppler, who, coming from Vienna, had started "Die Vehme" (1870) and after its demise "Puck" (1871). On the failure of "Puck" he came in 1873 to New York City, where in 1876 he established "Puck," a German weekly, which half a year later began to appear also in an English edition. Previous ventures had usually been modeled on "Punch." There was a full-page cartoon on the two middle pages, and usually a half-page drawing on the front page, reproduced by wood-engraving. "Puck" offered three cartoons in each number, produced by lithography. At first the cartoons were in black-and-white; then two tints—added from wood-blocks—were used. Finally came completer chromatic glory lithographically produced. It was uphill work at first; Keppler drew all three cartoons as well as some of the smaller illustrations and occasional advertisements. But success came, and "Puck" drew to itself the best talent in the land, as well as Karl Edler von Stur and F. Graetz from Vienna. Frederick Burr Opper developed remarkably while with "Puck." In "this funny world as Puck sees it" (1890) his humor drew its happiest inspiration from the life of the middle and laboring classes, the element of caricature entering with just enough force to accentuate the point of the joke. In his subsequent newspaper work drawing became subordinated to an almost elementary simplicity. T. Bernard Gillam, an Englishman by birth, who had cartooned for the "Graphic" and "Harper's Weekly," had a severity of manner reminiscent of Tenniel. Eugene Zimmerman showed a tendency to grotesquery apparently suppressed somewhat. James A. Wales, one of the few caricaturists of American birth in those days, could hit off a portrait with a sure touch. Dalrymple never did better work than under the guidance of Keppler,—"he is a born caricaturist," said the latter. And there were Ehrhart, a pen-artist of precise finish, and Syd B. Griffin, whose humor had an almost boyishly rollicking air. Charles J. Taylor, essentially an illustrator, good in his satires on society life, illustrated Philip G. Welch's "Tailor-made girl" dialogues, "In the Four Hundred and out," and works by H. C. Bunner and others. In its later years this journal enlisted also the services of Joseph Keppler the younger, L. M. Glackens, Albert Levering, Arthur Young (illustrator of "Hell up to Date," whose cartoons evidence serious convictions on social conditions), Gordon H. Grant, Will Crawford, Frank Nankivell, representing as many different styles and specialties.

During the early years of "Puck" there was a noticeably foreign tone in Keppler's cartoons, a somewhat Gallic freedom of expression. In the rather audacious conception, *Forbidding the Banns,* Garfield (in female garb) is about to be wedded to Uncle Sam, the officiating clergyman having a ballot-box for a head, Schurz and Reid standing by as bridesmaids. W. H. Barnum, bearing a baby labeled "Credit Mobilier," rushes in, vigorously protesting against continuation of the ceremony. "But it was such a little one," coyly remarks the blushing bride.

Keppler developed a partiality for large compositions with many figures; he was a sort of Makart in comic art.

His son scored telling hits with a minimum of figures, as in his résumé of the presidential campaign of 1908 with Roosevelt as John Alden and the Republican Party as Priscilla, Taft as Standish hovering in the rear. The mature coyness of the maid, the smile of self-satisfaction on the face of the vicarious suitor, are unmistakable. The title is, of course: *Why don't you speak for yourself?*

In 1887 "Judge" was founded. To it there came from "Puck" Wales, Gillam and Zimmerman; the last here developed to the full his predilection for exaggeration. Grant E. Hamilton grew into a manner of noteworthy ease, shown also in pen-drawings of lightly flowing stroke done for the "New York Herald." Frank Beard, J. H. Smith (cowboy scenes), F. Victor Gillam (who used the signature *F. Victor*), Penrhyn Stanlaws (i.e., P. S. Adamson), Flohri, James Montgomery Flagg are among the other artists whose work appeared in this weekly. *"Puck and Judge,"* say A. B. Maurice and F. T. Cooper, in their volume on caricature, "led to a distinct advance in political caricature in this country."

A third comic weekly, which maintained a foothold for a number of years, was the "Wasp," of San Francisco, where previously there had been "Puck," founded 1865, that "short-lived flower of Pacific Coast caricature." Other attempts to establish similar publications usually did not hold out long beyond the political campaign which called them into being. The Garfield-Hancock struggle of 1880 evolved "Chic," chief cartoonist C. Kendrick, better known as an illustrator of juveniles with colored pictures. Four years later Blaine was supported by

"Jingo," and by "Munsey's Weekly," for which A. R. Waud did cartoons. During that campaign of 1884 the strongest forces in caricature were arrayed on the other side. "Puck" offered a remarkable instance of sustained effort in its series of "plumed knight" and "tattooed man" conceits, mainly by Keppler and Gillam. The "tattooed" idea had been used in the German edition of "Puck" in 1876, Columbia appearing anything but a "gem," her body covered with the record of rings and frauds and political misdeeds. That idea, utilized in a political dime museum drawn by Gillam, in which Blaine appeared among the "freaks" as a tattooed man, was exploited with ingeniously varied insistence. Some of the cartoons were on a particularly high plane; so Gillam's *Phryne before the Chicago Tribunal* (Phryne being the tattooed man unveiled by Whitelaw Reid), a distinct appeal to the educated. The attacks on Cleveland were equally bitter, and in the two succeeding campaigns his figure, in grossly caricatured obesity, was incessantly held up to ridicule. In succeeding campaigns, Bryan came in for his share of attacks. Among many cartoons directed against him, one, usually free in conception, by Hamilton, represented him as the "Angel of Darkness" showing the American voter possibilities of power and wealth, as seen from a high mountain. *The Temptation* is its obvious title.

Shortly before the Spanish war, a cartoon by Victor Gillam, in which a diminutive Spaniard, looking into the mouth of an enormous American cannon, is admonished by Uncle Sam: *Be careful, it's loaded,* explained the state

of affairs with expressive simplicity. The Spanish caricatures issued during the war, usually variations on the
theme of the "American hog," may seem stupid enough,
but in Hamilton's *The Spanish Brute adds Mutilation to
Murder* there was an appeal to national prejudice not
pleasant to look upon. This war is already ancient history, which may be objectively studied in "Cartoons of
the War of 1898 with Spain, from leading foreign and
American papers" (1899). The World War brought
forth an enormous number of cartoons, of which a
hundred, by twenty-seven artists, were collected in a
volume "The War in Cartoons," compiled by George J.
Hecht.

There was established in 1883 a weekly devoted more
particularly to social caricature, and going back to black
and white. That was "Life." An interesting group of
artists have been in the service of this lively publication.
John Ames Mitchell, editor of the journal, spoke of the
"intellectual quality" of the delightful and droll conceits
of F. G. Attwood, of C. D. Gibson's "ability to draw a
lady," a not too common faculty, of the "lively fancy,
keen wit" of Oliver Herford. Further variations of outlook on the humorous side of our fellow-man were offered
in "Life" by W. A. Rogers, W. H. Hyde, Dan Beard,
Albert Sterner, S. W. Van Schaick, C. Gray Parker,
Palmer Cox, C. Kendrick, H. W. McVickar (illustrator
of "Daisy Miller"), Alfred Gillam, E. W. Kemble
("Thompson Street Poker Club" and other phases of
"Blackville" life, presented with understanding of negro
character, unexaggerated), John Ames Mitchell, author

of graceful pen-and-ink imaginings; Charles Broughton; T. S. Sullivant; Otho Cushing, who outlines heroically proportioned Junos, Venuses, Apollos, Jupiters and Dianas, both in classic garb and in modern dress; F. T. Richards, James Montgomery Flagg, whose humor has a spontaneous fling; and W. H. Walker, effective in the field of political satire.

Chip (F. P. W. Bellew, son of Frank Henry Temple Bellew) furnished many amusing little pictures to "Life"; Mitchell paid tribute to his "limitless invention." Ideas are very necessary to the caricaturist. The elder Bellew, who drew for "Punch," "Yankee Notions," "Harper's Weekly," "Texas Siftings," etc., had an inexhaustible fund of them, which never appeared to run short throughout his long career. F. M. Howarth's inventiveness was exploited in series of pictures, with large-headed, stare-eyed figures. In Bisbee and the bright and prolific James S. Goodwin (died 1890) this faculty mainly served as a basis for drawings by others, their own artistic talent being a negligible asset. "Idea mongers" some one has called these useful members of the craft.

The curious digger after facts may find yet more tombstones to note in the cemetery of comic journalism's blasted hopes. "The Free Lance," illustrated by Matt Morgan and others, was running in 1875, and "Tid Bits" (New York) and "Sam, the Scaramouch" (Cincinnati) in the eighties; "The Verdict" issued three volumes in 1898–1900;—but it would be an idle task to continue the list here. The power of the cartoon has been invoked even by religious journalism in the case of the "War

Cry," and by the "Ram's Horn" (Chicago) in its war on drink. The artist for the latter publication was Frank Beard, who came before the public in his "Chalk Talks."

Caricature of the past has its function also in preserving records of manners and customs. Figures that have disappeared from our streets,—the old apple woman, the mutton-pie man,—vagaries of fashion that had their little day, habits, such as whittling, that have lost their quality as national characteristics, these and other things were so much a matter of course that the pictorial press did not note them, but the eye and pencil of the comic artist held them incidentally to illustrate the point of some joke, or directly ridiculed them. Much of our social caricature, for a long while, was taken up with the doings of the more or less "upper ten." Not a little of the resultant work no doubt deserved Alfred Trumble's stricture that it consisted of "pretty drawings that mean nothing to fit text that means less."

But some of our best "comic artists" have given us mainly views of a life of simpler manners, homespun virtues and plain clothes. Frost's healthy and delightful humor, first shown in a tendency to grotesquery (as in "Stuff and Nonsense"), has become mellowed with years into an appreciative contemplation of the amiable weaknesses of his fellow-man. His later drawings of our rural compatriots and of our sporting brethren are friendly presentations of human traits. One of his colleagues has well said that "one of the greatest charms of Mr. Frost's work is the enjoyment the artist evidently takes in it himself."

E. W. Kemble has been best known as a delineator of negro life. W. L. Sheppard furnished many humorous drawings of the black man, with sympathetic truthfulness to nature. In that he was emulated for a while by Peter Newell, who later became well known through his "Topsys and Turveys," 1893, "The Hole Book" and similar grotesque conceptions, and by his illustrated quatrains of the "wild flower" type, with a quaintness of drawing and humor peculiarly his own. Sol Eytinge gave us kindly pictures of the black man in his happy moods. Thomas Worth, on the other hand, in gaudily colored Currier & Ives lithographs which once confronted one in shop windows, chronicled the doings of "Blackville" in distorted racial characteristics. He was identified for a while with "Texas Siftings" and illustrated the writings of "Bricktop," and Orpheus C. Kerr's "Smoked Glass" (1868).

Michael Angelo Woolf sketched what Leech called the "Children of the Mobility," ragged youngsters from the slums and the squatters' shanties of New York, sometimes in parody of adult life, and not infrequently in pathetic appeals on behalf of the unfortunate. A number of his drawings were collected as "Sketches of lowly Life in a great City" (1899).

Not a few of our illustrators were enlisted in the service of the comic art early in their career; Abbey, Reinhart, Church, Frost may be cited as conspicuous examples. Some turned to it after they had become known as illustrators: Bush, Rogers. The last two, identified with newspaper work, bring us to an interesting phase of the subject.

In our day the cartoon has become a prominent feature of the daily press, which has enlisted the services of some very clever artists. The thing began very soon after Gribayédoff did his series of humorous portraits, on the familiar plan of large heads and small bodies, in the N. Y. "World" in 1884. From that time on the "World" had among its cartoonists D. McCarthy, C. G. Bush, Charles R. Macauley, John Cassel, Rollin Kirby; the "N. Y. Herald," Grant Hamilton, Ch. Nelan and W. A. Rogers; the "Evening Telegram" (N. Y.), C. de Grimm (1884–87); the N. Y. "Recorder," Nast; the N. Y. "Press," Leon Barritt; the "Washington Star," Clifford K. Berryman, and so on, in ever-increasing number.

It is in the daily paper that political caricature in the United States to-day finds both its principal opportunity for expression and its directing influence. The spirit of journalism pervades cartooning. W. A. Rogers, long prominent in the field, has said: "After all, we cartoonists are merely reporters with a drawing-pen or brush instead of a pencil. . . . We must follow the news as closely as any editor. . . . I can't afford to miss the news of a single day." To which may be added the dictum of another member of the craft, C. L. Bartholomew: "The American cartoonist must anticipate the news." The news must be boiled down into the unequivocal directness of the cartoon. The result often appears on or opposite the editorial page, and is, in form and effect, a pictorial editorial. In its most satisfactory manifestation this product of newspaper art was characterized in the New York "Evening Post":

"The American cartoon, despite the undeniable amount of trash which its name has covered, is one of the most interesting manifestations of our art. There is less self-consciousness about it than many other outlets for artistic energy to-day can show. It has less pose, a characteristic honesty that is above question. It finds itself in that situation in which, perhaps, the best art of all fruitful periods is found, since it is art in service to an actual daily need of utterance and expression."

Not only must a cartoon be produced every day, but this daily output is of necessity effected under pressure. Yet in the case of our best cartoonists a review of this activity day after day, year, discloses an admirable average of elevated endeavor and intention. Papers in all parts of the country have adopted the cartoon feature. Each has its own artist. One cannot expect to find enough good ones to supply the demand. In the rush and flurry of the response to daily exigencies, an avalanche of ideas is pouring forth, on the whole remarkably good and varied despite much repetition. Some of these conceits are held again for a moment on the pages of magazines which make it a practice to reproduce these pictorial comments on current affairs, or in a monthly such as "Cartoons," quite devoted to this specialty. Then these cartoons, temporarily reviewed, also pass on to the limbo of the immediately forgotten. Noteworthy features in a large proportion of newspaper cartoons have been the very general good nature, the absence, on the whole, of vulgarity,—which cannot be said of all the non-political newspaper "comics"—the almost boyish delight in the fun of the thing, the good-humored clownishness. The prevailing spirit is that of kindliness, not of malignity. The great majority of newspaper cartoons bear the stamp of humor, not of satire. Even the sting of Frederick B. Opper's "Willie and his papa" series (1901) on William McKinley sugar-coated its bitterness with an air of innocuous drollery. His "Alphabet of joyous trusts" (1902), the best drawn of his newspaper series that I have seen, incites laughter rather than indignation, and seems to promote the American tendency toward *laissez-faire*. And, generally, the exaggeration of caricature, at least that of gross distortion, is wanting. In the majority of cases the artist draws as well as he knows how—often not very well—and with an unhesitating definiteness which to the mind of the average man takes the place of sureness of knowledge. The art of the newspaper cartoon has been to a large extent homespun and somewhat elementary. John T. McCutcheon says that it "might be considered as a sort of pictorial breakfast food and is popular with the cartoonist, who feels that his mission has been fulfilled if he succeeds in bringing a bit of cheerfulness to some one's heart and thereby makes the beginning of a day sunnier. Its excuse lies in the belief that people prefer to be amused than to be reformed. The cartoons of this class never rock the foundations of nations, but they probably make the world a little more cheery as it rolls along." This breathes the same spirit as the drawings of Mr. McCutcheon, whose healthy, artless humor, spontaneous and of the soil, is expressed more in pictures of social life than in political caricature. Similar inoffensive drollery and simplicity of method find varied individual expression in the products of other artists of this type, such as C. A. Briggs of the "N. Y. Tribune," whose general manner has already been stenciled by imitators.

The class of political cartoon just outlined goes back in its beginnings to Walt. H. McDougall, a pioneer in newspaper illustration, whose somewhat laborious artlessness was outstripped by his ideas. A number of cartoonists have since then tread in the path blazed by him, among them Charles L. Bartholomew ("Bart"), J. H. Donahey, John De Mar, and not a few others. In apparently joyous content with the technical means at their disposal, they exercise a simple, healthy humor in language "understanded of the people." Occasionally one will fairly surpass himself, as did Herbert Johnson in "Spanked," representing President Roosevelt as a Gargantuan, husky boy, rebuked by Congress as a diminutive daddy. The spirit of drollery pervading much of this work, in some quarters with a dash of the uncouth, is expressed by T. E. Powers with a more careful adjustment of pen-stroke, and by J. N. Darling ("Ding") with a slenderness of well-placed line that sometimes seems to accent a little too mildly the underlying idea.

Draughtsmanship is the obvious aid to the effective presentation of ideas. "To be a good cartoonist it is absolutely essential that one should be a good draughtsman," said C. G. Bush.

The noteworthy development of newspaper art has been made possible by the photo-processes. And the natural, most easily reproduced vehicle for the artist's ideas was for years pen-and-ink. In some cases the neat definiteness of the pen degenerated into a niggling preoccupation with unnecessary line-work. Recently the soft yet vigorous effect of the crayon is being wooed by the artist, as it once was by Gavarni, Daumier and others in France. They worked on the lithographic stone: to-day the drawings are reproduced by photomechanical process. But the possibility of the free, broad touch of the crayon line is there. The drawing is done with a soft pencil, or with a lithographic or similarly fatty carbon crayon, on grained paper. This grain slightly disintegrates the unctuous line, interrupting its continuity by minute staccato dots, giving it a feeling of palpitating life. This medium at its best is highly effective. At its best we get something of the bold characterization, the sweep and synthetic analysis for which Daumier stands as the great prototype. That this return to big principles in drawing should be exemplified notably in newspaper art is an interesting and significant circumstance. When these principles are joined to the power of indicating a likeness with a few strokes, and of summarizing fundamental traits of character throughout various expressions of mood and changing circumstance and fleeting mental attitude, we have the ideal equipment of the cartoonist. It is this quality, and its expression through the appropriate omission and accent which are the test of the draughtsman's tact, that give Boardman Robinson, for instance, a noteworthy position. To specify, his picture of Mayor Gaynor, myopic before municipal abuses, of Governor Dix ("Strictly constitutional"), or "The Sullivan Bill in Force" ("He's all right, Your Honor"), may serve as well as any other. "Beneath his art," wrote Charles Henry Meltzer, "is a deep sympathy for poor humanity. . . . In the 'Tribune' and in 'Harvey's Weekly' his drawings won him many friends and foes." One may study the application of this crayon manner in various degrees of power in the work of others, such as Cesare, Minor, Rollin Kirby, and John Sloan, who, predisposed to this movement, has addressed himself to a Socialist public. Pen artists such as Powers, C. R. Macauley and Nelson Harding, have also made occasional use of the crayon.

Through recurrence to a higher artistic point of view, the art of the daily does not lose; it can only gain. By simple directness of style, limitation of the design to few figures, elision of superfluous side issues, simplification of idea, so that the caption is sufficiently explanatory without looped speeches issuing from the mouths of the persons portrayed, always a device that smacks of the infantile, effectiveness becomes immeasurably stronger.

Cartooning in its highest type is a serious business. The caricaturist who can give expression to public opinion, and influence it, must have qualities of a high order, and seriousness and moral purpose in his convictions. "It is my belief that the serious cartoon will always be the most effective and the most enduring," said Homer Davenport, originator of the Mark Hanna $-mark suit of clothes. He himself was once called the "cartoonist dominated by moral ideas," as Nast was aptly described as "seriously and intensely in earnest," and C. G. Bush as "a man of serious convictions." Bush once referred in print to a danger that may easily beset the cartoonist. "In my opinion," said he, "the objectionable features of some cartoons published to-day are largely due to the attempt to make the cartoonist a mere tool in the hands of the editor or proprietor of the paper."

In the highest type of political caricature, humor is not likely to be of the cheaply obvious kind, but its quietly delivered satire cuts more deeply than does the whoop of the facile joke-maker. Comedy has its place, and a useful one, but in the exercise of the comic art as a political or social corrective, it is not the bouncing bladder of the clown nor the rattling slap-stick that scores the home-thrust.

In work by men of the stamp of C. G. Bush, Davenport, Rogers, the younger Keppler, Robinson, John H. Cassel, Robert Carter, D. R. Fitzpatrick, and Kirby, the product of reflection thoughtfully set down, one finds the reason for the effectiveness of political caricature when wielded with skill paired with conviction. The combination of seriousness of purpose and artistic knowledge produces the best results.

But it is not only the domain of political caricature that the daily paper has entered. It has come to cater extensively to humanity's willingness to laugh. Small doses of illustrated humor in daily issues, and more volumnious provision in special "comic" sections of those masses of printed sheets which overpower us on Sundays, offer a sort of continuous comic performance, where we formerly had it concentrated in an exclusively comic paper once a week. We are indeed carrying out Hudson's idea, cited before, that "no one can wait a week for a laugh; it must come in daily with our coffee," and we get it with our evening tea as well.

There has been much simple, clean, healthy humor, though not of a particularly high type, in these "comics." But the influence of the daily paper does not appear to have been invariably good. There is much childishness in conception and execution, and, what is worse, bad taste. There has been already a subtle but noticeable change since the days when R. F. Outcault presented *Buster Brown,* Carl E. Schultze ("Bunny") chronicled the escapades of *Foxy Grandpa,* and Winsor McCay dreamed with *Little Nemo.*

The "comic strip," with its daily record of the doings of stenciled personages, has in more than one case descended to an expression of unlettered vulgarity. And it is not art, but literature with rubber-stamp illustrations. The eternal ebullition of the all-dominating "kid," to the discomfiture of its elders, is not exactly a pleasing subject in the gaudy "Supplement" for which our children can hardly wait on Sunday.

Wallace Irwin, in the "New York Times" of October 22, 1911, characterized the colored comic supplements as "decidedly cockney, both in origin and method," and continued: "They are merely an American version of 'Alley Sloper's Half Holiday,' showing the same tendency to make Peck's Bad Boy the hero, to celebrate the dill pickle

as the classic model of wit, to weave the pun-draped
Daffydii, and to indicate Comedy as a gentleman with
green whiskers lying prone at the foot of a stairway with
a galaxy of stars swimming round his fractured skull."
It is no spirit of ultra-refinement that prompts this attitude, but the exercise of ordinary good taste. Public
taste has become somewhat vitiated by long continuance
of "evil associations." The antics of the "slap-stick"
element in comic art have dulled our powers of resistance
and we look, at the very least, indulgently on the most
vulgar vaudeville contortions in our daily and weekly
charges of pictorial humor.

Ambrose Bierce protests thus: "I wish that the American artists whose lot is cast in the pleasant domain of
caricature would learn something of the charm of moder-
ation and the strength of restraint. Their 'cartoons'
yell; one looks at them with one's fingers in one's ears.
. . . The American newspaper cartoonist . . . by in-
temperate exaggeration fails of his effect. His men are
not men at all, so it is impossible either to respect or
detest them, or to feel toward them any sentiment whatever. . . . His deformed and distorted creations are
entirely outside the range of human sympathy, antipathy,
or interest. They are not even amusing. They are dis-
gusting. . . . A peculiarity of American caricature is
that few of its 'masters' know how to draw."

The news of the voluntary abandonment of the comic
supplement by a Boston paper, some years ago, came like
a ray of hope. All of this may be said without reference
to any ethical viewpoint, in strict adherence to the domain

of art, with which the present book is concerned. The kindly, natural *Metropolitan Movies* of Gene Carr, the droll conceits of Fontaine Fox, the peculiar manner of Maurice Ketten, the sketches of C. A. Voight, are among the things that stand out like oases in this desert.

There has been an enormous increase in comic artists. Schools, even correspondence schools, for the art exist, and books on the art of cartooning, as if the true inwardness of pictorial satire could be taught by rote! But perhaps the kind which evidently pays so well as to have attracted special attention, can be.

CHAPTER XIV

THE BOOK-PLATE

THE spread of culture and the formation of collections of books brought about the use of the book-plate early in the eighteenth century. There were some in even earlier, that of John Cotton, 1674, being apparently the earliest discovered. This was merely a printed label, with a type border, the simplest indication of ownership apart from the name written by hand. The addition of an ornamental border, or an apt quotation, was quite natural, and thence grew decorative or pictorial embellishment. So our early engravers on silver and other metals, entering the field of line-engraving on copper, were called upon to produce ex-libris. Through the eighteenth century the following were more or less so employed: F. Dewing, M. G. Bruls, Henry Dawkins, Allyn Hyde, Nathaniel Hurd, Thomas Johnston, James Turner, Amos Doolittle, J. M. Furnass, E. Ruggles, Jr., Sparrow, Paul Revere, Elisha Gallaudet, Joseph Callender, Richard Brunton, Abraham Godwin, A. Billings, Abernethie (Charleston, 1785), Bull, James Smither, J. H. Seymour, Francis Shallus, James Akin, Nathaniel Dearborn, William Hamlin, James Trenchard, S. Harris, S. Hill, P. and P. R. Maverick (the latter "a most prolific worker in the 'Ribbon and Wreath' " style, writes C. D. Allen), Anderson, Wm. Rollinson, Vallance, Allardice, Thackara, Kearny and not a few others. Some of these lived well into the next century, in the first half of which Annin & Smith and C. G. Childs also executed such signs of bibliothecal proprietorship, as did Dr. John Syng Dorsey.

There was no particular originality in this work. Not only were English models followed, but some of the engravers were content to use the same design, with slight variation, for a number of plates. Hurd, for example, based the E. A. Holyoke, Thos. Dering (1749: the first plate by an American engraver that is both signed and dated), and other plates on the same design, in which figured, at the base of the escutcheon, a shell from which flowed water. Callender also repeated himself, and P. R. Maverick. These early men gave Chippendale, Jacobean and Ribbon and Wreath plates, according to their lights.

Of the early armorial plates, George Washington's is of paramount interest. It was printed from after the Civil War, and has been counterfeited, the spurious copy being utilized at a sale in Washington in the sixties to give a fictitious value to the books to be auctioned off. Like William Penn's, it was presumably engraved in England. Allen notes that in the Southern colonies, many men of cultivated tastes had their plates engraved in England, while in the North native talent was generally engaged. John A. Gade, in "Book-plates—old and new," states that Thomas Prince's (1704) was the earliest one actually executed in America.

The early book-plates were mainly armorial, and usually engraved in line on copper, although occasionally a

Book Plate of George Washington

woodcut was used. But the pictorial element also began to appear, to the extent of rows or piles of books, and the allegorical as well. Patriotism found vent in the employment of the American flag or the eagle, and T. Sparrow, in each of his few ex-libris on wood, introduced the thirteen stars of the new nation.

When our eighteenth century engravers broadened out from the scrollwork and scallops and conventional leaf designs (for which their practice as silversmiths had given them a certain fluency), the result is not always exactly happy. Note, for example, the wooden shepherd, shepherdess and lamb in Dawkins's plate for Benjamin Kissam. But it is difficult to keep purely artistic considerations unmixed with feelings of interest in the owners of the plates and in the spirit of time and place.

Neither the pictorial nor the allegorical seem to have been particularly numerous, and they were apparently more affected by associations than by individuals. The plate of the Society for Propagating the Gospel in Foreign Parts (1704) represents the savage Americans rushing to the shore to meet an incoming ship on which a missionary holds out a book. Later came the plates for Harvard College; Linonian Library, Yale College (1804) and Mechanics' Library, New Haven (two funny little cupids at an anvil, with the motto "improve the moment"), both by Doolittle; Massachusetts Medical Society (Æsculapius healing a wounded stag), Hasty Pudding Library (showing pot of pudding), American Academy of Arts and Sciences, all three by Callender; Harvard Porcellian Club (with a porker prominent);

Monthly Library of Farmington, 1795 (a crude and queer affair, *M. Bull's and T. Lee's sculp.*); Columbia College Library, Apprentices' Library, Typographical Society of New York, all three by Anderson; and New York State Agricultural Society (Ceres, with a sheaf of wheat). In such plates, owls, Minerva, Diana, Clio, lamps of knowledge, age guiding youth to the temple of learning, temples of honor, and similar devices add their pictorial lesson. For the New York Society Library a conception representing an Indian reverently receiving a volume from the hands of Minerva, was twice engraved by P. R. Maverick, another design having previously been cut by Elisha Gallaudet. Ann P. Shallus's Circulating Library, Philadelphia, is symbolized in the engraving by Francis Shallus by a female with a cornucopia. For an orphan asylum L. Simond designed, and Leney engraved, a picture of Christ blessing children.

Among private individuals who used similar emblematic ideas in their book-plates were Bloomfield McIlvaine (J. H. Seymour, engraver, from a design by J. J. Barralet); Williams and Samuel Walker (both musical instruments) and Henry Andrews (Minerva and owl), the first and last by S. Harris; Samuel Parker (Clio handing a book to a kneeling youth); J. B. Swett and John Green, Jr. (both reminiscent of the dissecting room); McMurtrie (book-pile and serpent of Æsculapius, *Fairman del., Kearny sc.*); and James Parker, an old railway conductor, who had an elaborate picture of the first railway train. P. R. Maverick depicted a young man reading, in his plate for Jacob Brown; a young woman

similarly employed figures in that of the Farmington
Village Library. Books, ink-pots and quills are of obvious applicability. The pile or row of books was occasionally used, by Doolittle and James Akin for instance;
the library interior served for Benjamin Ogle Tayloe's
plate. The American flag, cannon balls, an anchor and
a ship characterize the activities of Lieut. E. Trenchard,
and a soaring eagle figures in the plates of Brigham (engraved by writing-master Gershom Cobb), Abraham
Bancker (by Maverick) and others; in W. L. Stone's (by
R. Rawdon) the eagle is struggling with a serpent. In
Edward Livington's, by Maverick, the armorial design
is supplemented by a dog barking at a squirrel.

The plates of these early days, through the first quarter of the nineteenth century, bring before us a long list
of names noted in various walks of life. Presidents,
patriots of the Revolution, orators, signers of the Declaration of Independence, loyalists, merchants, preachers,
authors, lawyers, physicians, military officers, bound together in this pictorial representation by love and respect
for books. The book-plate, to a large extent, as we
have seen, reflected the importance of heraldry and was
an emblem of family dignity rather than an expression
of personal tastes. To-day the pictorial plate predominates, directly or symbolically illustrating a particular
individuality. That does not exclude the opportunity for
an unobtrusive introduction of heraldic devices. But
possibilities for a less hampered effort on the part of the
artist are immeasurably increased. The modern ex-libris
is based primarily on the individuality of the person for

whom it was made, the result of a natural impulse to indicate ownership in a book by some device that shall give indication of the owner's character and tastes.

In these little art products not only the skill and individual attitude of the artist are expressed; the personality and ideas of the one who orders the plate have a paramount influence on the result. Yet ultimately the artist's personality may be the dominating one. The factors in the composition of the book-plate, and its charm, are the relative mental attitudes of owner and artist, and the sympathy of each for the other's standpoint. Mottoes, allegorical allusions, the portrait of the owner, pictures of favorite places, the paraphernalia of sports or other hobbies, rows of books labeled with the names of preferred authors, allusions to personal achievement, wit good and poor, the downright pun,—such elements, with decorative setting, form material for ex-libris. Plenty of opportunity for the display of poor taste. An apparent anxiety to avoid running counter to the Scriptural admonition regarding bushel-covered lights may result in a parade of self-advertisement that weighs down the designer's freedom of expression. But if the owner may be too much in evidence, so, too, may the artist. An attempt to make a book-plate a compressed pictorial biography may prove fatuous, but it is equally unfortunate to make it a miniature mural decoration or poster, or to utilize it in the exploitation of super-advanced artistic idiotisms. Not necessarily absolute seriousness, but a certain dignity is called for here; vagaries are out of order. Appropriateness in conception, design and execution is a prime necessity.   Principles of taste hold good here as well.

The book-plate may indicate the owner's taste with no distinct reference to him, as when A. A. Hopkins adopts an illustration from the "Hypnerotomachia Poliphilii" (Florence, 1499), another a figure from Botticelli's "Spring," or Oliver Wendell Holmes's the chambered nautilus. The allusion may be more direct, as in Francis Wilson's court-jester lost amid old volumes while time goes on unheeded. Lawrence Barrett showed a mask of tragedy and an open book, Laurence Hutton's a statuette of Thackeray. The one designed for Brander Matthews by Edwin A. Abbey depicts an Indian looking at a huge Greek mask of Comedy, with the sentence *Que pensez-vous de cette comédie?* Daniel Maclise's sketch of Lamb served Frank Evans Marshall, Pan charming shepherd and nymphs with his pipes, with *le cœur au métier,* E. C. Stedman, and pen and sword, for George W. Childs. The library interior is a familiar form of indicating love of literature; the point is occasionally made more personal by showing the owner among his books. The influence of literature on life may also be expressed allegorically, as in E. Irenæus Stevenson's plate (serpent with the apple of knowledge) or John Herbert Corning's (by Henry Sandham) : Atlas supporting the world of letters.

Love of books and nature is indicated in a number of plates by a library interior with a window giving an outlook on fields and woods and brooks and sky: so in those of Georgia Medora Lee and Charlotte Anita Whitney.

Jack London's "Call of the Wild" is personified by the head of a wolf. In Alexander Melville Bell's, designed by himself, a pair of lips, a key and an open book play their symbolical part. There may be the reference to the owner's profession or occupation,—the bookbinders at work in E. D. French's plate for Henry Blackwell, the skull and microscope in that by J. H. Fincken for Dr. Edwin S. Potter, the engraver's tools embodied in Samuel P. Avery's plate, as in John Andrew's. The owner's hobbies or passions or pastimes form a favorite theme; for instance, in the angling plates of Dean Sage, Heckscher, Daniel B. Fearing, Howland or Joseph W. Simpson (both owner and designer). Birds figure in the plate of Olive Thorne Miller, by W. E. Fisher; a hornbook indicates George A. Plimpton's specializing, as a collector, in educational publications. A new form of the old admonition not to steal was employed by Dr. George L. Parmele, a trumpeting herald bearing a banner inscribed: *Verloren! Verloren! Ein Buch.* In such various ways the ex-libris gives some idea of the owner's tastes, theories, pastimes, studies, work and surroundings.

When a plate is to be made for a public or semi-public library, institutional aims are to be recorded. In such a case, expression in terms of stately impressiveness rather than of sympathetic grace is called for. Without insisting on the choice, it may be said that the problem was happily solved in such plates as French's for Harvard's Hohenzollern Collection, Princeton University and the American Institute of Electrical Engineers; Spenceley's for the University of Missouri, Harvard University,

By E. A. Abbey

By W. E. Fisher

By W. F. Hopson

By F. D. French

By S. L. Smith

By G. W. Edwards

A GROUP OF MODERN BOOK-PLATES
(Courtesy of Charles Scribner's Sons)

Boston Public Library, Davenport Academy of Sciences
and Library of the New Theater, New York City; Hopson's for the Blackstone Public Library, Branford,
Conn.; S. L. Smith's for the public libraries of Boston,
Lynn, Bangor and the District of Columbia, and for the
Massachusetts Historical Society; and Garrett's for the
Lowell City Library.

The preface to the catalogue of the exhibit of the Club
of Odd Volumes (Boston, 1898) stated that it included
"many uninteresting and even extremely ugly things"
gathered for the purpose of "showing how unsatisfactory
the great number of book-plates used by the public libraries, the libraries of colleges and of other institutions of
learning, is." Sheldon Cheney, in "Book-Plate Booklet"
for February, 1909, speaks of the "great number of utterly wretched book-plates used in our public libraries,"
but notes also some satisfactory ones. These latter are
found not only among those which have gained from the
stately formality of line-engraving. Not a few plates
reproduced by photo processes have shown artistic feeling joined to an appreciative understanding of the problem. They are numerous enough to make choice difficult;
a selection at random results in the naming of W. E.
Fisher's design for the Wadsworth Library, Geneseo,
N. Y., Mrs. A. R. Wheelan's for the University of California, and George W. Edwards's for the Public Library
of New London (nautical in spirit).

Among commercial undertakings one would not so
readily expect to find interesting material, but there are
the plates of the Alton Railway and of the New England

Telephone and Telegraph Co. (by W. C. Bamburgh).
Clubs offer opportunities for the designer, and we have
such plates as those for the Authors' Club and the Grolier
Club (the first one), both by George Wharton Edwards;
the Century Association, New York, by James D. Smillie;
University Club of Boston, by E. H. Garrett; University
Club of Washington, by Henry Sandham; Boston Brown-
ing Society, by F. T. Merrill; Chicago Woman's Club,
by Claude Bragdon, and Woman's Club, Wisconsin, by
J. W. Spenceley.

The ex-libris is a "document," a phase of human activity which repays study, and is of varied charm. It appeals through personal, historical or literary association,
and as an instance of art applied made an integral part of
daily life. Specifically the artist's province, when the
basic ideas have been decided on, is the design, the co-
ordination of the various elements into an orderly whole.
Over-elaboration is as objectionable as a slighting of
essential possibilities. One of the problems is the arrangement of name and motto. The medium employed
has also its distinct and important part in the result.
From the heraldic magnificence and stately formality of
the old line-engraving period we passed to the present-
day free expression of thought, or of passing mood or
whim. This expression, often transmitted by the immediateness of the photo-mechanical processes, frequently finds a medium also in the older method and in
wood-engraving as well, and in this very diversity of
means by which the modern viewpoint finds voice, lies

a reason for a wider appreciation of this specialty in graphic art.

The best traditions of line-engraving on copper were perpetuated by Edwin Davis French, who employed formalized foliage with a sure control of his particular decorative vein that drew endless diversity of effect from the same motive without striking a forced note. There is in his art a dignified beauty of decorative line, a calm nobility of expression that give it a commanding position, that have made him a classic. A happy combination of adaptativeness and individuality, of dignity and a certain free, etcher-like touch in landscapes, are the predominant characteristics in J. Winfred Spenceley's work. Similar notes of diversity are felt in the line-engravings of Sidney L. Smith and W. F. Hopson, who exhibit that combination of variety in treatment with dignity and restraint in expression which produces the happiest results in these marks of bibliophilic proprietorship. Hopson has exercised the mastery of the practised engraver also on the wood-block, which medium W. J. Linton, A. Allen Lewis, George Wolfe Plank, Lankes, Hugh M. Eaton and Rud. Ruzicka have likewise employed, as has William Miller, in a cut of noteworthy delicacy after a design by E. Hamilton Bell. J. H. Fincken (who uses also etching and stipple), Dr. A. J. Brown (working in the spirit of E. D. French), Frederick Spenceley, Arthur Engler and A. N. Macdonald also express themselves in the formal stateliness born of the union of burin and copper-plate. E. H. Garrett speaks in the freer language of the etching needle, which has served also W. H. H.

Bicknell, Roi Partridge, Preissig, and S. Hollyer (whose plate for Mary Anderson has been described as a "most charming bit of engraving"). There are also etchers who have turned aside to do a book-plate—usually their own only, rarely another for a friend,—C. F. W. Mielatz, E. L. Warner, Dr. L. M. Yale (for Dr. A. G. Gerster), Thomas Johnson, James D. Smillie.

The combination of graver and copper-plate imposes its limits and its distinction on the work of the engraver with a certain stamp of reserve. For the artist who draws for the photo-mechanical process the very facility of reproduction invites free expression and tempts those who have a tendency to go beyond proper artistic bounds. It is to the credit of our younger designers that their work, with so many opportunities for going astray, is so satisfactory. At its best it is simple and direct in intent and execution.

A number of designers have devoted themselves more or less habitually to this specialty: L. S. Ipsen, Wilbur Macey Stone (with preference for floral themes), George Wharton Edwards, Jay Chambers, William Edgar Fisher, Mrs. Albertine Randall Wheelan (an "artist thinker"; designs mostly symbolical, with a "western flavor"), Pauline Stone, D. McN. Stauffer, Louis J. Rhead (pictorial, with decorative poster reminiscences), Sheldon Cheney, Howard Sill, E. B. Bird, Gardner Teall, Hugh M. Eaton, H. C. Brown, and The Triptych. Simple lines and flat surfaces, with some employment of color, characterize this modern work.

While a number of able artists have devoted all or

much of their energy to this form of art, one notes with a shade of regret the comparatively few cases in which an American painter or other artist has turned aside from brush and canvas, or other media, to design an occasional plate. Some who have done so are: Elihu Vedder, E. H. Blashfield, W. H. Lippincott, Winslow Homer, Howard Pyle, Henry Sandham, James E. Kelly, C. R. Lamb, A. F. Jaccaci, George Gibbs, Joseph Lauber, Joe Evans (plate for Richard Hoe Lawrence, 1881), Thomson Willing, Victor S. Perard, Henry Mayer and A. F. Mathews. To them may be added the architects **Russell Sturgis** (Avery Architectural Library, Columbia University), Charles I. Berg, A. W. Brunner, George Fletcher Babb (Theodore L. De Vinne plate), Frank Chouteau Brown, Howard Van Doren Shaw, and Claude Bragdon (who made the pertinent statement that "a book-plate should be simple and personal"). We seem still too much dominated by the idea that art, "high art," is painting or sculpture, and that most other forms can be left to the artist-artizan or treated as a bit of byplay. Art should be the general application of principles of beauty in our daily life, and this application is not unworthy of the best talent.

The catalogue of the exhibit of the Club of Odd Volumes in Boston, 1898, summarized American achievement thus:

"Although America was one of the last of the nations to be affected by the book-plate revival, it has taken the lead in the matter of artistic plates and in the number of good plates produced. . . . With the encouragement of enthusiastic collectors, our book-plate engravers and designers have placed this country ahead of all others in quantity as well as quality of work."

The call of the book-plate has occasioned a voluminous literature, much of it due to the enthusiastic industry of collectors. Personal reasons, literary associations, the love of possession, and particularly the diversity of artistic individuality displayed in these little plates, which may tell so much within a small compass, have brought about a specialization, in this direction, of the collecting spirit, which has found organized expression in the American Book-Plate Society, and which has had various organs. These periodicals included "California Book-Plates," "Book-Plate Booklet," "Ex-Libran," "Book-Plate Annual," etc.

Exhibitions of book-plates have been held at the Grolier Club (1894), the Boston Museum of Art by the Club of Odd Volumes (1898), the Caxton Club, Chicago (1898), the Lynn Public Library (1907), Society of Colonial Dames (Colonial plates, 1908), the California Book-Plate Society (Berkeley, 1908), the New York Public Library (1910), the Avery Architectural Library of Columbia University, the library at Berkeley, California, the California State Library (traveling exhibit), and the Library of the University of California. "One-man shows" were devoted to E. D. French in Cleveland (1899), the New York Public Library (1907) and the Grolier Club (1909); to J. W. Spenceley at the last two named places; and to Mrs. A. R. Wheelan in San Francisco (1904). Book-plates appear also in New York at the exhibitions of the Architectural League, the National Arts Club and the Salmagundi Club.

There are permanent collections preserved in the New York Public Library, Columbia University, University of California (plates by California artists), the American Antiquarian Society, and elsewhere. In the British Museum is housed the large collection of British and American plates, brought together by Sir Augustus Wollaston Franks.

In the light of these recent dates, the opinion of Arlo Bates (writing to the "Book Buyer," Feb. 10, 1888) that "the book-plate collecting craze seems to have died out in Boston," looks a bit premature. But perhaps it is true, after all; a craze has died out, not the interest.

CHAPTER XV

APPLIED GRAPHIC ART: FROM BUSINESS CARD TO POSTER

OURS is the land of the advertiser. The results of his activity confront us at every step. In general, effect has been sought by repetition, by the force of unusual size, or brilliancy or garishness. However, the "ad" in good taste is becoming more common. We have yet to appreciate more generally that an advertisement may be effective both commercially and artistically. Not that there is a want of good drawing in many of the advertisements that we see in cars and elsewhere. But there is too often nothing beyond the dryest pictorial statement of fact. When you come across such a conceit as Edward Penfield's cover for a March "Harper,"—a young woman scurrying before a strong wind (which has whipped her copy of the magazine out of her hands), accompanied by a hare of sufficient, though self-contained, madness,—it strikes with the pleasant effect of the unusual. Whether the frequent display of a lack of particular concentration or thought or a stimulating inventiveness is due to artist or client or the public it would, perhaps, be idle to discuss here. Perhaps, too, there may be certain condescension on the part of some artists who occasionally turn to such "minor arts." A work will bear the mark of the spirit in which it was approached.

If treated as a "pot-boiler," it will appear as one; if undertaken with both the earnest desire and the ability to put all that was possible into it, the dignity of the intention ennobles the result. A beer-bottle label may rise to a height that many an easel painting does not attain. The designing of labels for boxes, bottles and tin cans, of business cards and advertisements, calls for knowledge and humility, for the exercise of the great virtue of appropriateness, just as does any form of art. The advertisement to-day is coming to be a highly significant phase of illustration with us, some of our best work being produced in the service of commerce. In this service Penfield, Maxfield Parrish, F. X. Leyendecker and others have entered with distinguished skill in the application of color and decorative effect. In black-and-white, leading naturally in some cases to consideration of the printed text and its office as a part of the design, a number of artists have more recently aimed at high standards. Earl Horter, F. G. Cooper (with drollery in conception and effectiveness in lettering), Wm. Oberhardt (who brings the element of characterization), Franklin Booth, Guy and Lawrence Rosa, are a few of them. To them must be added those mentioned in the chapter on "painter-wood-engraving." For the wood-block, by virtue of the appropriateness of its qualities, has been wedded to commercial art.

The strongly artistic element in our advertisements, and the importance of this phase of art, were well indicated by Frank Jewett Mather, Jr.: "And while our millionaires are wresting the accredited treasures of older art from aristocracy, in the most democratic fashion possible the illustrated magazine and even the advertisement are bringing a respectable and an improving grade of pictorial art to the millions. Here is a jumble of activities, vanities, cruder and finer desires, which shows at least that art is very alive in our civilization."

The "ads," displayed on cards in cars, are mainly text, with pictures thrown in by way of emphasis. They are usually statements of fact, pointed, sometimes humorous, printed on a card which is in part occupied by a picture. There is often no decorative relation between type and illustration. The display of humor is apt to run to caricature, as when Mrs. Grace G. Wiederseim's grotesque infants sing the praises of a certain product with the haunting persistence of droll appeal. Another set of car-posters, effective both in drawings and text, was the "Spotless Town" series of a certain cleaning compound.

It is a far cry from the few and unambitious efforts at pictorial advertising in the days of wood-engraving, to the superabundancy of such cleverly drawn material in these times. In the first half of the nineteenth century they did not go much beyond stock cuts such as railway trains, or ships, which puffed or sailed at the head of newspaper advertisements of transportation companies. A little later came the use of woodcuts of show fixtures bearing an assortment of hats or shoes (D. Haines engraved on copper, in 1822, a high hat on a stand on a card for Tweedy & Benedict, hatters). Then there were such conceits as an elephant rushing along triumphantly bearing aloft a pennant on which appeared the name of the firm advertised, or a sandwich man with similar information. In the advertising columns of the "Illustrated American News" of 1851, a thresher, a piano, a carriage, a horse, top offers of those articles. Such cuts were used also on business cards, a form of pictorial advertising not common now. In cigarette cards with portraits of actresses or pictures of military uniforms the pictures advertise indirectly. The same applies to the spool-cotton concern's cards with landscape sketches in color by Charles Graham,—"exquisite," as H. A. Ogden described them to me. During the later years of the eighteenth century and the earlier ones of the nineteenth, a number of our copper-plate engravers were turning an honest penny in producing card plates for business purposes. Paul Revere, Joseph Callender, William Hamlin (cards for his own nautical instrument business), St. Memin (a card for Peter Mourgeon, "copper-plate printer from Paris," of New York), Peter Maverick and Childs & Carpenter (1822) were among the engravers of such cards, sometimes with lettering only, again with added vignettes to illustrate for the man who ran. Pictorial billheads were done by Revere, Henry Dawkins, Hingston and Callender. And on the wood-block, Alexander Anderson and Abel Bowen did similar cards in the earlier years of the nineteenth century.

The poster was long the domain of the wood-cutter, the work done on planks of wood, basswood, usually. T. D. Sugden wrote: "J. Morse . . . working for Mr. Welch's circus on mahogany blocks." B. J. Lossing: "The Younger Lansing then [1838] engraved only the large coarse theater bills, using mahogany for the purpose." And W. J. Linton: "Joseph W. Morse, at that time with Strong, was, I believe, the first who engraved these on pine with an open graver, about 1840; and Strong first produced them, from designs by George Thomas, in combination of colors." Crude these things were, though effective in a simple way. The coloring was mainly on the chiaroscuro principle; a tint-block or two, with lights cut out in the shape of heavy white lines. Some were done by the Metropolitan Print Co., in one case designed by Robert Joste. These woodcut posters were used well into the eighties, A. S. Seer issuing many, as also Richardson & Foos. James Britton engraved some effective posters from his own designs about twenty years ago, with the simple tools used by the engravers of the Calhoun Co. (Hartford, Conn.), wood-carvers' tools ground down to the length of a boxwood graver, the blade grooved to prevent splitting in the wood, basswood, quite soft and free from knots.

Lithography long since seized on the specialty of the poster. Louis Maurer has recollection of posters designed by Peter Krämer as early as 1863 or '4. Mr. Maurer, who was then with Major & Knapp, thinks also that Krämer, who, as H. G. Plumb says, produced some of the best theatrical posters before 1870, did such work on large plates of zinc, adding that the use of zinc as a substitute for the lithographic stone long antedated that of aluminum.

Theatrical posters—both the large for billboards and the small for windows—were particularly numerous during the seventies and eighties. They were either portraits of individual actors (H. A. Thomas, Napoleon Sarony and Joseph E. Baker signed many) or illustrations of scenes in the play, the more startling and thrilling the better. As several posters were sometimes made for one play, the boy in those days of the melodramatic Bartley Campbell and the resplendently spectacular Kiralfy Brothers could often gain a fair idea of the delights in store by studying the pictures in the various shop windows. There was much poor work, with at best such smooth crayon-drawing as the rather monotonous and fuzzy portraits by Baker for J. H. Bufford and Forbes Co.

There came the influence of Matthew Somerville ("Matt") Morgan (1839–90), felt even in the later work of such a draughtsman as Vic. Arnold. He did illustrative (not decorative) posters with noteworthy skill, such as those for the Kiralfy Brothers' *Black Venus* and *Jay Rial's Ideal Uncle Tom's Cabin*. But he also executed portraits of actresses which left nothing to be desired in the way of smooth, flat, uninteresting reproduction of the photographic original. Much of Morgan's work was signed, and I found the monogram of Henry F. Farny on at least one poster, done for Bartley Campbell's *Galley Slave* and printed by the Strobridge Co. H. A. Ogden, who did a large number of the pictorial class, anonymously, signed his name to two done in 1896, for *Madame Sans-Gêne,* which are probably among his best, posters purely, and not illustrative.

The Strobridge Lithographic Co. (with which Morgan

was connected and for which H. A. Ogden has drawn scenes in many plays), A. S. Seer, Forbes Co. of Boston, Thomas and Wylie (Dan Smith was with Thomas about 1885, says Louis Maurer), W. J. Morgan & Co. were prominently identified with this period.

H. C. Bunner's graceful comments on America's part in the mural art of advertising were illustrated with an interesting series of reproductions of theatrical and circus posters by E. Potthast, Matt Morgan, Joseph E. Baker, Theodore Liebler, Hugo Ziegfeld (H. C. Miner-Springer Litho. Co.), F. M. Hutchins and one by A. Hoen & Co. Most of this was smooth, uninteresting work in which artistic originality had little chance.

Meanwhile, Cheret arose in France, but the influence of the principles which his work expressed was hardly felt here, except in frank imitations, such as the figure of a ballet girl announcing a revival of the *Black Crook* at the Academy of Music (New York) in 1892. C. B. Cochran (in "The Poster," London, July, 1898) states that the poster design was bought in Paris by Eugene Tompkins, and that this Cheret poster was followed by two by Jacobi for Kiralfy's Eldorado and Koster & Bial's Music Hall, respectively, and these by the designs of Scotson Clark. There are also such sporadic examples as Bradley's poster for *The Masqueraders*, F. A. Nankivell's Marie Hatton poster for Koster & Bial's—"indeed a thing of beauty," wrote Cochran—and Wm. Wallace Denslow (sometimes à la Bradley, sometimes broadly humorous, as W. S. Rogers says), Will R. Barnes and others are named.

Thus the merely illustrative poster did not hold the field entirely. Decorative possibilities began to be appreciated and efforts were made to establish harmony between lettering and design. This new spirit was felt less in theatrical posters than in those issued by magazines and newspapers. The result was not infrequently a revel in decorative effect without relation to the thing advertised. There was for a while (about 1894–95) a veritable poster craze. Collections were formed; for instance those of Charles Knowles Bolton, Alfred Bartlett, of Cornhill, William T. Peoples of New York, Wilbur Cherrier Whitehead, George Dudley Seymour, of New Haven, and Henry Lawrence Sparks, whose collecting activity embraces various lands and comes down to the present time. Exhibitions were held in 1895 and 1896 at the Brookline (Mass.) Public Library; the Union League Club, New York City; Pratt Institute; Denver; C. S. Pratt's, 169 6th Avenue, New York City; Mechanic's Institute, Boston (heralded by a poster by Claude Bragdon, after Willette); Boston ("Mechanic's Fair," 1895); Rhode Island School of Design, Providence, 1895; by the "Echo" of Chicago, 1896; and at the Mercantile Library, New York City. ("The Critic" of Feb. 23, 1895, found that the American designs did not carry so far as the French and therefore did better within four walls.) A little later (1899) there was an exhibit at the Fidelis Club, New York, where, according to Percival Pollard, 1,500 examples were shown. An earlier display at the Grolier Club, New York (1890), included only French work.

The theatrical poster, not particularly affected by this movement of the nineties, continued mainly in the beaten path of realistic representation, not infrequently attracting attention principally by its huge proportions.

The magazine and book publishers were the main support of this new spirit in its short-lived tide of conspicuous success. "Art in poster-making has in this country found its best inspiration, in most cases, from literature," said H. C. Bunner. The Harpers, the Century Co., the Scribners and others issued a series of posters (mostly small, for window display) advertising their magazines and books. The "Century Magazine" held a poster contest in Paris in 1895; Lucien Métivet won with his January, 1896, Napoleon poster. Another foreign-made poster advertising the "Century's" life of Napoleon was the equestrian one by Grasset, who later came before our billboard public again with his Bernhardt-Joan-of-Arc design. Boutet de Monvel was also laid under contribution by the "Century."

Home talent was widely enlisted and accomplished noteworthy results. Posters for books were designed by Henry McCarter (a green tree with purple birds for the Green Tree Library), Ethel Reed (A. M. Bagby's "Miss Träumerei," with a suggestion of the French romantiques), Will H. Bradley ("The Modern Poster," a peacock, effective in green, blue and white), E. A. Abbey ("Quest of the Holy Grail," lettering in harmony with drawing, "bold and impressive"), I. R. Wiles, Peter Newell, Maurice Brazil Prendergast, Abby E. Underwood (fashion artist for the New York Sun) and Will

P. Hooper (a poster each for "Chimmie Fadden"), C. D. Gibson, H. C. Christy, F. B. Smith ("Tom Grogan' and "The Delft Cat"), Thomas Buford Meteyard ("Songs of Vagabondia" and "The Ebb Tide"), Vierge ("On the Trail of Don Quixote"), Palmer Cox (for one of his "Brownie" books), E. W. Kemble ("Kemble's Coons"), Oliver Herford ("Artful Anticks"), and R. W. Chambers (for his "King in Yellow" and "Father Stafford"). Not a few of these artists thus advertised books written, or illustrated, or both, by themselves. It has been a not uncommon practice to transplant some illustration in a book directly to the poster for the same. John Sloan, who in those days was quite Beardsley-like in manner, did a few publishers' announcements, such as the characteristic one for "Cinder Path Tales," in black on brown paper. Both he (for "Philadelphia Inquirer" and "Philadelphia Press") and McCarter ("Lourdes," for the "New York Herald") designed illustrations for stories in the "poster style," as he says. Sloan describes his own as "black and white and gray in flat tints." McCarter's "Lourdes" illustrations R. W. Chambers characterized as "intensely sincere and decorative," adding that neither the "Herald" nor the public liked them.

Announcements for magazines, more than those for books, gave opportunity to poster artists. In these years, 1894–96, the "Century" issued designs by I. R. Wiles, George Wharton Edwards; Edward Penfield; Charles H. Woodbury; Louis Rhead; the three prize winners in the mid-summer poster competition, 1896: J. C. Leyendecker (1st prize), Maxfield Parrish (2d), Baron Arild Rosenkrantz (3d); E. Potthast (highly commended in the same competition); H. M. Rosenberg; E. B. Bird; H. M. Lawrence; and later F. Berkeley Smith. "St. Nicholas" used designs by Louis Rhead and Moores. "Scribner's" (for which H. C. Brown had drawn as early as 1891, and Victor S. Perard in 1892) employed L. L. Roush, Francis Day, Kenyon Cox (March, 1895, figure and lettering in effective harmony), Birch Will Carqueville, W. Granville Smith, L. J. Rhead, W. H. Low, W. T. Smedley, Sergeant Kendall (portraits of C. S. Reinhart and R. F. Blum), Geo. M. Reevs, H. McCarter, Hy Mayer ("Olympic Games" number). Furthermore, there were posters for "Harper's Bazar" by Rhead; "Lippincott's" by Will Carqueville and J. J. Gould, Jr.; "Atlantic" by R. R. Emerson (July, 1895); "Youth's Companion" by W. L. Taylor; "Illustrated American" by Archie Gunn; "Bookman" by Rhead and G. C. Parker; "Overland Magazine" by L. M. Dixon (1895) and E. B. Bird; "Quarterly Illustrator" by W. J. Yegel; "Outing" by H. S. Watson; "Truth" by Hy Mayer and E. Haskell; "Chap Book" by W. H. Bradley and E. B. Bird; "Black Cat" by E. B. Bird; "Inland Printer" by Will Bradley and E. B. Bird; "Bostonian" by A. G. Learned; and "Moods" (Philadelphia) by John Sloan, who describes this periodical as the "nearest attempt à la 'Yellow Book' done in this country," and states that it went through a couple of numbers.

The newspapers at this time (still 1894–95) used the poster in its new manifestation. Drawings by Miles C.

Gardner, Wm. M. Paxton, Charles M. Howard, Ethel Reed and E. H. Garrett were issued for the "Boston Sunday Herald"; by Rhead for the "Boston Transcript"; by Frank King, R. F. Outcault, M. de Lipman, Alder (had "all the go and deviltry and 'chic' that Guillaume possesses," said R. W. Chambers) for the "New York World," for which Dan Smith, in 1903, did a huge announcement of its anniversary number of May 10th; by Charles Hubbard Wright for the "New York Herald"; by de Yonghe for the "New York Times"; by Henry B. Eddy and E. Haskell for the Sunday issues of the "Journal" (New York); by Will H. Bradley for the Chicago Sunday "Tribune" and "Echo"; by Biorn and Nankivell for the "Chicago Echo"; by Will W. Denslow for the "Chronicle," "Herald" and "Times-Herald," all of Chicago; by Mrs. Alice R. Glenny for the woman's edition of the "Buffalo Courier"; by Claude Fayette Bragdon for the "Rochester Post-Express," and by Louis J. Rhead for the "New York Sun." The names of the many who were laid under contribution by the spirit of poster improvement emphasize the inclusiveness of the choice, though it did not always fall on those who showed peculiar fitness for the task. At least the designs were usually in good taste, and the individual artist was given some opportunity.

Bradley was one of those who attacked the problem with serious intent. He brought to the task some of the influence of Beardsley, more, perhaps, of the spirit of the old wood-engravers, and a decorative instinct quite his own. The bent toward ornamental fullness somewhat detracted at times from the absolute effectiveness of his posters in line work. The "Inland Printer" and "Chap Book" posters are noteworthy. His poster for the "Historical Musical Exhibition under the auspices of Chickering & Sons" (Boston, 1902) is somewhat Parrish-like, with an eighteenth-century woodcut effect, frequently exercised in this country, but not always with as good taste as here. Bradley even attempted a magazine for the "exclusive display of his various efforts in decorative art," with the title: "Bradley: His Book."

Simplicity and directness, two important factors in the attainment of the poster's prime function,—to attract attention and to hold it,—have marked the work of Edward Penfield, who has been particularly happy in some of his conceits. In one of his "Harper" posters a sportsman is so absorbed in his magazine that he overlooks two hares almost within reach of his hand. His work is strong in its emphatic directness of line and its broad, flat tints. Bunner used his "March hare" Harper design as a text for a little disquisition on native art: "In the lightness, freshness and purity of that humor, in the composition, free without license and unconventional without extravagance, in the striking yet inoffensive use of color, in the frankness and unaffected innocence and happy simplicity of the whole thing, I find a quality which, I am grateful to think, comes to the American artist as his natural and honest birthright." Penfield himself summarily states a basic principle: "A poster should tell its story at once—a design that needs study is not a poster, no matter how well it is executed."

The work of Louis Rhead, who was doing posters for the Harpers and the Century Co. as early as 1890–91, was striking, at times based on daring color schemes; it had not necessarily any relation to the thing advertised. Nor were the colors always those of nature. These qualities were quite apparent in that design of a young woman walking in a field, used by the "Sun." There was method in this outlandishness. Few lines, flat tints, simple composition were combined into a harmonious whole which, with a certain aloofness from material facts, attracted attention with a blare that had none of the shrillness of vulgar over-emphasis. In the "New York Times," February 23, 1896, Robert W. Chambers gave much space to Rhead and those who "out-Rheaded him."

To the names already cited may be added the following, listed by C. K. Bolton: S. Cruset, H. McVickar, Bertram Grosvenor Goodhue and Julius A. Schweinfurth (Boston Festival Orchestra, 1895). The curious may find still more in the book by W. S. Rogers. A considerable number of the posters by the artists mentioned were reproduced in "Some Posters reproduced by Wm. Troyon Higbee" (Cleveland, 1895) and in "Posters in Miniature, with an Introduction by Edward Penfield" (New York, 1896). Both books contained portraits of a number of the poster designers.

In the days of the poster excitement of 1895, even the art world was seized with the fever. The National Academy of Design and the American Water Color Society each used a poster designed by George Wharton Edwards, while Charles Herbert Woodbury is credited with one for the Society of Painters in Water Colors of Holland (exhibition in Chase's gallery). A poster, done in the eighties, for a "Grand concert of the Gotham Art Students" (New York), printed by Thomas & Wylie, but drawn or inspired quite evidently by artist or art student, illustrated a not uncommon error of the designer who has more respect for art than understanding of poster needs. The attempt to be artistic in the figure and in the lettering resulted in a colorless affair and was fatal to clearness. Subsequent noteworthy efforts to advertise art include the one by Britton for the Connecticut League of Art Students, and the simple, dignified performance of E. H. Blashfield for the twenty-fifth anniversary of the Art Students' League, of New York, in 1900. Some of the little posters of this same League's "Society of American Fakirs" are of an effective directness in their exuberant humor, for instance the one for the "fifteenth annual slam,"—Satan in black and red. The Society of American Artists used the figure designed for its catalogue cover by Will H. Low, and the National Academy of Design has similarly used its cover design.

An element that must not be overlooked is the impetus given by business. Even among old woodcut posters I came across an announcement of "gifts," issued by Paul & Curtis, 594 Broadway, with the traditional Santa Claus preparing to slide down the chimney. In 1896 the New York "Poster" reproduced various designs for the Columbia Bicycle, including Maxfield Parrish's, which won first prize. Charles D. Farrand also did a poster for this bicycle, and Bradley one for the "Victor," in those days of the cycling fever. "Pearline" (1895) and Lundborg's Perfumes were decoratively advertised by L. J. Rhead; Hood's Sarsaparilla by various artists, including Bradley, who also heralded "Narcoticura," while R. Wagner, it appears, was engaged by tobacco houses. "Aetna Dynamite" was dealt with by Penfield (his design showed an Italian with a red flag, with a suggestion of a volcano in the background), and the Hartford Building and Loan Association as well as the Millyer Institute, Hartford, by Wilbur Macey Stone. In recent years some of the drygoods houses as well as other business concerns have been testing the efficiency of the large poster on elevated and subway railroad stations. There may come such surprises as Jessie Willcox Smith's children in a home made cheerful by a certain brand of radiators.

We have long been accustomed to seeing the shop window turned into a portrait gallery of candidates in the weeks before an election. But the poster in the political field has been typographical in the main, and only exceptionally pictorial. In the latter case the vein of caricature is apt to appear; an effective newspaper cartoon may be reproduced on a large scale, or a pictorial skit drawn specially for the occasion, *vide* Tammany's "Spotter's Town" series in New York. In the campaign of 1903 in New York City the Citizens' Union in its fight for Seth Low against Tammany utilized designs by Chester Loomis and Ella Condie Lamb. Allegorical figures stood for the various departments of the city's government or for matters of vital public interest, and served as a sort of background for pithy printed statements and comparisons. These, as well as work by G. W. Edwards, James Preston, W. W. Fawcett, F. D. Steele, R. E. Gould Co. and O. J. Gude Co. were shown at an exhibition of artistic posters and advertising matter held by the Municipal Art Society of New York at the National Arts Club in 1906.

So we have come to more recent times. Since the advertising world swallowed the dose of '95, things have not been quite the same. Not that everything is rosy; the very diversity of racial antecedents, of training and environment, of esthetic and ethical viewpoint, in our land, especially in that congeries known as the metropolis, produces much that is objectionable in the general whoop to be heard. But the average artistic merit, and the average taste, of the pictorial advertisement is better and applied with more appropriateness and effectiveness than "before the poster war." And if, as was said at the beginning of the chapter, much of our poster and car advertising is typographical rather than pictorial, that may perhaps be due to the fact that our growing taste for better art has not yet overcome our national tendency to talk. Those who have used their artistic capabilities in this field include Robert J. Wildhack, F. G. Cooper, Orson Lowell, Walter Meyner, Gil Spear, Sydney Adamson, Dorwin Teague and others.

The circus poster has gone on its accustomed way of effective illustration of the alliterative and imaginative grandiloquence of the text. In recent years there has appeared occasionally, on very large theatrical posters, the use of a figure or two, life size or over, in combination with a minimum of text drawn in huge letters, the whole forming a not unpleasing effect. Once or twice, too, a welcome change from the mammoth illustrative poster has been found in the swirling lines of Hy Mayer or the vivaciousness of Archie Gunn. Ernest Haskell has drawn several studies of Mrs. Minnie Maddern Fiske which attracted attention by their very reticence, by the simplicity of means used, crayoned with an almost pertly incisive characterization. It was unusual to see a painter-lithograph actually appear on a billboard, the unaltered reproduction of the artist's own touch, not seen dimly through the intermediate work of the practised lithographer. S. de Ivanowski's almost life size full-length presentation of Nazimova attracted attention on similar grounds. There was dignity in the archer used for *Ulysses,* by Stephen Phillips (no signature but that of the Metropolitan Printing Co.). And some years ago the same printers signed an announcement of *The Ajax of Sophocles enacted by the Greeks of New York at Clinton Hall;* appropriate in style, modern, yet with a classic strain, with a suggestion of Greek vase decoration in its color. Different in style, with kinship to Forain, was the drawing by Boardman Robinson used by the Coburn Players at Columbia University in 1911. And there was that series of window posters put out one season by Francis Wilson, sketches, by various artists, of that actor of facile fun-making.

Posters and advertisements are being produced, which command attention by their good qualities. Some commercial ones have been mentioned incidentally while discussing earlier work.

More recently there has been seen an occasional effort to do something out of the ordinary in magazine posters. One recalls with amusement Frank A. Nankivell's "Mr. Bibliocrank" crowded out of his house by his books (done for the defunct "Literary Collector")—engraved on wood by the artist, and tinted from two color blocks etched on zinc. Arthur Wesley Dow's design for "Modern Art" edited by J. M. Bowles remains an interesting example of artistic feeling expressed with a simplicity of means in its uninvolved composition and color, a straightforward, effective response to the prime requisites in poster art. Generally, the magazine poster to-day is a printed list of contents for the current month with a noteworthy illustration of that issue thrown in, or a reproduction of the cover. For the cover of the magazine, changing each month, is a poster in itself, a striving for novelty, in fitful anxiety to be heard and seen. The unchanged cover, become a household word—like the old one for "Harper's," or the one by Vedder which long served the "Century"—is the exception. The cover is an "ad." Pictorial, too, like so many posters and advertisements, and often without the slightest reference to the nature of the magazine or the contents of the specific number. The thoughtless devotion to a type, the flourish of an "up-to-date" manner, is felt here as in illustration. In fact, cover designs are often enough simply illustration, slapped on below printed lettering to which it bears no relation. But there are always some which show that the artist really had something to say, that had to do with the matter in hand. The list of names that have appeared on cover designs include those of Will Bradley, Wm. Martin Johnson ("Harper's Bazar," 1893–95), Maxfield Parrish, George Wharton Edwards, Joseph C. and Frank X. Leyendecker, George F. Tobin, Guernsey Moore, Binner, Jessie Willcox Smith, Henry Hutt, John Cecil Clay, and Victor S. Perard.

The West has had its "Sunset" posters, often reproducing the cover design and often very good. Methfessel has done some of these, and particularly Maynard Dixon; there is quiet humor in the latter's design for December, 1904: Santa Claus with an Indian on one arm and a cowboy on the other. These "Sunset" drawings have a freshness and swing born of the soil and with no weakness of super-sensitive preciosity or swagger up-to-dateness.

The activities of the World War included an extensive use of the poster, C. B. Falls, Adolph Treidler and others contributing excellent material. More than one artist was awakened to the necessity of understanding the lithographic printer's problems in order to get the best results.

There has been a noteworthy improvement in the get-up of dealers' catalogues, an improvement with which the influence of such publications as "Printing Art" and "The Graphic Arts" has had something to do. This has extended also to some of the railway guide-books. Penfield, Haskell, Perard are among those who have decorated the catalogues of book-sellers and of various industrial concerns. Signatures, however, rarely appear on the products of this phase of art, which was dealt with in "Twentieth Century Cover Designs" (1902), a collection of nine essays issued by V. H. and E. L. Briggs. Cover designs, meaning, of course, paper covers, naturally suggest book-covers of cloth or leather. Those, however, are not quite within the province of our survey, and there must not be more than a mere reference to a specialty in which Walter C. Greenough, Alfred Brennan, Miss Amy Sacker of Boston, and very many others have done good work.

Since we have got away from the advertising atmosphere which has pervaded much of the present chapter, a few lines may be given to the holiday card. To-day that represents a form of activity extensive and commercialized. But that there are possibilities was proven by an exhibition of "Holiday cards by American Artists," held in the New York Public Library in 1922–23. Many of the cards shown were made by artists for their friends, others were drawn for firms. Some were by "commercial artists," others represented excursions from quite different fields of art in order to send personal greetings. But in each the result was individual and interesting. Nearly ninety artists were represented,—Charles Sarka, G. W. Plank, the Zorachs, A. A. Lewis, Ruzicka, F. T. Chapman, Walker Whitehead, Walter Meyner, R. M. Pearson, W. D. Teague, are but a few named to indicate the variety made possible in such an assemblage.

The earlier history of the Christmas card in this country is interesting on account of the names associated with it. The first ones, flower cards, were designed by Mrs. O. E. Whitney, who, it is said, based her idea on the decorated business card of Louis Prang, the lithographer, shown at the Vienna Exposition of 1873. Then came the impetus given by the Centennial Exhibition of 1876. In 1880, Prang arranged a competitive exhibition at the American Art Galleries, New York, Samuel Colman, Richard M. Hunt and E. C. Moore being the judges. The prizes were won by Rosina Emmet (1st), Alexander Sandler (2d), Alfred Fredericks (3d), and Anna G. Morse (4th). At a second competition in 1881, the judges being Samuel Colman, John La Farge, and Louis C. Tiffany, the first prize went to Elihu Vedder, the second to Dora Wheeler (later Mrs. Keith), the third to Charles Caryll Coleman, the fourth to Rosina Emmet (later Mrs. Sherwood). At a third competition, 1881, two groups of prizes were awarded, one by the ballot of artists and art critics, the other by popular vote. The first group went to Dora Wheeler (1st), Miss Lizbeth B. Humphrey (2d and 3d), Alfred Fredericks (4th). The "popular" prizes were won by Dora Wheeler (1st), Walter Satterlee (2d), Frederick Dielman (3d), Miss Florence Taber (4th). For the fourth competition, 1884, Mr. Prang commissioned twenty-two artists of standing to paint cards, which were then entered in a competition. The artists were J. Carroll Beckwith, E. H. Blashfield, Robert F. Bloodgood, I. H. Caliga, Thomas W. Dewing, Frederick Dielman, Rosina Emmet, Frederick W. Freer, Alfred Fredericks, I. M. Gaugengigl, W. St. John Harper, Lizbeth B. Humphrey, Will H. Low, Leon Moran, Percy Moran, Thomas Moran, H. Winthrop Pierce, A. M. Turner, Douglas Volk, J. Alden

Weir, C. D. Weldon, Dora Wheeler. The prizes were awarded by dealers' vote, and were taken by C. D. Weldon, Will H. Low, Thomas Moran and Frederick Dielman, in the order indicated.

To these names were added, in the same firm's Easter card list for 1887, those of Fidelia Bridges, Henry Sandham, Lizbeth B. Comins and others. A number of designs by these artists are reproduced in "Christmas cards and their chief Designers," by Gleeson White, who says of these cards: "The charm of the coloring is not to be attributed entirely to a larger number of color printings, or superior chromo-lithography; both these factors no doubt helped to give the peculiarly harmonious result; but one can feel beyond this, that the artists employed recognized from the first the limitation of all mechanical reproduction, however perfectly manipulated, and designed accordingly." A number of large scrapbooks, full of proof impressions of these cards, have found a home in the New York Public Library.

The story of these Prang competitions is told in the catalogue of the Prang sale (Boston, 1899) and in an article in the "Evening Post" (New York) for December 9, 1911, where attention is called to the "very real influence in the education of taste" exerted by these bits of pasteboard. It is for this last reason that I have given this matter so much space, and for the spirit of the projector who laid so many well-known or promising artists under contribution. Here was one example of the application of art to things near at hand, the entrance of art into daily life. The problem of such service on the part

of art without a loss of its ideals, a service just to both
parties, is always with us.

To indicate just two possible openings: cards of invitation and menus are pretty generally executed under the
name, and in the spirit, of large commercial houses. To

UPON THE ROOF GARDEN, IN
THE HEAT OF SUMMER, TEA OR
SUPPER MAY BE ENJOYED AMID
THE COOLING BREEZES FROM
THE EAST AND SOUTH

WOOD ENGRAVING   J. J. A. Murphy
(An Advertisement)

find an artist's signature—T. Sindelar's, for instance—on
the bill of fare of some banquet, is the exception. The
Kit-Kat and other clubs of artists have occasionally sent
out cards of invitation designed by members. And in the
eighties and nineties, exhibitions of the works of individual artists, arranged by dealers, were occasionally

advertised by cards designed by the artist in question. But such scattered instances do not, of course, indicate any general interest in an application of artistic principles, as a matter of course, to daily commercial needs.

Where the artists have an incentive to put their energies really to the task we get results that attract because they are attractive within the bounds of appropriateness. Always one reverts to the old truth that the medium, the object and the artist's personality must be considered in combination.

BIBLIOGRAPHY

This is a list of some important books and articles. The reader who wishes to go into the subject more deeply is referred to "A descriptive bibliography of the most important books in the English language relating to the art and history of engraving," by Howard C. Levis (London, 1912), to Wm. Dunlap's "History of the rise and progress of the arts of design in the U. S.," new edition, Boston, 1918 (vol. 3, pp. 346–377: Bibliography of American art and artists before 1835), and the card catalogues of large libraries, such as the New York Public Library. Some titles appear also in the body of the present book. Thus, this is a guide rather than a formal bibliography.

General works (including line and stipple engraving)

Boston. Museum of Fine Arts. Descriptive catalogue of an exhibition of early engraving in America. 1904.

The Boston Public Library published, on this occasion, a "List of books and magazine articles on American engraving, etching and lithography," in its "Monthly Bulletin" for Dec. 1904.

Gesellschaft für Vervielfältigende Kunst. Vienna. Vervielfältigende Kunst der Gegenwart. 1887–93.

Chapters on etching, wood-engraving and lithography in the U. S.

Stauffer, David M. American engravers upon copper and steel. Grolier Club. New York, 1907. 2 vols.

—— **Fielding,** Mantle. Supplement to Stauffer. Philadelphia, 1917.

Toppan, R. K. A hundred years of bank-note engraving in the U. S. New York, 1896.

Etching

American Art Review. Boston, 1879–82.

Cary, E. L. Collecting American etchings. (American Magazine of Art, May 1920.)

Cheney, Sheldon. Notable Western etchers. (Sunset, Dec. 1908.)

Dealers' catalogues. Klackner (1888); Wunderlich & Co.; Keppel & Co. (1908); Albert Roullier (1913).

Exhibitions. Catalogues: Boston Etching Club (1883); Boston Museum of Fine Arts, 1881, 1887 (etchings by women); New York Etching Club, 1882–1889 (illustrated with etchings); Philadelphia Society of Etchers, 1882 (illustrated with etchings); Union League Club, 1888 (etchings by women). Chicago Society of Etchers, Brooklyn Society of Etchers and California Society of Etchers are active today.

Hitchcock, J. Ripley W. Etching in America. New York, 1886.
Later artists dealt with in Scribner's Magazine, 1909, 1912, 1917.

Studio. Modern etchings and engravings. 1902. — Modern etchings, mezzotints and dry-points. 1913. London.
Chapters on American work.

Van Rensselaer, Mrs. M. G. American etchers. Reprinted from the Century Magazine, Feb. 1883. New York, 1886.
Victoria and Albert Museum. Catalogue of prints. Part 2: Modern etchings and aquatints of the British and American schools. London, 1906.
Wray, Henry R. Review of etching in the U. S. Philadelphia, 1893.

Wood-Engraving

Brown, Howell C. Block printing in the U. S. (American Magazine of Art, April 1923.)
By the secretary of the Print Makers Society of California.

Hamerton, P. G. The art of the American wood-engraver. New York, 1894. — Forty India proofs to accompany the text.
Bibliography by J. B. Carrington.

Linton, W. J. History of wood-engraving in America. Boston, 1882.
Portfolio of proof impressions selected from Scribner's Monthly and Saint Nicholas. 1879. — Second series, 1881. — Selected proofs from the first and second portfolios. 1881.
Society of American Wood Engravers. Engravings on wood, by members of the Society. . . . With . . . text by W. M. Laffan. New York, 1887.
The Society held exhibitions at the Kansas City Art Association, 1889; Chicago Art Institute; Museum of Fine Arts, Boston, 1890; Grolier Club, N. Y., 1890.

Weitenkampf, F. Wood-block printing to-day. (Scribner's Magazine, Nov. 1921.)
Whittle, G. H. Monographs on American wood-engravers. (Printing Art, 1917–18.)

Lithography

J. and E. R. Pennell's book on lithography includes American artists, and recent work was dealt with in Scribner's Magazine, May 1903, Jan. 1923.

Illustration

Smith, F. Hopkinson. American illustrators. New York, 1892.

Henry James had an article in "Harper's Weekly," June 14, 1890, V. Gribayédoff covered earlier newspaper art in the "Cosmopolitan," 1896, and J. Pennell's "Pen drawing and pen draughtsmen," 1920, has a chapter on the U. S.

The "Book Buyer," N. Y., published articles on: R. B. Birch (1892); R. F. Blum (1893); F. S. Church, Mary Hallock Foote, A. B. Frost, C. D. Gibson, E. W. Kemble, W. L. Metcalf, C. S. Reinhart, F. Remington, W. T. Smedley, A. E. Sterner, I. R. Wiles (1894); E. A. Abbey, B. W. Clinedinst, W. H. Drake, O. Herford, W. H. Low, T. de Thulstrup, E. Vedder (1895); Will H. Bradley, W. H. Gibson, W. M. Johnson, J. A. Mitchell, V. Perard, A. B. Wenzell (1896).

Volumes have been published of collected drawings by individual artists, among them A. B. Frost, C. D. Gibson, W. H. Gibson, Peter Newell, F. Remington, F. Richardson, C. H. Johnson, Harrison Fisher, and many others.

Caricature

Halsey, R. T. H. The Boston Port Bill as pictured by a contemporary London cartoonist. New York, Grolier Club, 1904.

Among publications on caricature of the Colonial and Revolutionary periods are such special ones as "The snake devices, 1754–76" (Cambridge, 1908), by Albert Matthews.

Magazine articles include: J. H. de Rosen's in "La Revue," Feb. 15, 1913; J. B. Bishop's in the "Century Magazine," June 1892, dealing particularly with the pre-Civil-War period; J. A. Mitchell's in "Scribner's," Dec. 1889, concerned with artists of the time; F. Weitenkampf's in the "Journalist" (1887) on artists of the day, in the "Critic," Aug. and Sept. 1905, on "Social history of the U. S. in caricature," and in the "Century," Jan. 1913, on "American cartoons of to-day."

Periodicals devoted to the comic art are "Cartoons Magazine" and "Cartoons." The "American Review of Reviews" and the "Literary Digest" make a feature of the reproduction of cartoons on current political affairs.

Collections of caricatures on noteworthy events or on particular individuals have been made in volumes on the Civil War (Currier & Ives prints), 1892; the War with Spain; the World War; Lincoln; and Roosevelt. Also, the work of individual artists has been republished in book form,—F. P. W. Bellew ("Chip"), Bud Fisher, Fontaine Fox, J. G. Francis, C. D. Gibson, Joseph Keppler, J. T. McCutcheon, Ch. Nelan, Frederick Opper, W. A. Rogers, and M. A. Woolf among the number.

Book Plates

Allen, Charles Dexter. American book-plates. New York, 1894; reprinted 1905.

Has list of periodical articles, as has W. G. Bowdoin's "Rise of the book-plate."

Banning, K. Book-plates designed, engraved and printed by the Triptych. New York, 1906.

Book-Plate Booklet during 1907–10 published articles on Claude Bragdon, Wm. E. Fisher, W. F. Hopson, J. W. and F. Spenceley.

British Museum. Catalogue of British and American book plates bequeathed by Sir Augustus W. Franks. By E. R. J. Gambier Howe. London, 1903–04. 3 vols.

Carver, C. N. Book-plates of well-known Americans. Princeton, N. J., 1911.

—— Book-plates of Princeton and Princetonians. Princeton, 1912.

Directory of bookplate artists. Kansas City. First issued in 1913.

Fincham, H. W. Artists and engravers of British and American book-plates. New York and London, 1897.

Prescott, Wm. Ward. A bibliography of book-plate literature. American Book-Plate Society, 1914.

Stone, W. M. Women designers of book-plates. New York: The Triptych, 1902.

Americans included are: A. R. Wheelan, B. M. Clute, Annie Hooper, Bessie Pease, Pamela Colman Smith, Misses Bonsall and Hallowell.

Troutsdale Press, Boston, appears on the title-pages of monographs on the following artists: Mrs. M. S. Frost, Herbert Gregson, I. J. Iorio, F. A. Jacobsen, Amy M. Sacker, Ralph F. Seymour (1903); — E. H. Garrett (1904); — Frank Chouteau Brown, Hugh M. and Margaret Eaton, F. G. Hall, J. W. Spenceley, D. McN. Stauffer (1905); — E. B. Bird, T. B. Hapgood, Louis Rhead (1907).

Individual artists, such as W. E. Fisher, R. M. Pearson and others, have issued portfolios of their plates.

Ward, Harry P. Some American college bookplates. Columbus, 1915.

White, Esther G. Indiana bookplates. Richmond, Ind., 1910.

Wyer, M. G. Bookplates in Iowa. Cedar Rapids, 1914.

Periodicals. "California Book-Plates," succeeded by the "Book-Plate Booklet" (organ of the California Book-Plate Society, edited by Sheldon Cheney, 1907–11), succeeded by the "Ex-Libran" (1912), continued as "Biblio" (1913), and that as "Miscellany" (1914 on); "Bookplate Booklet" (1919–20); "Ex-Libris" (1896–7), organ of the American Bookplate Society, as was the "Bookplate" (1914); "Bookplate Quarterly" (1917–8), superseded by the "Bookplate Bulletin" (1919) and that by the "Bookplate Chronicle." The "Bookplate Annual" has been published since 1921; it contains monographs on A. Allen Lewis and other artists.

Exhibitions were held, and catalogues published by, Grolier Club, N. Y., 1894; Caxton Club, Chicago, 1896; Club of Odd Volumes, Boston Museum, 1898; National Society of the Colonial Dames of America, 1908, the N. Y. Public Library, etc.

Posters

Books and articles are mentioned in Chap. XV. Chapters on American work appear in Charles Hiatt's "Picture poster" (London, 1895) and, by H. C. Bunner, in "The modern poster" (New York, 1895).

Special Subjects

In "Scribner's Magazine" appeared articles on "American sporting prints" (June 1920) and "The West in American prints" (April 1921); — in the "Print Connoisseur" articles on military (March 1921), early historical (March 1922) and naval (June 1923) prints; — in the "Century Magazine" on "American life in American art" (Dec. 1920); — in the "International Studio" on "American scenic prints" (July 1923); — in "Harper's Magazine" on "Country life" (1924); — in the "History Teacher's Magazine" on "Pictorial documents as illustrating American history" (Feb. 1917).

New York City forms the theme of several volumes, cherished by the collector, by William Loring Andrews: "New Amsterdam, New Orange and New York: a chronologically arranged account of engraved views of New York City" (1897), "Journal of the Iconophiles around New York in search of the historical and picturesque" (1897), "The Iconography of the Battery and Castle Garden" (1901), etc. The authoritative and definitive work on the subject is the "Iconography of Manhattan Island," by I. N. Phelps Stokes, of which vols. 1–4 (1915–22) have appeared. A list of Hudson River views appeared in the New York Public Library Bulletin, 1909.

Portraiture is dealt with in "Essay on the portraiture of the American Revolutionary War" (1896) by W. L. Andrews and Buford Samuel's "Index to American portraits" (Pennsylvania Magazine of History, 1901). Portraits of individuals are listed in monographs such as those on Washington by C. H. Hart (Grolier Club, 1904), Lincoln (Grolier Club, 1899) and those on Franklin (Jan. 1906) and Hawthorne (July 1904) published in the New York Public Library's "Bulletin."

Individual Artists

Only a few titles are mentioned here, mainly volumes devoted entirely to one artist. The list of periodical articles is long and is growing daily; for these the reader is referred to Poole's "Index to periodical literature" and to the "Reader's guide." The aim was to include mainly material that offered a record of the artist's work, especially catalogues.
See also Illustrators (chap. XI) and Book-Plates (chap. XIV) in the present book.

Aid, G. C.   Roullier (Chicago) Print Collector's Bulletin.
Anderson, Alexander.   Life by Frederick M. Burr. 1893. — Brief catalogue of books illustrated with engravings by Anderson. 1885.
Andrews, Joseph.   Boston Art Club. Memorial meeting. Biographical memoir by S. R. Koehler. 1873.

Anthony, A. V. S. S. G. W. Benjamin's "Our American artists," Boston, 1879, pp. 58–63.

Attwood, F. G. Boston. Museum of Fine Arts. Exhibition. 1901.

Bacher, O. H. Keppel & Co.'s Print Collector's Bulletin, 1908.

Benson, F. W. Paff, A. E. M. Etchings and drypoints by Benson. An illustrated and descriptive catalogue. Boston, 1917–23. 3 vols.

Blum, R. F. Exhibition of paintings and studies. Cincinnati Museum, 1905. (Etchings, pp. 7–9.)

Bowen, Abel. A sketch by W. H. Whitmore. Bostonian Society. 1884.

Brennan, Alfred. Catalogue of pen-and-ink drawings to be sold at auction. New York: Ortgies & Co., 1889.

Brunton, Richard. Bates, A. C. An early Connecticut engraver and his work. Hartford, 1906.

Criticized by James Terry in an "open letter"; *see* **Hyde.**

Burr, G. E. Articles in International Studio, Nov. 1914; Studio, 1922; Print Connoisseur, 1921.

Burt, Charles. Catalogue by Alice Burt. New York, 1893.

Chandler, G. W. Roullier (Chicago) Booklet.

Cheney, John and Seth Wells. Cheney, E. D. Memoir of John Cheney. Boston, 1889. — Memoir of S. W. Cheney. Boston, 1889.

—— Koehler, S. R. Catalogue of the engraved and lithographed work of J. and S. W. Cheney. Boston, 1891.

Clark, Walter Appleton. International Studio, 1907.

Cole, Timothy. Much of his work has been gathered in volumes devoted to British, Italian, Dutch and Spanish painters.

Dow, A. W. Boston Museum of Fine Arts. Special exhibition of color prints. Introduction by E. F. Fenollosa. 1895.

Durand, A. B. Life, by J. Durand. New York, 1894.

—— Grolier Club. Catalogue of the engraved work of Durand. New York, 1895.

Edwards, S. Arlent. Catalogues issued by the New York art dealers W. Clausen, 1893; Wunderlich & Co., 1900?; D. B. Butler, 1909?; Knoedler, 1910?.

Edwin, David. Catalogue, by Mantle Fielding. Philadelphia, 1905.

Fevret de Saint Memin, C. B. J. The St. Memin collection of portraits, photographed from proof impressions. New York: E. Dexter, 1862.

Foster, John: the earliest American engraver and the first Boston printer, by S. A. Green. Boston, 1909.

French, E. D.: a memorial [by I. H. Brainerd. With catalogue]. New York, 1898.

The Grolier Club published a catalogue of its exhibition held in 1909.

Frost, A. B. Harper's Magazine, Oct. 1892.

Gallagher, Sears, Etchings of Boston, by L. A. Holman. Boston, 1920.

Galton, Ada. Roullier (Chicago) Print Collector's Bulletin.

Gleeson, C. K. Special exhibition catalogue. City Art Museum of St. Louis. 1910. — Roullier (Chicago) Booklet.

Haskell, Ernest. International Studio, 1911; Century, July 1919. — A. E. Gallatin's "Whistler's pastels" (1912) contains an article on Haskell.

Higgins, Eugene. Arts and Decoration, Feb. 1915.

Hopson, W. F., Book-plates of. By C. D. Allen. Berkeley, 1910.

Hornby, L. G. Art and Progress, 1914. — Roullier (Chicago) Booklet.

Hyde, Allyn, of Ellington, Conn., together with a review of "An early Connecticut engraver and his work." By James Terry. Hartford, 1906.

Hyde, Helen, and her work. By Bertha Jaques. Chicago.

Juengling, F. Biographical sketch and catalogue of his proofs . . . to be sold . . . 1890. Salmagundi Club, New York. — F. Juengling, by S. R. Koehler. Roxbury, Mass., 1890.

Kingsley, Elbridge. Catalogue [by M. E. Dwight]. Mt. Holyoke College, 1901.

Lafarge, John, Illustrator. Print Collector's Quarterly, 1915.

Lankes, J. J.: his wood-cut book-plates. By W. M. Stone. Gardenville, N. Y., 1922.

Lum, Bertha. International Studio, Dec. 1912.

MacLaughlan, D. S. Keppel & Co.'s Print Collector's Bulletin, 1908. — Roullier (Chicago) Booklet.

Mielatz, C. F. W. International Studio, Sept. 1911. — City Art Museum, St. Louis. Special exhibition, 1910.

Moran, Peter. Catalogue of the etched work of. Keppel & Co. New York, 1888.

Moran, Thomas. Catalogue of the complete etched work of T. and M. N. Moran, on exhibition at Klackner's, New York, 1889.

Nast, Thomas, by A. B. Paine. New York, 1904.

Newsam, Albert. Memoir by J. O. Pyatt. Philadelphia, 1868. — Lithographic portraits. [Catalogue.] By D. M. Stauffer. 1901.

Nordfeldt, B. J. Olsson. Roullier (Chicago) Print Collector's Bulletin.

Norman, John, Some notes concerning, by C. H. Hart. Cambridge, 1904. — Remarks on the Boston Magazine and . . . Norman. By S. A. Green, Cambridge, 1904.

Parrish, Stephen. Catalogue of etchings, 1877–83. Philadelphia [188–?].

Pelham, Peter, Notes concerning, by W. H. Whitmore. Cambridge, 1867.

Pennell, J. [Typewritten catalogue. New York Public Library. Print Room.] — Graphische Künste, Vienna, 1910.

Plank, G. W. Arts and Decoration, July 1913.

Platt, C. A. Descriptive catalogue. By R. A. Rice. 1889.

Revere, Paul, and his engraving, by W. L. Andrews. New York, 1901. — List of works of Revere, by C. S. Brigham, in Boston Transcript, Jan. 17, 1912.

Robinson, Boardman. Arts and Decoration, Aug. 1921.

Roth, E. D. Print Collector's Quarterly, Oct. 1911. — Arts and Decoration, 1916.

Ruzicka, R. Arts and Decoration, July 1922.

Sartain, John. Reminiscences of a very old man. New York, 1899.

Savage, Edward, and his unfinished copper-plate of "The Congress voting Independence." With a catalogue of his engraved work. By C. H. Hart. Boston, 1905.

Schneider, O. J. Roullier (Chicago) Print Collector's Bulletin.

Sensensey, G. Keppel & Co.'s Print Collector's Bulletin, 1908.

Sloan, John. Catalogue. In A. E. Gallatin's "Certain contemporaries," New York, 1916.

Smillie, J. D. Some works by Smillie. Century Association, New York, 1910. — City Art Museum, St. Louis. Memorial Collection. 1910.

Smith, J. André. Roullier (Chicago) booklet.

Smith, S. L., Bookplates by. By Gardner Teall. Kansas City, 1921.

Spenceley, J. W., his etchings and engravings in the form of bookplates. By J. M. Andreini. New York, 1910.

Washburn, C. International Studio, 1912. — Keppel & Co.'s Print Collector's Bulletin, 1908. — Roullier (Chicago) Booklet.

Webster, H. A. Art and Progress, Aug. 1911. — International Studio, 1911, 1912. — Gazette des Beaux-Arts, 1920. — Keppel & Co.'s Print Collector's Bulletin, 1908. — Roullier (Chicago) Booklet.

Weir, J. Alden. A catalogue of Weir's etchings was published by the Metropolitan Museum, New York, 1923.

Whistler, J. A. M. The etched work of Whistler, illustrated by reproductions in collotype of the different states of the plates. Compiled by E. G. Kennedy. Grolier Club, New York, 1910. 1 vol. text, 5 vols. plates.

—— A descriptive catalogue of the etchings and drypoints of Whistler. By Howard Mansfield. Caxton Club, Chicago, 1908.

White, C. H. Roullier (Chicago) Print Collector's Bulletin.

Wolf, Henry. Keppel & Co. Print Collector's Bulletin, 1908.

Yale, L. M. [Manuscript catalogue, 1906, in New York Public Library.]

Young, Mahonri. American Magazine of Art, April 1922.

INDEX

Abbey, E. A., 7, 170, 191, 192, 193, 232, 240, 257
Abbott, Jacob, "Rollo" books, 186
Abernethie, 53, 251
Abolition, 217, 219, 224. *See also* Slavery
Academy of Design. *See* National Academy
Academy of Fine Arts, 115
Academy of Natural Sciences, 66
Adams, John Wolcott, 204
Adams, Joseph Alexander, 74, 117, 118, 119
Adamson, P. S. ("Penrhyn Stanlaws"), 235
Adamson, Sydney, 282
Advertisements, chap. XV (especially 266–269, 283–284), 65, 147, 164, 233. *See also* Cards; Posters
Aid, George C., 36, 295
Aikman, Walter M., 8, 85, 138, 139
Aitken, Robert, 48, 52, 53, 58
Akin, James, 55, 160, 215, 251, 255
Alder, 277
"Aldine, or Art Journal of America," 123
Alexander, F., 155
Alexander, John W., 135, 195
Allard view of New York, 44
Allardice, Samuel, 66, 251
Allen, James, 46
Allingham, Mrs., 190
Allston, W., 81
Alsatian lithographers, 159, 165
Aluminum, in lithography, 270
American Antiquarian Society, 51
"American Art Review," 16, 20, 106, 291

American Art Union, 71, 94, 181
American Bank-Note Co., 77, 78
American Book-Plate Society, 264, 294
American Gallery of Art, 93
American Lithographic Co., 164
"American Magazine," 47
"American Monthly Review of Reviews," 293
American Press Association, 187
American Society of Painter Lithographers, 168
American Sunday School Union, 117, 162
American Tract Society, 120
"American Turf Register," 155
"American Universal Magazine," 58
American Water Color Society, 7, 97, 110, 279
"American Whig Review," 95
"Analectic Magazine," 61, 101
Anderson, Alexander, 295; engravings on copper, 58, 76, 254; on wood, 114–5, 116, 269; caricatures, 212; portrait of, 184
Anderson, Anna, 115
Anderson, I., 68
Andreini, J. M., 298
Andrew, John, 119, 122, 258
Andrews, Joseph, 70, 72, 75, 81, 295; Andrews & Co., 115–6
Andrews, Wm. Loring, 85, 295, 298; frequently cited in chap. III
Animal subjects, 11, 33–35, 133, 154, 162, 191, 193–4
Annin, Wm. B., 120, 122; Annin & Smith, 104, 252; Annin & Smith Senefelder Lithographic Co., 104, 160

Annuals ("Keepsakes," "Tokens," etc.), 80, 81, 92, 93, 94, 180
Anthony, A. V. S., 117, 122, 228, 296
Apollo Association, 71, 79, 94
Appleton, Thomas G., 4
"Appleton's Journal," 189
Aquatint, chapter VI; also 13, 25, 40, 48, 214
Archer, John, 67
Architectural League, N. Y., 265
Architectural subjects in etching, 15, 27, 30, 37, 38, 169, 175; lithography, 169, 175. *See also* City views
Arizona views, 28
Armington, Frank M. and Caroline H., 37
Armistead, Robert, 35
Arms, John Taylor, 27, 30, 108
Arnold, Vic., 271
"Art, L'," 20, 134
"Art Amateur," 168
Art Club, N. Y., 109
"Art Journal," 123
Art Students' League, N. Y., 24, 280
Art Union. *See* Apollo Association; American Art Union; Western Art Union
Art Union of Philadelphia, 71, 94
Arthurs, Stanley M., 202
Artist-authors, 184–5, 194, 198
Aston Collection, 137
"Atlas," 187
Attwood, Francis G., 8, 237, 295
Atwater, 163
Atwood, John M., 55
Audubon, J. J., 104, 159, 166
Avery, Samuel Putnam, 18, 120, 258
Avery Architectural Library, 263, 264
Avignon. *See* D'Avignon
Aylward, W. J., 202

Babb, George Fletcher, 263
Bacher, Otto H., 4, 15, 108, 109, 195, 295
Bachmann, 156–7

Bacon, Peggy, 34
Baer, H. M., 149
Bailey, Vernon Howe, 173, 175, 203
Baker, John, 2
Baker, Joseph E., 8, 223, 225, 271, 272
Balch, Vistus, 81, 160
Ball, W., 155
Ballads (Sheet), 114
Ballou, Maturin M., 186
Baltimore views, 103, 104
Bamburgh, W. C., 260
Bank-note engraving, 3, 44, 50, 61, 65, 76–8, 82, 84, 133, 291; vignettes, 116, 183
Banning, K., 294
Barber, Alice (Mrs. Stephens), 190
Barber, John-Warner, 51, 117
Barker, William, 46
Barnard & Dick, 66
Barnes, Will R., 272
Barnum, Phineas T., 186
Barralet, John James, 58, 66, 67, 76, 254
Barritt (Lossing & Barritt), 117
Barritt, Leon, 241
Barry, August, 21
Barry, Charles A., 185
Bartholomew, Charles L. ("Bart"), 241, 244
Bartlett, Wm. Henry, 82
Barton, Emery H., 8
Bassett, W. H., 65
Basswood, in wood engraving, 146, 269, 270
Bauer, W. C., 9
Baulch, A V., 82
Baumann, Gustave, 141, 149
Bauncou, J, 157
Beal, W. Goodrich, 9
Beard, Dan C., 185, 238
Beard, Frank (Thomas Francis), 189, 222, 235, 239
Beard, James Carter, 193
Beardsley, Aubrey, influence of, 275, 277

Beatty, John W., 10
Becker, Joseph, 186
Beckwith, H. E., 84
Beckwith, J. Carroll, 17, 168, 287
Belgian artists in the U. S., 39, 159
Bell, E. Hamilton, 261
Bellew, Frank Henry Temple ("The Triangle"), 3, 184, 186, 224, 228, 230, 232, 238
Bellew, F. P. W. ("Chip"), 238, 293
Bellows, Albert F., 70
Bellows, George, 173, 174, 177
Benecke, Th., 157
Bennett, Wm. James, 74, 102, 103
Bensell, E. B., 189
Benson, Frank W., 35, 296
Berg, Charles I., 263
Berghaus, Albert, 186
Berlett, 122
Bernstein, Therese, 32
Bernström, Victor, 131, 136, 140
Berryman, Clifford K., 241
Best, E. S., 72
Bewick, Thomas, influence of, 112, 114, 116
Bible illustrations, 49, 59, 114, 117, 118, 119, 181–2
"Biblio," 294
Bibliophile Society, Boston, 18, 85
Bicknell, Albion Harris, 17
Bicknell, W. H. W., 18, 31, 85, 261–2
Biddle, George, 145
Bien, Julius, 162, 166
Bierstadt, Albert, 69, 70, 82
Billheads, 47, 269
Billings, A., 251
Billings, Hammatt, 116, 182
Billings, Joseph, 50
Bingham, G. C., 94
Binner, 285
Biorn, Emil, 277
Birch, Reginald Bathurst, 195, 293
Birch, Thomas, 67
Birch, William, 2, 63, 68
Bird, Charles, 97

Bird, E. B., 35, 133, 149, 154, 156, 160, 262, 276, 294
Bisbee, 238
Bisbee, John, 155
Bisbing, Henry, 189
Bishop, Joseph B., 220–1, 293
Bishop, Wm. H., 185
Bishop Collection: Jade, 166
Bispham, H., 180
"Black Cat," 276
Blada, V. (A. Volck), 226
Blaine, James G., in caricature, 236
Blake, William, influence of, 145, 146, 174
"Blanket sheets," 121, 188
Blashfield, Edwin Howland, 196, 263, 280, 287
Bloodgood, Robert F., 287
Blum, Robert F., 16, 195, 276, 293, 296
Blumenschein, Ernest L., 202
Blyth, Benjamin, 88
Bobbett, Albert, 118, 119, 120; Bobbett & Edmonds, Bobbett & Hooper, 120
Bogardus, James, 76
Bogert, J. A., 120, 122, 125
Bohemian etchers in the U. S. See: Preissig, Ruzicka, Vondrous
Bolton, Charles Knowles, 273
Bona del., 55
Bonds, Government, 84
Bonner, Capt. John, 46
Bonsall, Miss, 294
Book bindings, 197, 203, 286. See also Covers
Bookhout, E., 118
Book-plates, chap. XIV; 47, 84–5, 147, 293–4; periodicals, 264, 294
Booth, Edwin, portraits, 189
Booth, Franklin, 202, 267
Booth, T. D., 71
Borein, Edward, 28, 176
Borg, Carl Oscar, 144
Borglum, Gutzon, 142

Boston views and plans, in etching, 5, 26, 297; copper engraving, 43, 46, 47, 50, 51, 52, 85; aquatint, 100, 103; mezzotint, 88; wood-engraving, 116

Boston Etching Club, 8, 291

"Boston Evening Post," 208

"Boston Gazette," 208

"Boston Magazine," 58

Boston Massacre, 50-1, 209

Boston Museum of Fine Arts, 4, 8, 14, 137, 264, 291, 292, 295, 296

"Boston News Letter," 208

Boston Port Bill, 207, 293

Bourne, publisher, 66

Boutet de Monvel, 274

Bouvé, E. W., 165

Bouvier, 156

Bowen, Abel, 62, 116, 269, 296

Bowen, J. T., 161

Bower, J., 101

Bowes, Joseph, 48, 58

Bowlend, George B., 230

Boyd, 120

Boyd, John, 62, 63

Bradish, A., 94

Bradley, Will H., 197, 203, 265, 293; posters, 272, 274, 276, 277-8, 280, 281

Bradley, William Aspenwall, 138-9

Brady, daguerreotypes, 159

Bragdon, Claude Fayette, 197, 260, 263, 273, 277, 294

Brainerd (D'Avignon & Brainerd), 159

Brennan, Alfred, 10, 191, 194, 195, 286, 296

Breuer, H. J., 203

Bridges, Fidelia, 288

Bridgman, L. J., 190

Bridport, Hugh, 63, 157

Briggs, Clare A., 244

British books in American editions, 116

British engravers in the U. S., 58, 63; wood-engravers, 119, 122-3, 124

British influence in book-plates, 252; in illustration, 3, 66; line engraving, 45, 49, 66; mezzotint, 93; wood-engraving, 118, 119

British mezzotint portraits of Americans, 90

Britton, James, 146, 270, 280

Brodsky, Horace, 141, 145, 146

Bromley & Co., 225

Brooklyn Scratchers' Club, 8

Brooklyn Society of Etchers, 24, 291

"Brother Jonathan: Great Pictorial Battle Sheet" (1847), 188

Brougham, John, 229

Broughton, Charles, 195, 238

Brown, Dr. Alfred Jerome, 261

Brown, Bolton, 173-4

Brown, C. J., 186

Brown, E., 180

Brown, Frank Chouteau, 263, 294

Brown, George Loring, 3, 6, 79, 81, 116

Brown, Harold Haven, 143

Brown, Howell C., 262, 276, 292

Brown, John George, 168

Brown, M. E. D., 158

Browne, George Elmer, 174

Brueckner, 164

Bruls, Michelson Godhart de, 46, 251

Brunner, Arnold W., 263

Brunton, Richard, 50, 251, 296

Bry, T. de, 43

Bryan, Wm. Jennings, in caricatures, 236

"Bubble, The," 229

Buccaneers, 198

Buchanan, James, in caricature, 218, 219, 220

Buechner, G. J., 136

Buell, Abel, 46, 50

Buffalo views, 103

Bufford, J. H., 156, 159, 271

Bull, M., 251, 254

Bull-fights, 38

Bunker Hill, 1, 51, 52

"Bunny" (C. E. Schultze), 248
Burgess, Gelett, 197
Burgis, William, 46, 88
Burnet, John, 100
Burney, 66
Burnisher, in aquatint, 108
Burns, Michael J., 17, 193
Burr, George Elbert, 28, 40, 296
Burt, Charles, 64, 71, 72, 73, 75, 79, 85, 296
Burton, C., 66, 80
Burton, C. W., 156
Burton & Edmunds, 77
Bush, Charles G., 189, 240, 241, 244, 247
Bush-Brown, Mrs. H. K., 14
Butler & Long, 102-3
Buttons, engraved, 44, 75
Buttre, John Chester, 82, 84, 95
Buxton, 45, 56

Cadart, A., 5
Calhoun Co., 270
Calico printing, 44, 113
California Book-Plate Society, 264, 294
California Society of Etchers, 24, 291
California State Library, 264
"Californian, The," 185, 203
Californian book-plates, 265; caricaturists, 235; etchers, 8, 28; illustrators, 184, 203; lithographs, 167; magazines, 184; posters, 285
Caliga, Isaac Henry, 287
Callender, Joseph, 48, 58, 251, 252, 253, 269
Calyo, Nicolino, 103
Canadian subjects, 195
Canot, 44
Canova, 157
Cards, 64, 192; business, 1, 47, 48, 65, 114, 267, 268, 269, 287; holiday, 147, 164, 286-289; invitation, 84, 289-290; playing (wrappers), 114; visiting, 64. See also Tickets

Caricature, Chap. XII, XIII; etchings, 3; mezzotints, 89-90; aquatints, 102; wood-engravings, 113, 182; lithographs, 162-3, 168, 170, 178; in advertisements, 268; in political posters, 281; British and other foreign, Revolutionary War, 206, 207, 293; bibliography, 293
"Carl" (G. W. Carleton), 228
Carleton, Clifford, 202
Carmiencke, Hermann, 4
Carpenter (Childs & Carpenter), 269
"Carpet Bag, The," 229
Carqueville, Birch Will, 276
Carr, Gene, 250
Carter, Robert ("Frank Leslie"). See Leslie
Carter, Robert, cartoonist, 247
Carter, Andrews & Co., 115-6
Cartoons. See Caricature
"Cartoons," 242, 293
"Cartoons Magazine," 293
Cary, W. M., 189
Casilear, John W., 69, 79; Casilear, Durand, Barton & Edmunds, 77
Cassatt, Mary, 13, 14, 107, 170
Cassel, John H., 178, 241, 247
Castaigne, André, 196
Catherwood, F., 104
Catlin, George, 154
Cauldwell, Leslie, 110
Caxton Club, Chicago, 4, 264, 294, 298
Cemeteries, books on, 81
Centennial Exhibition, Philadelphia, 6
"Century Magazine," illustrations, 132, 144-5, 191; cover, 284; posters, 274, 275, 279
Certificates, 47, 64, 84, 100, 167
Cesare, O. E., 178, 246
Chambers, Jay, 262. See also Triptych
Chambers, Robert W., 275, 277, 279
Champlain's "Voyages," 43
Champney, J. Wells, 17
Chandler, G. Walter, 38, 39, 296

"Chap Book," 197, 276, 278
Chapin, John R., 180, 183, 184, 186
Chapman, Carlton T., 10
Chapman, F. T., 147, 286
Chapman, John Gadsby, 3, 4, 81, 103, 118, 181-2
Chappel, Alonzo, 83, 180
Charles, William, 2, 3, 102, 211, 213-4
Chase, William M., 16, 109, 135
Cheney, John, 76, 81, 160, 296
Cheney, Seth Wells, 74, 296
Cheney, Sheldon, 262
Cheret, Jules, 272
Chiaroscuro wood engraving, 120, 148, 270
"Chic," 235
Chicago views, 26-27, 28, 29, 177
Chicago Society of Etchers, 24, 38, 291
Child subjects, 14, 32, 33, 34, 40, 190, 281
"Child's Paper," 184
Children, books for, 120, 186, 235
Childs, Benjamin F., 116, 119, 120
Childs, Cephas G., engravings, 66, 68, 252; lithographs, 153, 154, 158, 160, 215; caricatured, 215; Childs & Carpenter, 269; Childs & Inman, 154, 156, 157; Childs & Lehman, 164; Pendleton, Kearny & Childs, 158, 164
"Chip." See Bellew
Chippendale style, 47, 252
Christmas cards. See Cards (Holiday)
Christy, Howard Chandler, 275
Chromo-lithography, chromos. See Color printing
Church, F. E., 69, 70, 73
Church, Frederick S., 10, 133, 134, 232, 240, 293
Ciconi, I., 109
Cigar box labels, 164
Cigarette cards, 164, 269
Cincinnati views, 27
Cincinnati Etchers' Club, 8

City views, in etching, 12, 25, 26-27, 35, 36, 39; engraving, 67, 68; aquatint, 103, 104, 105; lithography, 161, 174. See also cities: Baltimore, Boston, Buffalo, Chicago, Cincinnati, Florence, Gloucester, London, Nantucket, New Orleans, New York, Paris, Philadelphia, Pittsburgh, Provincetown, Troy, Venice
Civil War, in etching, 5, 6, 82; wood-engraving, 121, 188; lithography, 82, 161, 163, 167, 168; illustration, 183, 185, 198; caricature, 216, 218-26, 227, 229-31, 293
Clark, A. (Rawdon, Clark & Co.), 66
Clark, Roland, 35
Clark, Scotson, 272
Clark, Walter Appleton, 202, 296
Clark, William, 115, 117
Clarke, Thomas, 58, 59
Claudius, 136
Clay, Edward W., 215, 217, 219
Clay, John Cecil, 203, 285
Claypoole, James, Jr., 47, 48, 84, 208
Cleland, T. M., 203
Clements, Gabrielle D., 14, 17
Cleveland, Grover, portrait, 18; caricature, 236
Clinedinst, B. West, 195, 293
Clonney, J. G., 71, 154-5
Closson, W. B., 122, 133, 139
Club of Odd Volumes, Boston, 259, 263, 264, 294
Clubs, book-plates of, 260
Clute, Beulah, M., 294
Cobb, Gershom, 255
Cochin, C. N., 54
Coffin, Frederick M., 183, 184
Cogswell, Charlotte B., 132
Cole (18th century), 88
Cole, Miss, 14
Cole, J. Foxcroft, 1, 5, 11, 168
Cole, Thomas, 68-9, 73, 81, 155
Cole, Timothy, 124, 126, 128, 129, 134-5, 136, 138, 296

Coleman, Charles Caryll, 287
Coll, J. C., 204
College Book-plates, 294
Colleges, prints of, 30, 46–7
Collyer, Vincent, 160
Colman, Samuel, 12, 18, 287
Colon, J. H., 156
Colonial history, 18, 90, 199, 206, 207.
  See also Revolutionary War
Colonial Society of America, 18
Color printing, in etching, 13, 25, 40;
  mezzotint, 89, 96, 97; aquatint, 105,
  106, 107, 110; monotypes, 108, 109,
  110; wood-engraving, 139, 140, 141,
  148–50, 270; lithographs, 156, 162,
  164–6, 169, 172, 176, 233; illustra-
  tion, 181; holiday cards, 288;
  posters, 270, 278, 279, 284
Color (hand-coloring), in engraving on
  copper, 47, 50, 51, 63; aquatint, 101,
  102, 103, 104; lithography, 156
Colorado views, 40
Columbia Bank Note Co., 76
"Columbian Magazine," 58, 80
Colwell, Elizabeth, 150
Comic papers, chap. XIII; 121, 162–
  163, 164
"Comic strips," 216, 243, 248–9
Comic supplements (Sunday), 247, 248
Comins, Lizbeth B., 288
Commercial art, 147, 153; chap. XV.
  See also Advertisements; Posters
Commercialization, in engraving on
  steel, 82–3, 84, 85, 93, 95; etching,
  19, 22; lithography, 166, 171; wood-
  engraving, 120; holiday cards, 286
Comstock, Anna Botsford, 132
Concord, Engagement at, 51
Cone, Joseph, 63, 84
Confederate caricatures, 225–6; pub-
  lications, 186–7, 230
Congdon, Thomas Raphael and Ade-
  laide Vose, 37
Conny, or Cony, John, 44, 45
Cooke, R., 155

Cooper, F. G., 267, 282
Cooper Institute, 132
Copeland, Charles, 195
Copley, John Singleton, 88
Corbould, Henry, 66
Cordoba, Mathilde de, 33–4, 40
Cornwallis, Surrender of, 52
Corot, J. B. C., 133, 135
Corwin, Charles A., 15
Cotton, John, book-plate of, 251
Coultous, Henry C., 187
Counterfeiting, 50, 76, 208
Country life in prints, 70, 71, 193, 295
Covers, book, 165, 286; catalogue,
  280, 285; magazine, 169, 284, 285
Covey, Arthur, 39
Cowboys, 194, 235
Cox (Richardson & Cox), 120
Cox, Kenyon, 195, 196, 276
Cox, Palmer, 185, 237, 275
Coxe, John Redman, 2
Coxe, Reginald Cleveland, 17, 168
Cozzens, Frederick Schiller, 193, 230
Craig, W. M., 66
Cranston, 122
Crawford, Will, 234
Crawley, John, Jr., 155
Crehen, Charles G., 159
Creifeld, 153
Cremona, T., 109
Crests, engravers of, 44
Criblee manner, 114
Croome, William, 78, 116, 180, 182
Cropsey, J. F., 167
Cruikshank, George, imitated, 3, 214,
  215
Cruset, S., 279
Curran, Charles Courtney, 17
Currier, Nathaniel, 163, 218
Currier & Ives, 161, 163, 216, 221,
  223, 240, 293
Curtis, Jessie (Mrs. Shepherd), 189
Cusachs, Philip G., 187
Cushing, Otho, 238
Cyclopedia illustrations, 2, 59

Daguerreotypes, mezzotints after, 95; lithographs, 159
"Daily Graphic," 187, 231, 233
Daingerfield, Elliott, 17
Dakin, J. H., 66
Dallas, Jacob A., 180, 183, 184, 186, 228
Dalrymple, L., 234
Dancers, in etching, 34
Danforth, Mosely Isaac, 66, 74, 75, 81; Danforth, Perkins & Co., 77
Daniels, John H., 6, 51
Darley, Felix Octavius Carr, 72, 78, 82, 119, 162, 180, 181, 182–3, 184, 189
Darling, J. N. ("Ding"), 244
Daubigny, C., 131
Daumier, Honoré, influence, 178, 245
Davenport, Homer C., 246, 247
Davenport, William H., 184
Davidson, Julian O., 193
Davies, Arthur B., 107–8, 144, 175–6
D'Avignon, F., 158–9; D'Avignon & Brainerd, 159
Davis, Alexander Jackson, 80, 154
Davis, Georgiana A., 186
Davis, Jefferson, portrait, 157; caricatures, 215, 222, 224
Davis, John Parker, 122, 132, 134; Davis & Spier, 124
Davis, Theodore R., 188
Dawkins, Henry, 47, 48, 50, 113, 208, 251, 253, 269
Day, Benjamin, 222, 229; Ben Day process, 187
Day, Francis, 196, 276
Dearborn, Nathaniel, 48, 53, 116, 251
Declaration of Independence. See Independence
De Hass. See Haas
Dehn, Adoph, 177–8
Delaplaine, Joseph, 61, 74
Delessard, A., 167
"Delineator, The," 139
Del'Orme, Edward H., 131

De Maine, Harry, 149
DeMar, John, 244
Deming, E. W., 196
Denman, Herbert, 195
Denslow, Wm. Wallace, 272, 277
Derby, George H. ("John Phoenix"), 185
Derby Gallery, 5
Detwiller, F. K., 26, 108
Devereux, George Thomas, 116, 186
Deville, Henry, 27
Dewing, Francis, 44, 46, 113, 251
Dewing, Thomas Wilmer, 287
De Yonghe, 277
Diaz, 133
Dick, Archibald L. (Barnard & Dick), 66
Dickens, Charles, 3, 82, 180, 182, 183, 189
Diederich, Hunt, 145, 146
Dielman, Frederick, 21, 195, 287, 288
Dies, die-plates, 65, 77
Dillaye, Blanche, 14
Ding (J. N. Darling), 244
Diplomas, 84, 114
Dixon, L. Maynard, 203, 276, 285
Dodson, Richard W., 74, 75
Doepler, Carl Emil, 104, 184, 186
Dog collars, engraved, 44, 65
Domenichino, 76
Donahey, J. H., 244
Doney, Thomas, 94, 95
Donoho, Ruger, 168
Doolittle, Amos, 48, 49, 51, 52, 53, 58, 59; caricature, 214; book-plates, 251, 253, 255
Door-plates, engraved, 44, 65
Doré, Gustave, 136
Dorsey, Dr. John Syng, 252
Dougherty, Paul, 31
Doughty, Thomas, 81, 153, 154
Dow, Arthur Wesley, 141, 148, 284, 296
Drake, Alexander W., 134, 191
Drake, William Henry, 195, 293

Draper, John (Murray, Draper, Fairman & Co.), 77
Drayton, J., 102
Dry-point, 12, 14, 25, 29, 35, 107, 131
DuCreux, 43
Duncan, B., 225
Duncan, W. J., 176, 177, 204
Dunes, etchings of, 29, 31
Dunlap, William, 1, 3, 4, 57, 65, 91, 96, 155, 291
Duplessis, J. S., 54, 75
Duponchel, F., 157
Duran, Carolus, 133
Durand, Asher Brown, 72, 296; engravings, 48, 68, 69, 73, 74, 75, 76, 79, 81, 83, 85; mezzotint, 91; bank-notes, 78; portrait of, 55, 75
Durand, Cyrus, 76
Durand & Co., 77, 83; Durand, Perkins & Co., 77
Durkin, John, 187
Du Simitière, P. E., 53–4
Duval, P. S., 156, 157, 159, 165; P. S. Duval & Co., 164; P. S. Duval's Lithographic & Color Printing Establishment, 165–6; Lehman & Duval, 158, 164
Duveneck, Frank, 15, 27, 109, 128
Dwiggins, W. A., 143, 203, 204

Earle, Ralph, 51
Easter cards. See Cards (Holiday)
Eastman, H., 184
Eaton, Charles H., 17
Eaton, Charles Warren, 109, 110
Eaton, Hugh M., 149, 261, 262, 294
Eaton, Margaret, 294
Eaton, Wyatt, 6
Eby, Kerr, 33, 173, 204
Eckstein, John, 63
Eddy, Henry B., 277
Edmonds, Charles, 120
Edmonds, Francis W., 70, 71
Edmunds, 77
Edwards, E. B., 203

Edwards, George Wharton, 185, 197, 259, 260, 262, 275, 279, 282, 285
Edwards, Harry C., 195
Edwards, S. Arlent, 96–7, 296
Edwards, Thomas, 155
Edwin, David, 57, 61, 62, 296
Egbert, 186
Eggleston, Allegra, 190
Ehninger, John Whetton, 162, 181
Ehrhardt, I., 234
Electrotypes of wood-engraving and half-tone compared, 138
Elliot, 186
Ellis, George B., 81
Elten. See Kruseman
Emerson, R. R., 276
Emmes, Thomas, 45
Emmet, Rosina, 287
Emmet, Thomas Addis, 83
Emporium of Arts and Sciences, 2, 61
Encyclopedia illustrations, 2, 59
End papers, 197, 203
Endicott, 164; Endicott & Co., 155; Endicott & Swett, 155, 164
Engler, Arthur, 261
English. See British
Engravers (British). See British
Engraving (Line: copper and steel), 291; chap. III, IV; in advertisements, 268–9; book-plates, 251–5, 258, 259, 260, 261–2; caricature, 206–11, 214; illustration, 113, 179, 180; combined with mezzotint, 93; imitated in wood-engraving, 115, 118–9, 128. See also Bank-note, British engravers, Etching, Mixed manner, Stipple
Engraving on wood. See Woodengraving
Envelopes, Civil War caricatures on, 221–2
Etching, chap. I, II; basis for engraving, 2, 3, 6, 73, 75, 83; with mezzotint, 97; soft-ground, 2, 13, 25, 28, 32, 39, 40, 107; reproductive etching,

2, 3, 10, 11, 12, 19–22, 106; book-plates, 261–2, 291–2; illustrations, 291; caricatures, 213–5, 217; reproduced in wood-engraving, 131; double needle, 13; classes, 8; limitation of editions, 18
Ettlinger (Schumacher & Ettlinger), 164
European War. *See* War
Evans, Joe, 263
Evans, John W., 131
"Evening Post," 212
"Evening Telegram," 241
"Every Saturday," 189
Exilious, John, 68
Ex-libris. *See* Book-plates
Eytinge, Sol, Jr., 186, 189, 240

Faber, Hermann, 8, 18
Fabronius, D., 159
Fagan, James, 10, 18, 21
Fairchild, 117
Fairman, Gideon, 66, 67, 74, 76; Murray, Draper, Fairman & Co., 77
Fairmount Park Art Association, 7
"Fakes." *See* Frauds
Falconer, J. M., 1, 5
Falls, Charles Buckles, 147, 285
"Family Magazine," 179
Fanning, J. B., 63
Farmer in prints, 70–1
Farny, Henry F., 8, 191, 195, 271
Farrand, Charles D., 280
Farrer, Henry, 5–6, 7, 10, 13
Fasel, George W., 156
Fawcett, W. W., 282
"Federal Republican," 212
Fenderich, Charles, 158
Fenn, Harry, 188
Fenner & Sears, 66
Ferris, Stephen J., 5, 6, 8, 13, 19–20
Fevret de St. Memin. *See* St. Memin
Field, Edward Loyal, 17
Field, Robert, 58
"Fifth Avenue Journal," 232

Figure subjects, in etching, 10, 11, 14, 25, 31–5; engraving, 64, 70–3; lithography, 176
Fillmore, Martin, portrait of, 218
Filmer, 122
Fincham, H. W., 294
Fincken, James H., 258, 261
Firemen, 162, 163
Fisher, Bud, 293
Fisher, Harrison, 200, 293
Fisher, Wm. Edgar, 258, 259, 262, 294
Fiske, W., 229, 230
Fitzpatrick, D. R., 247
Flagg, James Montgomery, 200–1, 235, 238
Flohri, 235
Florence views, 38
Flowers, in prints, 12, 97; 105, 286
Fogarty, Thomas, 202
Folwell, Samuel, 101
Foos (Richardson & Foos), 270
Foote, Mary Hallock, 185, 189, 190, 293
Forbes, Edwin, 1, 5, 6, 189
Forbes Co., 166, 271, 272
"Foreign Semi-Monthly," 92
Forester, Frank (H. W. Herbert), 182, 185
Forrest, Ion B., 62
Forster (Kimmel & Forster), 161
Fortuny, 20; influence, 194, 195
Fossette, H., 66
Foster, John, 112–3, 296
Foul biting, 108
Fox, Fontaine, 250, 293
Fox, Gilbert, 2
Framing prints, 70–1, 85, 94, 183
Francis, J. G., 232, 293
"Frank Leslie's." *See* Leslie
Franklin, Benjamin, as a caricaturist, 113, 208–9; portraits of, 18, 53, 54, 55, 56, 72, 75, 89, 295
Franklin Institute, 152
Franks, Sir Augustus Wollaston, 265, 294

Franquinet, W., 4
Fraser, C., 103
Fraser, W. Lewis, 192
Frauds, 54–5, 113, 188, 252
Fredericks, Alfred, 191, 195, 287
"Free Lance," 238
Freer, Frederick W., 10, 287
Fremont, John C., 159, 218, 219, 220
French, Edwin Davis, 85, 258, 261, 264, 296
French, Frank, 131, 136, 140, 185
French influence in etching, 5; wood-engraving, 130; lithography, 157, 160; posters, 272, 273, 274
French lithographers in the U. S., 157, 159, 160; plate printer, 1
Frenzeny, Paul, 189
Fritsch, F. J., 156
Fritz, Mildred, 149
Frizzell, S. S., 167
Frontiersmen, 194
Frost, Arthur Burdett, 193, 232, 239, 240, 293, 297
Frost, Marguerite Scribner, 294
Fuchs, Emil, 34
Fuller, George, 122, 133
"Fun," 231
Furnass, J. M., 251

Gallagher, Sears, 27–8, 31, 174, 297
Galland, John, 58
Gallaudet, Edward, 81, 100
Gallaudet, Elisha, 251, 254
Galton, Ada, 297
Gardiner, Elizabeth, 149
Gardner, Miles C., 276–7
Garfield, James A., in caricature, 234, 235
Garneray, 104
Garrett, Edmund Henry, 8, 195, 259, 260, 261, 277, 294
Gaugengigl, Ignaz Marcel, 10, 287
Gaul, Gilbert, 194
Gavit, John E., 103, 161
Gay, Henry B., 4

Genre art, 57, 70, 71
German lithographers in the U. S., 157; wood-engravers, 124, 131, 133; illustrators, 186
Gerrymander, 211
Getchell, Edith Loring Pierce, 14
Gibbs, George, 185, 263
Gibson, Charles Dana, 199–200, 238, 293
Gibson, Wm. Hamilton, 133, 185, 194, 293
Gifford, R. Swain, 7, 12, 69, 134, 189
Gilbert (wood-engraver), 117
Gilbert, C. Allan, 202
Gilbert, Sir John, 120, 191
Gildemeister, Charles, 156
Gillam, Alfred, 237
Gillam, F. Victor, 235, 236
Gillam, T. Bernard, 233, 236
Gillray, James, influence, 213, 214
Gimber, Stephen H., 66, 95, 103, 160
Gimbrede, Joseph Napoleon, 62–3
Gimbrede, Thomas, 61, 62, 63
Girardet, P., 104
Girsch, F., 84
Glackens, L. M., 234
Glackens, William J., 32, 177, 203
Glasgow, D., 161
Glass, J. W., 73
Glass, etching on, 2
"Gleason's Pictorial," 186
Gleeson, Charles K., 39, 297
Glennie, J., 68
Glenny, Alice R., 277
Gloucester views, 29
Goater, John H., 186, 220, 229
Gobrecht, Christian, 62
Godey's Lady's Book, 80, 165, 179–80
Godwin, Abraham, 48, 59, 251
Goldthwaite, Anne, 34
Goodhue, Bertram Grosvenor, 203, 279
Goodman, Charles (Goodman & Piggot), 62
Goodwin, James S., 238
Gottschalk, Otto H. von, 187

Gould, J. J., Jr., 276
Gould, R. E., Co., 282
Graetz, F., 232, 233
Graham, Charles, 195, 269
Graham, George, 63, 91
"Graham's Magazine," 74, 80, 92
Grant, C. R., 21
Grant, Gordon H., 203, 234
Grant, Ulysses S., 79, 163, 224
"Graphic, Daily," 187, 231, 233
"Graphic Arts, The," 285
Graphotype, 224
Grassby, Percy A., 147
Grasset, Eugene, 274
Greatorex, Eliza, 14
Greeley, Horace, in caricature, 219, 220, 225, 231
Green, Elizabeth Shippen, 190
Green, Valentine, 90
Greenough, Walter C., 286
Greenwood, John, 89
Gregory, Frank M., 10, 195
Gregson, Herbert, 294
Grennell, 217
Gribayédoff, Valerian, 187, 241, 293
Griffin, Syd B., 234
Grimm, Constantin de, 241
Grolier Club, 4, 264, 273, 292, 293, 294, 295, 296, 298
Gross, J., 62
Grozelier, Leopold, 159
Gruger, Frederick R., 202
"Grundy, Mrs.," 229
Gude, O. J., Co., 282
Guerin, Jules, 202
Gunn, Archie, 276, 283
Gunn, Thomas Butler, 185, 228
Guy, Seymour J., 21, 167

Haas, M. F. H. de, 10, 79
Haid, J. C., 54
Haider, M., 131
Haines, D., 268
Haines, W., 62
Hale, Walter, 28

Half-tone process, 114, 138-9, 179, 187, 198
Hall, F. G., 31, 294
Hall, Henry Bryan, 18, 55, 82, 83, 161
Hall, John J., 115-6
Halliwell, 122
Hallock, Mary A. See Foote
Hallowell, Miss, 294
Halpin, Frederick, 55, 64
Hals, Frans, 20, 88, 96, 134, 135
Halsey, R. T. Haines, 206, 293
Hambidge, Jay, 202
Hamerton, Philip Gilbert, 9, 292
Hamilton, Grant E., 231, 235, 236, 237, 241
Hamilton, Hamilton, 21
Hamilton, James, 82, 180
Hamlin, William, 48, 61, 65, 89-90, 100, 251, 269
Hapgood, T. B., 294
Harding, Charlotte, 190
Harding, Chester, 75, 154
Harding, Nelson, 246
Hardtmuth, 157
Harley, 122
Harlow, Louis K., 17
Harmer, Alexander F., 185, 203
Harper, Robert G., 210
Harper, Wm. St. John, 17, 197, 287
Harper Brothers, Bible, 117, 118, 119, 181-2; "Harper's Bazar," 276, 285; "Harper's Magazine," 26, 133, 184; covers and posters, 266, 274, 278, 279, 284; "Harper's Weekly," 126, 186, 233, 238; Nast caricatures, 222, 230, 231, 232
Harral, Alfred, 122
Harris, George, 164
Harris, I., 46
Harris, S., 61, 251, 254
Harrison, William, Jr., 58
Harshe, Robert B., 28
Hart, George ("Pop"), 31
Hart, James M., 69

Hart, Thomas, 90
Hart, William, 69, 119
Hartgers view of New York City, 52
Hartman, C. Bertram, 144
"Harvey's Weekly," 246
Haskell, Ernest, 285, 297; etchings, 30–1; lithographs, 163, 174–5, 176; monotypes, 110; posters, 276, 277, 283
Hassam, Childe, 27, 30, 143, 147–8, 174, 196
Hatch, George W., 77; Hatch & Smillie, 66
Havell, Robert, 104
Hawthorne, Nathaniel, portraits, 132, 295
Hayden, Sir Francis Seymour, 9, 15
Hayes, 120, 122
Hayward, George, 164
Hazenplug, Frank, 197
Healy, George P. A., 75
Heath, Charles, 77
Heath, J., 62
Heil, Charles E., 35
Heine, W., 104, 162
Heinemann, Ernst, 134
Heintzelman, Arthur W., 33
Held, John, Jr., 146
Helmick, H., 229
Hennessy, William J., 189
Heppenheimer & Maurer, 164
Herbert, Henry Wm. ("Frank Forester"), 182, 185
Herford, Oliver, 201, 238, 275, 293
Herrick, Henry W., 118, 119, 120, 185
Herring, James, 62, 64, 74, 83
Herter, Albert, 197
Hewitt, 68
Hicks, Thomas, 95
Higgins, Eugene, 32, 110–11, 297
Hill, J., 189
Hill, John, 102–3
Hill, John Henry, 11, 97, 102, 106
Hill, John William, 11, 102, 103, 104, 155

Hill, Samuel, 58, 67, 251
Hiller, Joseph, Jr., 1
Himely, Sigmund, 104
Hingston, 269
Hinsdale, 184
Hinshelwood, R., 69–70, 71, 72, 79, 82, 84
Historical prints. See U. S. History
Hitchcock, DeWitt C., 120, 184, 186, 228
Hitchcock, J. Ripley W., repeatedly quoted, chap. I
Hitchcock, Lucius W., 203
Hoas, P., 155
Hoen, A., & Co., 272
Hoffmann, G. A., 31
Hoffy, A., 156
Hogan, Thomas, 189
Holland, views, 39, 106, 170
Hollyer, S., 18, 82, 262
Holme, F., 150
Homer, Winslow, 10, 20, 167, 168, 188, 189, 263
Homer-Lee Bank Note Co., 77
Hoogland, W., 74, 155
Hooper, Annie, 294
Hooper, Edward (Bobbett & Hooper), 120
Hooper, Will P., 274–5
Hopkins, Edna Boies, 150
Hopkins, George E., 15
Hopkins, Livingston, 185, 232
Hopper, Edward, 32
Hoppin, Augustus, 119, 184, 185, 186, 228, 230
Hopson, Wm. Fowler, 85, 106, 147, 259, 261, 294, 297
Horgan, Stephen H., 187
Hornby, Lester G., 37, 107, 297
Horner, T., 102
Horter, Earl, 29, 38, 267
Horton, 117
Hoskin, Robert, 122, 123, 136
Hough, 222
Houghton Mifflin & Co., 136

"Hour, The," 232
Houston, H., 58
Hovenden, Thomas, 11, 21, 137
Howard, Charles M., 277
Howard, Justin H., 183, 225, 228, 230
Howarth, F. M., 238
Howdell, 44
Howell, 186
Howland, W., 118, 120
Hows, John A., 189
Hoyt, Henry Martin, 39
Hubard, 156
Huber, Konrad, 162
Hudson River Scenery, 100, 102, 103, 117, 156, 184, 295
Hudson River Portfolio, 100, 102
"Hudson River School," 69
Huffington, J. M., 22
Humphrey, Lizbeth B., 190, 287
Humphreys, Maud, 190
Hunt, Leigh H., 17
Hunt, Richard M., 287
Hunt, Samuel Valentine, 70
Hunt, Wm. Morris, 20, 79, 167
Hunter, F. Leo, 17
Huntington, Daniel, 20, 69, 72, 73, 79, 95
Hurd, Nathaniel, 48, 84, 88, 208, 251, 252
Hurley, Edward Timothy, 27
Hutchins, F. M., 272
"Hutchins' California Magazine," 184
Hutt, Henry, 200, 285
Hyde, Allyn, 251, 297
Hyde, Helen, 106, 149, 297
Hyde, Wm. Henry, 237

Iconographic Society, Boston, 85
Iconophiles. See Society of Iconophiles
Illman, Thomas, 80; Illman & Sons, Illman & Pilbrow, 95
"Illustrated American News," 186, 269
"Illustrated News," 186

Illustration, chap. XI; 234, 293; in aquatint, 102, 103; etching, 2, 3, 18, 21, 22, 214; line engraving, 48–49, 61, 65–8, 79–82, 85, 112, 180; mezzotint, 92, 180; stipple, 58–9; wood-engraving, 112, 116–25, 130, 147, 181; lithography, 162, 181; harmony between illustration and type, 147, 181, 190, 191, 196, 197, 203–5, 267–8 (advertisements), 273–76 (posters), 284 (magazine covers); magazines, 58–9, 61, 80–1, 92, 103, 114, 121, 179–80, 183, 184, 191, 196, 203, 268; weeklies, 121, 186–7; newspapers, 113, 114, 121, 187–8, 208–9, 212, 233, 241–50, 268, 293
Imbert, Anthony, 67, 153, 154, 155, 157, 160, 216
Independence, Declaration of, 52, 73, 78, 298
Indian subjects, 70–1, 90, 156, 164, 165, 181, 194
Indiana book-plates, 294
Ink, in mezzotint, 95, 96; aquatint, 106
"Inland Printer," 276, 278
Inman, Henry, 66, 68, 71, 103, 153; Childs & Inman, 154, 156, 157
Inness, George, 8, 167
Insects illustrated, 122, 133
Intaglio & Graphotype Co., 224
"International Monthly," 183
Iorio, I. J., 294
Iowa book-plates, 294
Ipsen, Ludvig Sandoe, 197, 262
Ivanowski, Sigismund de, 283
Ives, James M., 220–1; see also Currier & Ives
Ivins, Mrs. Wm. M., Jr., 149

Jaccaci, August F., 185, 263
Jackson, Andrew, portraits, 62, 101, 156; caricatures, 216–7
Jacobi, 272
Jacobs, Wm. L., 202

Jacobsen, F. A., 294
Japanese influence, 106, 140, 148, 149, 194
Jacques, Bertha E., 38, 297
Jarvis, John Wesley, 58, 91, 212
Jefferson, Joseph, 109, 195
Jefferson, Thomas, portraits and caricatures, 18, 53, 210
Jennys, Richard, 88
Jerome, Irene E., 190
"Jingo," 236
Jocelyn (Jocelyn & Annin), 120
Jocelyn, Nathaniel, 69
"John Donkey," 229
Johnson, C. H., 293
Johnson, David, 69
Johnson, Eastman, 21, 167, 168
Johnson, Herbert, 244
Johnson, Thomas. *See* Johnston
Johnson, Thomas, 18, 132, 262
Johnson, Wm. Martin, 197, 285, 293
Johnson, Fry & Co., 180
Johnston, David Claypoole, 3, 4, 154, 214
Johnston, Thomas, 46, 48, 87–8, 251
"Jolly Joker," 229
Jones, Alfred, 71, 72, 73, 74, 78, 85
Jones, Benjamin, 48
Jones, E., 155
Jones, Hugh Bolton, 17
Jones, Haydon, 33
Jones, W. R., 62, 63
Jordan, William. *See* Triptych
Joste, Robert, 270
"Journal," N. Y., 277
"Judge," 162, 235
Juengling, Frederick, 124, 126–7, 128, 136, 137, 191, 297
Juengling, J. F., 131
Junius Junior, 217

Kansas City Art Association, 292
Kappes, Alfred, 189
Karst, John, 117, 122

Kearny, Francis, 1, 64, 67, 77, 252, 254; Pendleton, Kearny & Childs, 158, 164
"Keepsakes." *See* Annuals
Keith, Dora Wheeler, 287
Keith, W., 185
Keller, Arthur I., 202
Kellogg, D. W., 164
Kellogg, E. B. & E. C., 222
Kelly, James Edward, 126, 127, 191, 263
Kelly, Thomas, 74, 75
Kelly, W., 155
Kemble, Edward Winsor, 193, 232, 237, 240, 275, 293
Kendall, Sergeant, 276
Kendrick, Charles, 235, 237
Kennedy, Edward G., 4, 298; catalogue of Whistler's lithographs, published by Kennedy & Co. in 1914
Kennedy & Lucas, 164
Kensett, John F., 64, 69, 70
Kent, Rockwell, 145, 174, 176
Keppel & Co., 291, pamphlets on individual artists, 295–8
Keppler, Joseph, 166, 231, 232, 233, 234, 236, 293
Keppler, Joseph, Jr., 234, 235, 247
Ketten, Maurice, 250
Kidder, J., 100
Kilburn, S. S., 116, 131; Kilburn & Mallory, 122
Kimball, Katherine, 37, 39
Kimmel & Co., 103
Kimmel & Forster, 161
King, C. B., 27
King, Francis Scott, 85, 133, 136, 138
King, Frank, 277
King, James S., 18–9, 20, 97, 106
Kingdon & Boyd, 120
Kingsley, Elbridge, 133, 137, 139, 297
Kinnersley, Henry, 118, 120
Kinney, Troy, 34; The Kinneys (Troy and Margaret West), 202

Kirby, Rollin, 178, 241, 246, 247
Kit-Kat Club, 289
Klackner, C., 291, 297
Kleboe, Bernhardt, 145
Kneass, William, 101
Knickerbocker, J., 187
"Knight Errant," 197
Koehler, Robert, 10
Koehler, Sylvester Rosa, 16; repeat-
edly cited, chap. I, VIII, etc.
Koopman, Augustus, 109
Koppel, C., 157
Kraemer, Peter, 163, 270
Knapp, Joseph, 162, 270
Krimmel, John Lewis, 71
Kruell, Gustav, 132, 136
Kruseman van Elten, Hendrick Dirk,
11, 13
Kummer, J., 104
Kuntze, Edward J., 4

Labels, 267
Labor subjects in prints, 26, 32, 33,
231
Lacour, Peter, 52
"Ladies' Companion," 80
"Ladies' National Magazine," 80
"Ladies' Repository," 80
"Lady's Cabinet Album," 81
LaFarge, John, 124–5, 190, 287, 297
Lafayette, portraits, 53, 58, 67
Laffan, Wm. Mackay, 185, 292
Lamb, Charles Rollinson, 263
Lamb, Ella Condie, 281
Lambdin, J. R., 154
Lander, Benjamin, 8, 11
Landscape, 295; in etching, chap. I,
II; line and stipple engraving, chap.
III, IV; mezzotint, 89, 97; aquatint,
chap. VI; wood-engraving, 116, 121,
123, 142, 185, 188–9; lithography,
161, 174; book-plates, 261; adver-
tisements, 269
Langridge, 122
Lankes, Julius J., 142, 143, 261, 297

Lansing, Garret, 115; "the younger
Lansing," 269–70
"Lantern, The," 182, 229
"Lark," 197
Lathework in engraving, 78
Lauber, Joseph, 10, 263
Lawrence, H. M., 276
Lawrence, Sir Thomas, 93, 153
Lawson, Alexander, 2, 66, 67, 70–1, 91
Learned, Arthur G., 34, 276
Ledyard, Addie, 189, 232
Lee, Homer, 77
Lee, T., 254
Le Fevre, W. J., 8
Lehman, G., 103, 156; Lehman &
Duval, 158, 164; Childs & Lehman,
164
Leigh, Howard, 173, 175
Le Moyne, Jacques, 43
Leney, Wm. Satchwell, 58, 62
Lesley, Margaret W. (Mrs. H. K.
Bush-Brown), 14
Leslie, Charles Robert, 73, 75, 81
Leslie, Frank (Robert Carter), 119;
"Frank Leslie's Illustrated News-
paper," 186, 188, 231
Leutze, Emanuel, 4, 73, 94
Lever, Hayley, 29
Levering, Albert, 234
Levis, Howard C., 114, 291
Levy, W. Auerbach, 34
Lewis, Arthur Allen, 32–3, 204, 286;
wood-engravings, 143, 145, 147, 148,
261, 294
Lewis, J. O., 164
Lexington, Battle of, 51
Leyendecker, Frank X., 267, 285
Leyendecker, Joseph Christian, 275–6,
285
Libraries, public, book-plates for, 253,
254, 255, 258–9
Liebler, Theodore, 272
"Life," 10, 237, 238
Lincoln, Abraham, 222–3; portraits,
18, 34, 55, 79, 133, 142, 163, 295;

caricatures, 220, 221, 222, 223, 224, 225, 226, 293
Lindenmuth, Tod, 141, 142
Line drawing, in harmony with printing type, 191, 203, 204
Linoleum prints, 139, 144
Linson, Corwin Knapp, 202
Linton, Henry, 122
Linton, William James, 123, 132, 136, 189, 261 (book-plate), 292; cited throughout chap. VII, VIII; 270
Lion, J., 159
Lipman, M. de, 277
Lippincott, Wm. Henry, 21, 263
"Literary Digest," 293
Lithography, chap. X; 104, 291, 292; caricature, chap. XII (216–27), 233; holiday cards, 287–8; posters, chap. XV (270 et seq).
Lithotints, 156, 165, 169
Little, Philip, 29, 31
Loeb, Louis, 109, 202
Logan, Robert F., 37
London views, 36, 39
Long (Butler & Long), 102–3
Long Island views, 13, 14, 27, 29
Longacre, James Barton, 62, 64, 74, 83
Longworth, David, 59
Loomis, Chester, 281
Lopez, 163
Lord, Caroline, 8
Lossing, Benson John, 114, 117, 183, 184, 209, 212, 214, 269–70; Lossing & Barritt, 117
Lossing, Helen Rosa ("H. Rosa"), 190
Lotos Club, N. Y., 137
Low, Will Hicok, 84, 189, 196, 197, 276, 280, 287, 288, 293
Lowell, Orson, 202, 282
Lucas (Kennedy & Lucas), 164
Luks, George, 107
Lum, Bertha, 149, 297
Lumley, Arthur, 186, 188
Lungren, Fernand Harvey, 195
Luquiens, Huc Mazelot, 30

Macauley, Charles R., 241, 246
McCarter, Henry, 274, 275, 276
McCarthy, Daniel, 241
McCay, Winsor, 248
McClellan, George B., in caricature, 223, 224–5
McCormick, Howard, 142
McCutcheon, John Tinney, 243–4, 293
Macdonald, A. N., 261
McDermott, Jessie, 190
McDonough, 186
McDougall, Walter H., 185, 244
McEntee, Jervis, 69
Machine Ruling, 3, 74, 77, 78, 93
McKinley, William, portrait, 18; caricature, 243
MacLaughlan, Donald Shaw, 36, 297
McLaughlin, M. Louise, 8
McLenan, John, 228–9
McMillen, Mildred, 141
McNevin, J., 189
McQueen, 104
McRae, John C., 95
McVickar, Henry W., 237, 279
Madison, James, portrait, 57
Magazines, covers, 284, 285; posters, 273, 274–6, 278, 284, 285; illustration, see Illustration
Magee, John L., 163, 186, 223, 228
Magrath, William, 131
Mahogany in wood engraving, 269, 270
Main, William, 64, 74
Maine views, 27, 31, 38
Majer, A., 145
Major, Richard, 155, 160–1, 162, 218, 270
Mallory, 116; Kilburn & Mallory, 122
Manet, E., 135
Manley, Thomas R., 9
Manners and customs in caricature, 239
Mansfield, Howard, 4, 298
Maps and plans, 44, 46, 53, 56, 59, 88, 113, 179

Marin, John, 28, 38
Marine subjects, 10, 31. *See also* Naval prints; Ships
Marks, Montague, 168
Mars, Ethel, 150
Marsh, Henry, 122, 124, 133
Marshall, Wm. Edgar, 79
Marsiglia, Girlando, 154
Martin, Charles, 228
Martin, Homer, 136
Martin, J. B., 160
Mason, Abraham J., 117-8
Mason, William, 117
"Massachusetts Magazine," 58, 67-8
Masson, 186
Mather portraits: Cotton, 87; Increase, 45, 87-8; Richard, 112
Mathews, Arthur Frank, 185, 203, 263
Matteson, T. H., 82, 182
Maurer, Louis, 163, 219, 221, 222, 270, 272; Heppenheimer & Maurer, 164
Maverick, Andrew, 65, 102
Maverick, Peter, engravings, 48, 58, 65, 66, 68, 74, 80, 83, 251, 269; lithographs, 65, 153, 160
Maverick, Peter Rushton, 48, 58, 59, 68, 74, 251, 252, 254, 255
Maverick, Samuel, 67
Mayer, Ferdinand, & Sons, 164
Mayer, Frank Blackwell, 167, 185
Mayer, Henry, 263, 276, 283
Measom, 122
Medium, limits of, 41; in etching, 24, 25, 31; lithography, 169, 172-3; wood-engraving, 128-31, 141, 149, 150, 151, 206; cards, posters, commercial art, 285, 288, 290
Megarey, Henry I., 102
Menus, 84, 289-90
"Mercury," 187
Merrill, Frank Thayer, 8, 195, 230, 260
Merrill, Katherine, 28
Merritt, Anna Lea, 14, 18
Meryon, Charles, influence, 35, 36

Mesier, 155
Metcalf, Willard Leroy, 196, 293
Meteyard, Thomas Buford, 275
Methfessel, 285
Métivet, Lucien, 274
Metropolitan Print Co., 270
Metropolitan Printing Co., 283
Mexican subjects, 38, 142
Mexican War, 71, 188; caricatures, 217-8
Meyner, Walter, 282, 286
Mezzotint, chap. V; in "mixed manner," 74; in illustration, 93, 180; British caricatures, 207; sandpaper mezzotint, 106, 108
Michelin & Creifeld, 155
Michigan, Lake, in etching, 29
Middleton, Stanley, 8
Middleton, Thomas, 2
Mielatz, Charles Frederick William, 24, 97, 297; etchings, 5, 10, 12-3, 105, 106, 107, 262; aquatints, 105, 106, 107; monotypes, 110; lithographs, 169
Mielziner, Leo, 173
Military prints, 71, 156, 164, 194, 215, 269
"Military Magazine," 156
Miller, Addison Thomas, 13, 28, 39, 106
Miller, Dr. Charles Henry, 5, 9, 21, 109
Miller, Kenneth Hayes, 34
Miller, W. R., 186
Miller, William, 131, 261
Millet, Frank Davis, 185
Miner (H. C.) - Springer Litho Co., 272
Minor (caricaturist), 246
Minor, Robert C., 17, 21
Mirall, 232
Miranda, Fernando, 232
Mitchell, J., 88
Mitchell, John Ames, 10, 237, 238, 293

Mitchill, Dr. Samuel Latham, 152
"Mixed manner," 64, 74, 93, 95
Molthrop, 101
Momberger, William, 189
"Momus," 229
Money, Paper. *See* Bank-note
Monks, John Austin Sands, 11
Monotypes, 108–9
Monroe, James, 63
Montanus view of New York, 44
Moore, E. C., 287
Moore, Guernsey, 285
Moore, Humphrey, 195
Moore, T., 164
Moores, 276
Mora, F. Luis, 202, 204
Moran, Leon, 21, 287
Moran, Mary Nimmo, 13, 14, 297
Moran, Percy, 287
Moran, Peter, 6, 7, 8, 11, 20, 109, 297
Moran, Thomas, 136, 287, 288; etchings, 5, 10, 11, 13, 21, 297; lithographs, 167–8; illustrations, 122, 125, 188
Morgan, Matthew Somerville ("Matt"), 163, 166, 231, 238, 271, 272
Morgan, W. J., & Co., 163, 272
Morgan, Wallace, 204
Morgan, William, 115
Morghen, Raphael, 64
Morse, Anna G., 287
Morse, J., 269
Morse, Nathaniel, 47–8
Morse, Joseph W., 270
Morse, William H., 120, 122, 131
Morton, John Ludlow, 101
Mount, William Sidney, 70, 71, 159
Mourgeon, Peter, 1, 269
Mueller (Wegner, Brueckner & Mueller), 164
Mullen, E. F., 184, 229, 232
Muller, Richard Alexander, 131, 136
"Munsey's Weekly," 236
Murphy, Cecil Buller, 143

Murphy, J. J. A., 141, 143, 147, 289
Murray, Draper, Fairman & Co., 67, 77
Music engravers, 47; music covers and titles, 47, 163–4
Myers, Jerome, 32, 177
Mygatt, Robertson K., 17

Nagel & Weingartner, 157, 159
Nahl, A., 167
Nahl, Charles, 184
Nankivell, Frank A., 39, 234, 272, 277, 284
Nantucket views, 29
Nast, Thomas, illustrations, 186, 189, 297; caricatures, 222–3, 229, 230, 231, 232, 241, 247
National Academy of Design, 3, 7, 24, 74, 109, 279, 280; engravers members, 115, 117
National Arts Club, 173, 265, 282
"National Gallery of American Landscape," 69
"National Magazine," 183
"National Portrait Gallery" (Longacre-Herring), 62, 64, 74, 83; (Duyckinck), 83, 180
Naval prints, 67, 99, 100, 213, 214, 295. *See also* Marine subjects; Ships
Neagle, John, 55, 74, 92, 158
Neagle, John B., 64, 65, 66, 74, 81
Neal, David D., 167
Neale, John, 102
Neale, William, 102
Neely, J., Jr., 8
Negro subjects, 11, 186, 189, 193, 232, 237; caricatures, 162, 219, 225, 227, 237, 240. *See also* Abolition; Slavery
Nehlig, Victor, 5
Nelan, Charles, 241, 293
New Jersey views, 9, 29
"New Mirror," 103
New Orleans views, 26, 29, **144**

New Orleans, Battle of, 2
New York City views, 193, 295; in etching, 1, 5, 7, 12, 13, 14, 18, 26, 27, 28, 30, 32; engraving, 43–4, 46, 47, 52, 56, 66, 68, 79, 85, 156; aquatint, 100–6; monotype, 110; wood-engraving, 140, 144; lithography, 153, 154, 156, 157, 160, 161, 162, 163, 169, 177
New York Etching Club, 1, 7, 17, 22, 24, 291
"New York Herald," caricatures, 235, 241; posters, 275, 277; illustrations, 121, 187
"New York Illustrated News," 186
"New York Magazine," 58, 68
"New York Mirror," 80, 179
New York Public Library print collection, 7, 69, 72, 83, 114, 137, 188, 265, 288, 291, 295, 298; exhibitions, 173, 264, 286, 294
New York State views, 68, 100, 103, 106, 154, 155, 161, 174. See also New York City; Hudson River; Long Island
"New York Tribune," 244, 246
Newell, Peter, 240, 274, 293
Newsam, Albert, 157–8, 297
Newspapers, caricatures, chap. XIII; posters, 273, 275, 276–7; illustration, see Illustration
Nichols, George Ward, 167
Nichols, Juliette S., 149
Nicoll, James Craig, 10, 13
Niemeyer, John Henry, 17
Nordell, Carl J., 29
Nordfeldt, B. J. Olsson, 26, 35, 149, 297
Norman, John, 47, 48, 49, 51, 52, 53, 55, 58, 59, 64, 297
Nourse, Elizabeth, 8
Nursery rhymes, 162

Oakes, William, 161
Oakford, Ellen, 14

Oakley, Thornton, 173
Oakley, Violet, 177, 190
Oberhardt, William, 176, 267
O'Brien, Robert, 132
Oertel, Johannes Adam, 69, 184
Ogden, H. A., 163, 194, 267, 269, 271, 272
Okey, Samuel, 88
O'Neill, Rose Cecil, 190
Opper, Frederick Burr, 232, 233, 243, 293
Oriental subjects and views, 12, 33, 35, 39, 149, 162; Japan, 39, 149, 162
Ormsby, Waterman Lilly, 76–7
Orr, John William and Nathaniel, 120, 122
Orr, Louis, 36–7
Osborne, Milo, 82
Osgood, James A., 117, 122
Osgood, Henry Haviland, 28, 35
Ostertag, Blanche, 190
Otis, Bass, 90, 91, 100, 152
Ottman, J., 164
"Our Young Folks," 189
Outcault, Richard Felton, 248, 277

Page, William, 94
Paine, Thomas, caricatured, 210
Painter Gravers of America, 24, 150
Paintings reproduced, in aquatint, 100, 101; etching, 2, 3, 10, 11, 12, 19–22, 106; engraving, 70–3; mezzotint, chap. V; wood-engraving, chap. VIII; lithography, 152, 154, 157, 166. See also names of painters
Palmer, 122
Palmer, Frances F. (Palmer, F. & S.), 161
Pape, Eric, 195
Papprill, Henry, 104
Paradise, John Wesley, 74
Paris views, 10, 35, 36, 37, 38
Parker, C. Gray, 237
Parker, G. C., 276

Parker, George, 62
Parrish, Maxfield, 267, 276, 280, 285
Parrish, Stephen, 7, 8, 9, 10, 13, 21, 297
Parrish, Thomas C., 11
Parsons, Charles, 161–2, 163, 192
Parte sculp., 55
Partridge, Roi, 28, 37, 262
Pate, William, 103; W. Pate & Co., 69
Patterson, F. B., 7
Patterson, Margaret, 150
Paxton, William M., 277
Peale, Charles Willson, 56, 88–9
Peale, Rembrandt, 152–3
Pearson, Ralph M., 26, 28, 29, 286, 294
Pease, Bessie, 294
Pease, Joseph Ives, 64, 69, 71, 75–6, 101
Pease, R. H., 164
Peckwell, Henry W., 131
Peixotto, Ernest C., 109, 203
Pekenino, Michele, 55
Pelham, Henry, 51
Pelham, Peter, 87, 88, 297
Pen-and-ink drawing, in illustration, chap. XI (pp. 190–204), 293; caricature, 225, 234, 235, 238, 240–6; etching, 16; lithography, 152, 159, 171, 172
Pendleton, John, 153, 154, 155, 156, 157, 162, 164
Pendleton's Lithography, 162
Pendleton, Kearny & Childs, 158, 164
Pendleton, W. S., 160
Penfield, Edward, 266, 267, 275, 278, 279, 281, 285
Penman, Edith, 21
Penn, William, 47, 252; fictitious portrait, 54;
Pennell, Joseph, 24, 176, 298; etchings, 5, 8, 10, 12, 26, 41; aquatints, 106–8; illustrations, 191–2; lithographs, 169–70, 171, 173, 175
Penniman, J. R., 155, 156

"Pennsylvania Gazette," 208
"Pennsylvania Journal," 208
"Pennsylvania Magazine," 47, 58
Pennsylvania views, 100, 155
Perard, Victor Semon, 203, 263, 276, 285, 293
Perine, George E., 95
Perkins, Charles C., 185
Perkins, Granville, 123, 189
Perkins, Jacob, 76, 77, 155
Pettrick, Ferdinand, 165
Pewter, engravers on, 44
Pfau, Gustavus, 157
Philadelphia, in etching, etc., 2, 28, 68, 161, 165, 182, 215; caricature, 208, 215
"Philadelphia Gazette," 47
Philadelphia Sketch Club, 8
Philadelphia Society of Etchers, 8, 291
Phoenix, John (G. H. Derby), 185
Photographs re-drawn for illustration, 195
Photography, use in wood-engraving, 124, 129, 130, 198; used directly in illustration, 181
Photomechanical processes, 67, 138, 203, 245, 259, 260, 262; photo-engraving for illustration in line, 204; photo-lithography in newspaper illustration, 187. *See also* Half-tone
"Phunny Phellow," 229
Physionotrace, 54
Piazzoni, Gottardo, 28
Picart, B., 210
"Picayune, The," 229
"Picture Gallery," 179
"Picturesque America," 70, 122, 123, 188
Pierce, Edith Loring, 14
Pierce, Franklin, portrait of, 218
Pierce, H. Winthrop, 287
Pierson, R. B., 117
Pigalle, 1
Piggot, Robert, 62

Pilbrow, 95

Pine wood, in wood-engraving, 270

Pioneers, 70, 122

Pittsburgh in etching, 26, 29

"Pittsburgh Telegraph," 187

Plank, George Wolfe, 143, 147, 261, 286, 297

Plans. *See* Maps

Plant life, 6, 194

Plate printers. *See* Printers

Platt, Charles Adams, 9, 10, 18, 297

Political caricatures, chap. XII, XIII; posters, 281

"Polyanthos," 61, 100

Poore, Henry Rankin, 8

Pope, Marion Holden, 28

"Port-Folio," 57, 61, 68, 100, 101, 115

Porte Crayon (D. H. Strother), 184, 185

Porter, R. K., 54

Portraits, 295; in etching, 1, 18-9, 34; line and stipple engraving, chap. III, IV; mezzotint, chap. V; aquatint, 101, 102, 103; wood-engraving, 112, 113, 132, 133, 183-4; lithography, chap. X; illustration, 195; caricature, 232; posters, 271, 276, 281, 283

Postage stamps, 84

Posters, 295, chap. XV; in wood-engraving, 112, 146-7; lithography, 163, 164, 172, 173, 177; for books, 274-5; magazines, 273, 274-6, 278, 284, 285; newspapers, 273, 275, 276-7; theatrical, 270-2, 273, 274, 282-3; circus, 269, 272, 282; political, 281-2; harmony between picture and type, 273-6

"Potomac," 223, 224

Pottery, Staffordshire, 106

Potthast, Edward Henry, 272, 276

Poupard, James, 48, 58, 64

Powell, Caroline A., 131, 132

Powers, T. E., 244, 246

Prang, Louis, 159, 166, 287-8; L. Prang & Co., 167, 168

Pranischnikoff, I., 189

Preissig, Vojtech, 24, 107, 262

Prendergast, Maurice Brazil, 274

"Press, The," New York, 241

"Press, The," Philadelphia, 275

Preston, James, 282

Preston, May Wilson, 190

Prevost, B. L., 53-4

Price, William, 47

Primers, 114

Prince, Thomas, his book-plate, 252

Princeton book-plates, 258, 294

Print dealers and publishers, 6-7, 19, 20, 22, 24 (*see also* Huffington, Keppel, Kennedy, Klackner, Megarey, Patterson, Roullier, Seitz); engraver-publishers, 56, 88, 91 (*see also* Adams, J. A., Barber, J. W., Bowen, Charles, Hurd, Karst, Okey, Sartain, J., Savage, Smith, J. R., Strong, T. W.)

Print Makers' Society, California, 292

Printers, copper-plate, 1, 8, 65; *See also* Butler & Long, Daniels, J. E. Gavit, Kimmel & Co., Maverick, A., Mourgeon, Neale, Pate, Ritchie, G. W. H., Rollinson

Printers, Lithographic, 152-6

Printers' ornaments, 47, 113

Printing, of etchings, 5, 6, 8, 9, 13, 25, 39, 41; mezzotints, 91-2, 95, 96; aquatints, 106; wood-engravings, 115, 119, 137, 139; lithographs, 174

"Printing Art," 285

Probst, John Michael, 54

Prohibition, in caricature, 218

Proofs, in etching, for the "amateur," 16-7; in wood-engraving, 137; "touched," 72, 83

Provincetown views, 27

"Provincetown Group," 150

Prud'homme, John Francis Eugene, 62, 64, 74, 81

Publishers. *See* Print dealers
"Puck," St. Louis, 232-3
"Puck," New York, 162, 231, 232, 233, 234, 235, 236
"Puck," San Francisco, 235
Pullinger, Herbert, 145, 173
"Punch," 226
"Punchinello," 230
"Punster," 229
Purcell, E., 186
Pursell, Henry, 44
Putnam, F. W., 131
Putnam, G. P., 119-20
Putnam, Stephen Greeley, 131
Pyle, Howard, 190, 198-9, 232, 263

Quartley, F. O., 122
Quinlan, Will J., 27

Rajon, Paul, 6
"Ram's Horn," 239
Ranger, Henry Ward, 168
Ranney, William, 70, 71, 72
Raubichek, Frank, 21
Rawdon, Ralph, 48, 255
Rawdon, Clark & Co., 66; Rawdon, Wright, Hatch & Smillie, 77, 81
Rayner, R. J., 156
"Recorder," New York, 241
Redding, 120
Redwood, Allen C., 185
Reed, Abner, 45, 58, 101
Reed, Earl H., 29
Reed, Ethel, 274, 277
Reevs, George M., 276
Reich, Jacques, 18, 34
Reinagle, Hugh, 67, 153-4
Reindel, W. G., 29, 144
Reinhart, Charles Stanley, 7, 126, 185, 191, 192, 231, 240, 276, 293
Remarques, 17
Rembrandt, 20, 96; etchings copied, 2
Remington, Frederic, 185, 194, 293
Renault, J. F., 52
"Repository," Delaplaine's, 61-2, 74

Restrikes, 50
Retroussage, 6, 25
Reuterdahl, Henry, 202
Revere, Paul, 47, 48, 50-1, 53, 54, 58, 64, 251, 264, 298; caricatures, 207-8
Revolutionary War, in work on copper, 1, 2, 50-4, 58-9, 83, 88-9, 90; wood-engraving, 117, 126; lithography, 159; illustration, 179, 184, 194, 198, 199; caricatures, 206-9
Reynolds, Frederick, 97
Reynolds, Sir Joshua, 89
Rhead, George W., Frederick and Louis, 197
Rhead, Louis, 197, 262, 275, 276, 277, 279, 281, 294
Rhode Island views, 100
"Rhode Island Literary Repository," 61
Ribot, Theodule, 134
Richards, Frederick Thompson, 238
Richards, John H., 165
Richards, Thomas Addison, 81, 184, 185
Richardson, Frederick, 197, 293
Richardson, James H., 119, 120, 122; Richardson & Co., Richardson & Cox, 120; Richardson & Foos, 270
Ridinger, 114
Rimmer, William, 133
Riordan, Roger, 185
Ritchie, Alexander Hay, 55, 72, 94-5
Ritchie, George Wistar Hodge, 8, 22
"Riverside Magazine," 189
Roberts, Charles, 158
Roberts, J. M., 155
Roberts, John, 91
Roberts, W. M., 120
Robertson, Alexander, 68
Robertson, Archibald, 91, 154
Robinson, Boardman, 178, 245-6, 247, 283, 298
Robinson, H. D., 210
Robinson, H. R., 216, 217
Rodgers, 74

Rogers, William Allen, 195, 238, 240, 241, 247, 272, 279, 293
Rollinson, William, 44, 58, 59, 66, 75, 76, 84, 100–1, 102 (printer), 251
Romans, Bernard, 46, 48, 52, 53
Rondel, Frederic, 167
Rood, Roland, 17
Roosevelt, Theodore, portrait, 19; caricatures, 235, 244, 293
Rosa, Guy and Lawrence, 267
Rosa, H. (H. R. Lossing), 190
Rosenberg, C. G., 229
Rosenberg, H. M., 15, 276
Rosenberg, Louis C., 35
Rosenkrantz, Baron Arild, 276
Rosenmeyer, Bernard Jacob, 163
Rosenthal, Albert, 18
Rosenthal, L. N., 159, 165
Rosenthal, Max, 18, 96, 159, 165
Roth, Ernest D., 38, 298
Rothermel, Peter F., 72, 94, 95, 180
Roulette, in etching, 2, 13, 19, 54; mezzotint, 90, 93; "mixed manner," 74; aquatint, 107
Roullier, Albert, 291; pamphlets on individual artists, 295–8
Roush, L. L., 276
Rousseau, Th., 133
Rowlandson, Thomas, 102
Rowse, Samuel Worcester, 79
"Royal American Magazine," 51, 58, 208
Royal Society of Painter Etchers, 8
Ruggles, E., Jr., 251
Ruling machine, 3, 74, 77, 78, 93
Runge, 185
Ruzicka, Rudolph, 141, 143, 144, 147, 148, 204, 261, 286, 298
Ryerson, Margaret, 33–4

Sabin, J. Percy, 88 .
Sabin, Joseph F., 17
Sacker, Amy, 286, 294
Sackett & Wilhelms, 164
Sadd, H. S., 82, 95

St. Memin, C. B. J. Fevret de, 1, 53–4, 101, 269, 296
"St. Nicholas," 125, 136, 222, 276, 292
Saintin, Jules Emile, 160
Salvation Army, 186
"Sam, the Scaramouch," 238
Sandham, Henry, 18, 195, 257, 260, 263, 288
Sandler, Alexander, 287
Sandpaper mezzotint, 106, 108
Sanford, Issac, 47
Sandzén, Birger, 141, 142, 174
Santee, Rose, 28
Sargent, Henry, 91
Sargent, John Singer, 170
Sarka, Charles, 204, 286
Sarony, Napoleon, 166–7, 217, 271; Sarony & Major, 155, 160–1, 218; Sarony, Major & Knapp, 162
Sartain, John, 5, 91–3, 94, 95, 96, 298
Sartain, Samuel, 95
Sartain, William, 17, 96
Satin, impressions on, 56
Satterlee, Walter, 287
Savage, Edward, 52, 56, 57, 89, 91, 95, 99, 101, 298
Sawyer, Philip, 28
Scacki, Francis, 2
Schell, F. B., 188
Schell, Frank H., 189
Schelling, R., 136
Schilling, Alexander, 9
Schladitz, Ernst, 131
Schlecht, Charles, 84
Schneider, Otto J., 34, 298
Schoff, Stephen Alonzo, 17, 18, 20, 79, 82
School books, 117, 120–1, 181, 186 (Southern), 191
Schultze, Carl E. ("Bunny"), 248
Schumacher & Ettlinger, 164
Schussele, Christian, 72, 94, 96, 165–6, 180, 188
Schweinfurth, Julius A., 279
Scoles, John, 58, 59

Scot, Robert, 48

Scot & Allardice, 66

Scotch stone, 13, 108

Scraper, in aquatint, 108; in lithography, 158, 167, 168, 170, 171, 174

Scratchers' Club, Brooklyn, 8

"Scribner's Monthly," 126, 127, 133, 134, 136, 144, 189, 191, 232, 274, 292

Seals, in wood-engraving, 1672, 112

Sears (Fenner & Sears), 66

Sebron, H., 104

Seer, Alfred S., 163, 270, 272

Seitz, Emil, 6, 156

Senat, Prosper L., 9

Senefelder Co., 160

Senseney, George, 13, 107, 298

Sewell, Robert van Vorst, 17

Seymour, Joseph M., 49, 59, 66, 251, 254

Seymour, Ralph Fletcher, 28, 294

Shakespeare illustrations, 73, 115, 180, 182, 183, 192

Shallus, Francis, 101, 251, 254

Share, H. Pruett, 21

Sharp, William, 45

Sharp, W., & Co., 164

Shattuck, Aaron Draper, 69

Shaver, J. R., 202

Shaw, Howard Van Doren, 263

Shaw, Joshua, 65, 102

Shaw, Robert, 18

Sheldon, Rufus, 109

Shelton, Wm. Henry, 185, 194

Shepherd, Jessie Curtis, 189

Sheppard, William L., 189, 230, 240

Sherwin, J. H., 157

Sherwood, Rosina Emmet, 287

Sherwood, William A., 27, 40

Shinn, Earl (Edward Strahan), 185

Shinn, Everett, 110

Shinplaster caricature, 217

Ships, 26, 30, 31, 103, 108, 123, 162, 163, 175, 193

Shirlaw, Walter, 11, 21, 69, 78, 196

Shope, Henry B., 27, 30

Sill, Howland, 262

Silversmiths, 44

Simmons, Will, 34-5

Simon, 90

Simond, L., 254

Simpson, John W., 258

Simpson, R., 44

Sinclair, T. S., 162, 164

Sindelar, T., 289

Slader, 122

Slavery controversy, in caricature, 218, 219, 223, 226. See also Abolition

Sloan, John, 32, 177, 197, 246, 275, 276, 298

Smedley, Wm. Thomas, 191, 192-3, 276, 293

Smillie, James, 3, 66, 69, 72, 73, 74, 75, 77, 78, 81, 82, 85, 160

Smillie, James David, 298; etchings, 7, 12, 13, 20, 22, 24; engravings, 69, 78, 82; mezzotints, 97; aquatints, 105; lithographs, 163; bookplates, 260, 262

Smirke, Robert, 66

Smith, B. E., 68

Smith, Dan, 272, 277

Smith, F. Berkeley, 275, 276

Smith, Francis Hopkinson, 168, 193, 198, 202

Smith, George Girdler, 63; Annin & Smith, 104, 160, 252

Smith, Hezekiah Wright, 82, 95

Smith, J. André, 27, 35, 298

Smith, J. H., 235

Smith, Jessie Willcox, 190, 281, 285

Smith, John Rubens, 63, 65, 91, 100, 154, 160

Smith, Pamela Colman, 294

Smith, Sidney L., 6, 18-9, 20-1, 50, 51, 85, 259, 261, 298

Smith, W. D., 66

Smith, W. Granville, 195-6, 276

Smither, J., 46, 47, 48, 53, 58, 251

Smithwick, John G., 126, 127, 131
Snyder, H. W., 61
Socialism, in caricature, 219, 234, 246
Society of American Etchers, 17–8
Society of American Wood Engravers, 134, 136, 292
Society of Iconophiles of New York, 85, 106, 110, 169, 295
Soft-ground etching. *See* Etching
Soft metal process, 187
Sonntag, William Louis, 69
"Southern Illustrated News," 186
Southern illustrators, 187
Southern life, 182, 185
"Southern Punch," 230
Spain views, 169, 170, 192
Spanish-American War, caricatures, 236–7, 293
Sparks, Henry Lawrence, 273
Sparks, Will, 28
Sparrow, Thomas, 45, 113, 251, 253
Spear, Gil, 282
Spenceley, Frederick, 261, 294
Spenceley, J. Winfred, 258–9, 260, 261, 264, 294, 298
Spencer, Lily Martin, 180
Spier (Davis & Spier), 124
Sporting prints, 35, 163, 185, 193, 239, 256, 295
Sprague, Isaac, 161
Squire, Maud Hunt, 40
Staffordshire pottery, views on, 106
Stamp act, 207, 208
Stanlaws, Penrhyn (P. S. Adamson), 235
Stansbury, A. I., 66
States' rights, caricatures, 218
Staudenbaur, R., 136
Stauffer, David McNeely, 158, 222, 262, 291, 294, 297; repeatedly cited, chap. III, etc.
Steel, James W., 75
Steel engraving, chap. IV
Steel plates, 77
Steele, Frederic Dorr, 202, 282

Steeper, John, 47
Stephens, Alice Barber, 190
Stephens, Henry L., 162, 180, 184, 229, 230
Sterner, Albert Edward, 109, 110, 176, 202, 237, 293
Stetson, Charles Walter, 21
Stevens, Thomas Wood and Helen B., 29–30
Stevens, William Dodge, 202
Still life etchings, 25
Stipple engraving, chap. III, IV; in etching, 13, 19; aquatint, 101; mezzotint, 90, 93; lithography, 172; book-plates, 261; new mode invented by J. Roberts, 91
Stokes, I. N. Phelps, 44, 295
Stone, Pauline, 262
Stone, Wilbur Macey, 262, 281, 294, 297. *See also* Triptych, The
"Stopping out," in aquatint, 107
Storrs, John, 145
Story, Thomas C. (Story & Atwood), 55
Stothard, Thomas, 66
Strahan, Edward ("Earl Shinn"), 185
Strickland, William, 101
Strobridge Lithographic Co., 163, 271
Strong, Thomas W., wood engravings, 117, 132, 186, 220, 225, 228, 270; lithographs, 218, 219
Strother, David Hunter ("Porte Crayon"), 184, 185
Stuart, Gilbert, 56, 57, 59, 61, 96, 156, 211
"Studio," New York, 21
Stur, Karl Edler von, 233
Sturges, Dwight C., 33
Sturgis, Russell, 263
Sugden, Thomas D., 132, 189, 269
Sullivant, T. S., 238
Sully, Thomas, lithographs, 153; paintings, 62, 63, 67, 75, 93, 94, 157
Sulphur tint, 108

"Sun, The," New York, 187, 277, 279
"Sunset," 285
Swett, Moses, 155, 164
Szekessy, Curt, 28

Taber, Florence, 287
Taft, William Howard, in caricature, 235
Tallmadge, Thomas E., 26
Tanner, Benjamin, 52, 57, 58, 66, 67
Tanner, Henry, 76
Tanner, Vallance, Kearny & Co., 77
Tarbell, Edmund C., 135
Taylor, Charles Jay, 234
Taylor, F. Walter, 176
Taylor, J. E., 194
Taylor, William Ladd, 197, 276
Teague, Walter Dorwin, 282, 286
Teall, Gardner C., 197, 262, 298
Teniers, 115
Tennant, W., 47
Tenniel, Sir John, 226
Terry, James, 297
"Texas Siftings," 238, 240
Thackara, James, 65, 251
Thayer, B. W., & Co., 161, 163, 164
Thomas, George, 270
Thomas, George H., 119
Thomas, Henry A., 163, 271; Thomas & Wylie, 272, 280
Thompson, E. Seton, 185
Thompson, John, 115, 118
Thorpe, Thomas Bangs, 183, 185
Thulstrup, Thure de, 194, 195, 293
Thurston, John, 66, 115
Thurwanger, Martin, 159
Thwaites, William H., 184
Tickets of admission, 48, 65
"Tid-Bits," 238
Tiebout, Cornelius, 51, 56, 58, 59, 66, 68
Tietze, Richard George, 131, 136
Tiffany, Louis C., 287
Tinker, E. L., 144
Tinkey, John, 122

Tint blocks, in wood-engraving, 120, 143, 148, 233, 270, 284
Tint stone, in lithography, 155, 162, 165, 181
Tisdale, Elkanah, 51, 58, 59, 65, 209
Title-pages, 1, 47, 66, 165
Tittle, Walter, 34
Tobacconists' devices, 114
Tobin, George F., 285
"Tokens." See Annuals
Toppan, Charles, 155
Toppan, Robert Noxon, 291
Townsend, Harry, 147, 173
Transfer paper, in lithography, 170, 171, 172
Transfer press, 74
Trappers, in prints, 70-1
Treidler, Adolph, 147, 174, 285
Trenchard, James, 58, 251
"Triangle, The." See Bellew
Tripoli, war with, 100
Triptych, The (W. M. Stone, Jay Chambers, W. Jordan), 262, 294
Trowbridge, Vaughan, 27, 107
Troy views, 103
Trumbull, John, painter, 51, 73, 74
"Truth," 187
Tryon, Dwight William, 133
Tucker, William E., 80
Turner, A. M., 287
Turner, Charles Yardley, 21
Turner, James, 45, 46, 47, 48, 251
Turner, J. M. W., 97
Twachtman, John H., 16; Mrs. Twachtman, 14
Type-metal cuts, 47, 50, 51, 113, 114 116

Uhle, B., 8
Underwood, Abby E., 274
Union League Club, New York, 14, 273, 291
United States history, 63, 72, 99, 295. See also Civil War; Colonial History; Mexican War; Revolutionary

War; Spanish-American War; Tripoli, War with; War of 1812; War, European
"United States Magazine," 183
University of California, 264, 265

Vallance, John, 48, 63, 77, 251
Van Buren, Martin, in caricature, 218
Vanderburgh, Walter H., 144
Vanderhoof, Charles A., 9, 13, 106, 168–9, 195
Vanderlyn, John, 63, 73, 79
Van Elten. *See* Kruseman
Van Ingen, W. B., 177
"Vanity Fair," 229
Van Ness, 131
Van Schaick, S. W., 237
Varian, George, 202
Vedder, Elihu, 184, 196, 230, 263, 284, 287, 293
"Vehme, Die," 232
Velazquez, 135
Venice, in etching, 4, 11, 14, 36, 38, 39
"Verdict, The," 238
Verger, P. C., 52
Ver Meer, 135, 136
Verrées, J. Paul, 39
Victor, F. (F. V. Gillam), 235, 236
Victoria and Albert Museum, 292
Vierge, Daniel, 194, 275
Views. *See* City views; Landscape; and names of individual countries and states
Virginia, 103, 185
Visscher view of New York, 44
Voight, C. A., 250
Volck, Adalbert (V. Blada), 226
Volk, Douglas, 287
Volkmar, Charles, 6, 17
Vondrous, John C., 27, 35

Wagner, Robert, 197, 281
Wagner, T. S., 164
Walcott, Jessie McDermott, 190
Waldo & Jewett, 83

Wales, George E., 31
Wales, James Albert, 232, 234
Walker, Charles A., 21
Walker, Charles H., 109
Walker, Horatio, 135
Walker, William H., 238
Wall, William G., 68, 102
Waller, Frank, 17
Wallin, Samuel, 183–4, 186
Walter, Adam B., 63, 95
Walters, William T., 166
War, European, 33, 108, 172, 173, 237, 285, 293
War of 1812, 2, 67, 101, 117, 184; caricatures, 102, 211–4
"War Cry," 186, 238–9
Warner, Everett Longley, 36, 262
Warner, William, 94
Warren, A. Coolidge, 189
Warren, A. W., 1, 5, 6
Washburn, Cadwallader, 27, 38–9, 177, 298
Washington, George, portraits, 295; in etching, 1, 18; engraving, 45, 49, 53, 54, 55, 56, 75, 79, 83; mezzotint, 89, 90, 91, 95, 96; aquatint, 101; lithography, 152, 153, 154, 156, 165; scenes in his life, 2, 52, 72; caricatures, 209–10; his book-plate, 252; engraved buttons, 45; owned book on engraving, 2
"Washington Star," 241
"Wasp, The," 162, 235
Watson, E., 177
Watson, Henry Sumner, 276
Watson, M. L. D., 190
Watt, William G., 138, 140
Waud, Alfred R., 186, 188, 236
Waud, William, 188
Waugh, Ida, 190
Webb, Alonzo E., 37
Weber, E., 165
Weber, Frederick T., 29
Weber, Otis, 97
Weber, Sarah S. Stilwell, 190

Webster, Herman Armour, 27, 36, 298
Weeklies, illustrated. *See* Illustration
Weeks, W. W., 4
Wegner, A. D. (Wegner, Brueckner & Mueller), 164
Weingartner (Nagel & Weingartner), 157, 159
Weir, Julian Alden, 135; etchings, 16, 25, 298; engraving, 85; lithographs, 168; holiday cards, 287–8
Weir, Robert Walter, 2, 3, 4, 19, 80
Welch, Thomas B., 62, 63, 64, 95
Weldon, Charles Dater, 231–2, 288
Wellington, Frank H., 131, 139
Wellmore, E., 62
Wellstood, John Geikie, 76
Wellstood, William, 68, 69–70, 72
Welsh, H. Devitt, 32
Wenban, Sion Longley, 15
Wendel, Theodore M., 15
Wenzell, Albert Beck, 200, 293
West, Benjamin, 2, 94, 152
West, Raphael, 152
West, The, in prints, 70, 174, 182, 189, 194, 295
Westall, Richard, 66
Western Art Union, 71
Western etchers, 28, 291. *See also* Californian
Western Methodist Book Concern, 71–2
Wheelan, Albertine Randall, 203, 259, 262, 264, 294
Wheeler, Dora, 287
Whelpley, P. M., 95
Whistler, J. A. M., 131, 135, 136, 139, 151; etchings, 4, 13, 15, 41, 298; lithographs, 169, 170, 175, 176 (a catalogue, with reproductions of all the lithographs, was issued by Kennedy & Co. in 1914); influence of, 4, 25, 30, 38
White, Charles Henry, 26, 298
White, Edwin, 4, 167
White, George G., 180, 185, 191

White, John, 43
White, John Blake, 94
"White line" in wood-engraving, 114, 115, 116, 118, 125, 143
Whitechurch, Robert, 72, 95
Whitefield, E., 161
Whitehead, Walker, 286
Whitney, Elias J., 119, 120, 183
Whitney, J. H. E., 131
Whitney, Mrs. O. E., 286
Whittemore, Charles E., 10
Wickenden, Robert J., 170
Wiederseim, Grace Gebbie, 268
Wiggins, Carleton, 8
Wilcox, John A. J., 84
Wild, J. C., 161
Wildhack, Robert J., 282
Wiles, Irving Ramsey, 195, 196, 274, 275, 293
Wilford, L. F., 145
Wilhelms (Sackett & Wilhelms), 164
Will, August, 184
Willette, 273
Williams, Virgil, 8
Willing, John Thomson, 263
Wilmer, W. A., 62, 64
Wilson, Francis, 257, 283
Wilson, Rose Cecil O'Neill, 190
Wilson, William, 4
Wilson, Woodrow, portrait of, 97
Winkler, John W., 30
Winslow, Henry, 27, 35
Witkowski, Charles, 203
Wolf, Henry, 134, 135–6, 137, 138, 140, 298
Women artists: in etching, 8, 13, 14, 17, 18, 21, 28, 29, 30, 33–4, 37, 38, 39, 40, 291, 297; aquatint, 106, 107; wood-engraving, 115, 131–2, 141, 143, 145, 146, 149, 150, 297; lithography, 161, 170; illustration, 180, 186, 189–90, 202, 203; caricature, 232; book-plates, 259, 262, 264, 294; advertisements, 268; posters, 274, 277, 281; cards, 286, 287, 288

Wood, Joseph, 61, 63, 101
Wood, Samuel, 114
Wood, Thomas Waterman, 11
Wood-engraving, 44, 96, 291, 292, chap. VII–IX; illustration, chap. VII, VIII, XI (especially, p. 181–191), 204–5; newspaper illustration, 187; caricature, 212, 220, 221, 225, 229–33; book-plates, 260, 261; posters, 163, 269–70, 280, 284; advertisements, 267, 268, 269; paper money, 113; school, 118; imitation of engraving on copper, 115, 118–9, 128
Woodbury, Charles Herbert, 31, 275, 279–80
Woodbury, C. O., 145
Woodville, R. Caton, 70, 71
Woodward, John D., 188, 189
Woodward, Stanley W., 31
Woolf, Michael Angelo, 228, 232, 240, 293
Woolf, S. J., 176
"World, The," New York, 187, 241, 277
Worth, Thomas, 162, 222, 227, 228, 240
Wray, Henry Russell, 5, 20, 22, 292
Wright, wood-engraver, 118
Wright, Charles Hubbard, 277

Wright, Charles Cushing, 74, 77, 81
Wright, George, 202
Wright, Joseph, 1
Wunderlich & Co., 291, 296
Wust, Theodore, 17, 231
Wyeth, N. C., 203
Wylie (Thomas & Wylie), 272

Yale, Dr. Leroy Milton, 7, 13, 262, 298
"Yankee Doodle," 228
"Yankee Notions," 117, 228, 238
Yeager, Joseph, 3
Yegel, W. J., 276
Yohn, Frederick C., 202
Yorktown, Battle of, 52
Young, Arthur, 234
Young, C. Jac., 29
Young, Mahonri, 28–9, 177, 298
"Young America," 177, 229

Zeke, 225
Ziegfeld, Hugo, 272
Zimmermann, Eugene, 233–4, 235
Zimmermann, W., 136
Zinc etching, 204
Zinc plates, in lithography, 270
Zogbaum, Rufus Fairchild, 194
Zorach, William and Marguerite, 145, 146, 286